I0111777

Death is the Ultimate Orgasm

Handbook on How to Live and Die

How to Come and Go at the Same Time

Robin Wheeler

DEATH IS THE ULTIMATE ORGASM
Handbook on How to Live and Die

Copyright © Robin Wheeler 2018

ISBN: 978-0-6399591-0-8 **print**
       978-0-6399591-1-5 **eBook**
       978-0-6399591-2-2 **mobi**
       978-0-6399591-3-9 **audiobook**

BEntrepreneurING Books
Box 875, Bedfordview, 2008, South Africa

www.bentrepreneuring.com

Layout & typesetting : Robin Wheeler
Photography : Resheka Mahadow
Proofreading : Amanda Ghigini and Resheka Mahadow
Cover : Happy Self Publishing

Thank you Resheka Mahadow for your love, companionship, support, backing and insight along the way. What a trip it's turning out to be. Thank you Amanda Ghigini for your instinct, love, friendship, support and insight along the way. What an adventure we are on. Thank you both, too, for being there with me step-by-step, for your early reading, for nurturing me through the nodes, for helping with the editing and polishing, and for sharing in the incremental highs. The best a man could ask for.

Thank you Frank Wheeler for all you do for and with me. Didn't know you'd be in a book, did you? Thank you George Michael for showing us how it's done. Thank you Simon Napier-Bell for coming to take us to lunch. Thank you Greg Marucchi for decades of friendship, keeping me on course when it counted, and world class fun. Thank you waitresses at Hudsons Bedfordview for the inspiration. Thank you England, South Africa and Thailand for being my homes. Thank you life for making it all possible. Thank you love for being the way.

This is for the earth and

all of its dwellers

Contents:

Chapter 1:	Father Figure....................................	1
Interlude 1:	*You Know That I Want To.................*	10
Chapter 2:	Edge of Heaven..............................	18
Chapter 3:	Fastlove...	25
Chapter 4:	Outside..	36
Chapter 5:	An Easier Affair............................	45
Interlude 2:	*I'm Your Man.................................*	50
Chapter 6:	To Be Forgiven..............................	60
Chapter 7:	Amazing...	65
Chapter 8:	Faith...	68
Chapter 9:	Flawless (Go to the City)...................	72
Chapter 10:	White Light.....................................	80
Chapter 11:	Older..	91
Interlude 3:	*Last Christmas...............................*	95
Chapter 12:	Round Here.....................................	101
Chapter 13:	A Different Corner...........................	112
Chapter 14:	Freedom..	115
Chapter 15:	Heal the Pain..................................	118
Chapter 16:	John and Elvis are Dead..................	123
Chapter 17:	Fantasy...	129
Chapter 18:	Waiting for that Day.......................	135
Chapter 19:	I Want Your Sex..............................	139
Chapter 20:	Free..	143
Chapter 21:	Hard Day...	146

Chapter 22:   One More Try.................................   153

Chapter 23:   Like a Baby.................................   158

Interlude 4:   *Something to Save.............................*   163

Chapter 24:   Please Send Me Someone

(Anselmo's Song)............................   170

Chapter 25:   Jesus to a Child...............................   176

Chapter 26:   Praying for Time..............................   181

Chapter 27:   Club Tropicana...............................   190

Chapter 28:   Cowboys and Angels.......................   193

Chapter 29:   Heartbeat.....................................   200

Chapter 30:   Patience.......................................   204

Chapter 31:   Move On.......................................   208

Chapter 32:   Soul Free......................................   213

Chapter 33:   Nothing Looks the Same in the Light..   219

Chapter 34:   Happy..   223

Chapter 35:   You Have Been Loved......................   228

Chapter 36:   Do You Really Want To Know............   235

Chapter 37:   If You Were There...........................   241

Chapter 38:   Precious Box..................................   247

Chapter 39:   Cars and Trains.............................   256

Chapter 40:   Battlestations................................   263

Chapter 41:   Star People....................................   273

Chapter 42:   Everything She Wants......................   281

Chapter 43:   Come On!......................................   290

Chapter 44:   Where Did Your Heart Go?...............   301

Chapter 45:   Blue (Armed with Love).....................   310

Chapter 46:   It Doesn't Really Matter....................   319

Chapter 47:   Hand to Mouth...............................   331

Interlude 5:   *The Strangest Thing*.........................   337

Chapter 48:   Look at Your Hands.........................   344

Chapter 49:   Kissing a Fool...............................   353

Interlude 6:   *Understand*.....................................   363

Chapter 50:   A Ray of Sunshine...........................   368

A Last Request (I Want You Sex Part III).................   380

Waiting (Reprise)...   389

Chapter 1:

Father Figure

"I've put money aside for that assisted suicide facility in Switzerland," he said to me matter-of-factly as he drove us through Pattaya. Always the pragmatist, he was sharing his stiff-upper-lip yet intelligent take on one of many aspects of life, business and spirituality that we would discuss, although he was soon to dispute the meaning and fervently refute the use of the word 'spiritual'. He'd call his perspective logical rather than mystical, I would come to see from our ensuing discussions, and he'd not be wrong, but he was pushing away the very side of life that he sought. Practicality and transcendence meet in that place where you don't think but simply do or be, but you also have to embrace the mystery. Doubting dogma is essential but you have to outgrow the rejection, especially as death approaches. Ultimately this happens in truth, which calls for acceptance and surrender.

We'd met only an hour before his revealing statement, in the lobby of the hotel I was staying in with my girlfriend, Resheka, with the two of us having flown into town for the meeting and a weekend in the notorious city of sin. Pattaya, which lies on the coast of the Gulf of Thailand, ninety kilometres east of Bangkok, began as a getaway for the capital's wealthy and evolved into an entertainment mecca famous for its freedom-from-taboo. The three of us had hit it off instantly, as hoped, and were on our way in his SUV to a transformative day and evening together, already making the most of our mutual intrigue for what we knew about each other so far. The topic of death had already come up a few times, as had sex, and our respective testing of the waters had shown that there was nothing to avoid or leave out. We hadn't come this far to hold back either, plus it was neither his nor my style. The two outspoken men had that in common, and a lot more, while Resheka, who was traditionally more reserved, rolled with it silently in the back seat.

I had first heard his name thirty five years before, in my early teens in the mid-eighties, in two British pop music magazines that I lived to receive via sea freight in South Africa a few weeks after issue, and read with far more relish than anything scholastic, absorbing every detail and nuance in my free time. Simon Napier-Bell, manager for Wham!, the man who helped them out of their restrictive record contract naively signed in their teens, and the intrepid and flamboyant character who engineered their historic tour to China that shot them to international stardom. I'd hardly forgotten his name but not heard or used it for decades while he had moved on to managing other artists, authoring a few landmark books about the music industry, and making movies. My friend and fervent supporter across town in Johannesburg, and fellow music fanatic, Amanda, had found herself spurred by George Michael's death in December 2016 to reread her copy of Simon's *I'm Coming to Take You to Lunch: A Fantastic Tale of Boys, Booze and how Wham! were Sold to China (2006)*, and this revisit reminded her of how she found his style reminiscent of mine. And so she sent the book to me to experience for the first time in early 2017.

It helped lift me out of a slump I'd been struggling with for some time, despite writing two or three books a year, by rekindling my flair and enthusiasm for punchy public relations and ballsy storytelling from my entrepreneurial adventures and giving me a taste of going global. It also rewired me to those heady teenage days when Wham! made it big and George Michael leapt into my life as a fantastic star and instant hero five years my senior showing all the talent, courage and confidence I felt inside but needed somewhere to shine. Catholic all-boys high school was not the place, although I gave it a good go there nonetheless. I needed much more, the world stage, and someone from London, where I was born, had shown me how. Simon's book took me back to where it began and, twenty one years into being myself for a living, helped relight my way forward.

I'd then found his profile page on Facebook and shared a moving and insightful post of his that showed how George was an exceptional example of someone being himself for a living, adding for my online friends (and whoever might be reading) that Simon was the kind of collaborator and manager I needed. I also saw on his personal profile that he lived in my beloved Thailand. To my surprise, I woke the next morning to a message from the man himself:

3

Hi Robin. Your concept appeals to me greatly. The problem being, as you obviously know too well, that people have to find out who they are before they can make money from being it. Presumably your seminar helps them with that.

After sharing it with Amanda and calming down (long before she did), and letting Resheka know too, I sent a considered reply:

Hi Simon

Super to get your message. I am delighted to hear that the concept speaks to you. You personify it.

Finding who we are is the core of the issue, the place to start, especially as the world changes so fast. We are being pushed into it and we are choosing it. All my work hinges on it and people tell me that my books inspire and push them to be who they really are. This is the journey we are on as individuals and a species shifting into a new realm. Most challenging and exciting.

I have been doing this since 1996 when I had an epiphany that it was both my calling and the future for humanity. I have developed and built the brand, spread the message, and created tools that implement it for various markets. So there are keynote talks, public seminars, a management consulting product, the INSIGHTS series of books, and more. I have put out six books so far, largely locally, and have another fourteen lined up, if you include the one I am writing at the moment, making twenty in total, ready to go really large around the world. I also wrote my autobiography last year.

There is much to share, like that I first heard your name in 1982 when Wham! broke and I used to get Smash Hits and No.1 magazines two weeks late here in South Africa, like that music is my great love and George has always been an artistic inspiration and long-distance mentor (and doppelganger), like that I fell in love with Thailand seven years ago and am making my way to be based there, like that I have struggled largely alone to get this BEING thing all in place, and like that someone gave me 'I'm coming to take you to lunch...' earlier this year and it reminded of those special '80s days while rekindling my broken enthusiasm for marketing and publicity and gave me a fresh sense of my global plans. I still don't like hangovers, but you helped me appreciate happiness with less regret.

I recently wrote an article for the corporate world about handling crisis using George as a shining example. It's lengthy, so perhaps I should email it to you rather. I am sure it would make him proud, and that his spirit has a hand in us being in touch here.

Look forward to speaking further, Simon.

This was in July. I didn't hear from him again but sent him the article anyway, sensing intuitively that the connection was sound and growing. When Resheka and I set the dates for a five week holiday in Thailand in December, I wrote to him again and he replied, scheduling loosely to meet up in Pattaya if a trip there from Phuket materialised. On the first of January I'd checked in with him again and set up a visit that weekend, assigning the whole Saturday together if all went well. All would go well, I knew.

The scheduled occasion had arrived, the two of us were in his town, and he'd driven across the city and met us in our hotel lobby to break the ice. A warm reception and immediate resonance later and the three of us had jumped into his car for a drive through the central sights for a coffee on the pool deck of the Intercontinental Hotel and then some Thai food out on the south side of the coast, close to his home. I'd paid for the coffee and he'd got the meal. As the title of his book had predicted, he had come to take us to lunch. Life has a wonderful way of working out with aplomb.

Simon was eloquent and outspoken, with plenty to say, probing questions to pose and a propensity to be provocative, especially with a mischievous youngster for company. I played comfortable second fiddle to that, while holding my own kind of dominance through acute hearing, voicing in the gaps and my knowing presence, and Resheka adopted a largely listening position out of respect for what was going down that fateful day. Not shy to speak her mind at the right time, she is also happy to be receptive and reverent. The three of us conversed and absorbed in our respective styles, building the banter based on the bank of topics discussed and insights shared, and having sincere and solid fun. Simon is a wildly worldly man twenty nine and a half years my senior and born six weeks before my father, Frank, who would have been his age had he not died ten years ago. This symbolic synchronicity was not lost on me. They are strikingly different in temperament, though, and a wholesome mix when taken together, which is what I needed at the time. Whereas my dad, a chartered accountant, was cautious, analytical and reserved, and principally illiterate when it came to emotions and entrepreneurship, Simon is creative, artistic, irreverent and fearlessly enterprising. Whereas Frank had worked in an office his whole life and travelled very little, Simon did business and pleasure in one, usually somewhere extravagant or decadent or both over an expensive bottle of wine or three, and still spends half the month away from home. Just before our get together he had been to three countries in two weeks. Frank went to three in his whole life. The two me depicted sides of me.

There had been that implied idea of Simon managing me, from my first sharing of his online post about George Michael through my written message and inherently in my trip to see him, but that was neither my agenda nor his plan. It was just seen as a mutually enriching day together sharing and connecting, "a labour of love" as he put it on New Year's Day, which seemed understandably to have a growing sense of fatherliness from him as it happened. Being gay, or bisexual but mostly gay, he has never had children, which weighs on his mind enough to even have said early on in the hotel lobby that he would do so if he had his life again. His Thai partner, Yo, is thirty two years his junior, so maybe there is a streak of parental affection in there too. They met when Simon was roughly my age now, on New Year's Eve just after the Wham! era ended, and have been together for twenty eight years, which is

7

another indication of the bohemian nature of his orientation. There's much more to life than the nuclear family, although that, too, has its charms, even to the creative types.

As an artist myself, and someone seeking to shift up a level, did I not want Simon's mentorship, help or at least input? Perhaps, even probably. I was, however, already liberated by the break at the end of a challenging year, unattached to outcomes, acting on instinct, following intuition, and going with the flow. I was there for the adventure, connection and certain inspiration, and Resheka was supportively along for the enriching ride. In the sea before we left Phuket she had said that she didn't want to miss it. Who would? It was an opportunity brimming with promise at a turning point in our lives.

Twenty books into my INSIGHTS series, I was ready for a new voice, and she knows a vein of gold when she sees one. I needed a fresh spark to kick-start a fuller fire in being myself for a living, and she is on her version of the same journey. Perhaps Simon was also seeking something special and spirited. It certainly seemed so as we came to know each other. And George? As a fine example of 'my concept', and in absentia, he was palpably present, perhaps arranging if not orchestrating the whole song. Frank, too, had his eye on the numbers and an encouraging hand in the calculated risk.

It all worked well from the start and even better as the hours passed, six and a half of them over the afternoon. At that point

Simon said that needed to attend to some work and Sheke and I needed to rest and refresh, and so we went to our respective residences for a break and a shower with the plan to reconvene in the heart of the city to see it at night have dinner somewhere in well-known Walking Street. That then took us even higher for another four and a half hours to eventually end the intense encounter with Simon summoning a cab in Thai for Sheke and me, and, with a quick goodbye in the gentle midnight rain, hurrying us heartily into the back seat like a scene from Casablanca.

Just before that, between a litre of Italian dry white wine with three perfect pastas and some reserva grappas, we had stumbled upon this book title. With Amanda five hours behind back home intuitively tracking the meeting she had triggered, Simon was prodding and advising me on how to write a market-cracking book following his dipping into the copy of SEXIER INSIGHTS that I had given him earlier. The two of us were like mentors to each other, old friends and brothers. Death and sex were still dancing together in the liberated and lubricated encounter when I responded to one of his incisive chirps with, "Well, death is the ultimate orgasm!"
He leapt on it, saying, "There's the title of your best-seller."

I knew there and then that he was right. I felt the whole book hovering in the ether and begin to descent as we spoke. I could have turned to the keyboard and begun but kept flowing in the conversation. Resheka, who was sitting across the table from the two inspired and mirrored writers jumped up to take photographs of the magic unfolding before her eyes.

9

Interlude 1:

I Know That You Want To

In March of 2017, before I read Simon's Wham! book, I was inspired, with an edge of frustration, to pen a piece for the corporate market that confronted the rampant corruption around the world, offered a solution, and indirectly promoted my management consulting product called 'Fully Booked', which I had been doing valiantly for nearly ten years. The combined transformation and branding tool is a stroke of genius that, I had come to accept, was ahead of its time, despite its simplicity and accessibility. Through it I facilitate a shift in the organisation towards everyone being themselves for a living, and then bring about a book written collectively by key contributors, which becomes a multi-purpose management device and marketing tool. Instead of presenting it as a way of leading the future, as I had been doing for a decade, I positioned as a crisis management device, because it is that too, and because people and organisations usually need desperation to wake up and make sincere change.

I had not written for the South African media for years following eventual disgust at their myopia and disrespect, and wanted to pitch something much higher in the market to take my work to a fitting level. A rush of rage in me produced a powerful burst of saying-it-like-it-is, and I groomed the outcome to perfection so that I could send it to some big players in New York and London. After reading through their extensive submission instructions online, following their arrogant stipulations, and awaiting their reply that never came, I left both cities to their devices and sank into a trusting surrender, albeit disheartened, knowing that the right route for the article would surely emerge at the right time.

A corruption scandal broke in the local news with the chairman in waiting for one of the big finance houses resigning as a result, and I emailed him and the existing incumbent the redemptive piece with my offer to help. No response, of course. Then KPMG South Africa were thrust into the spotlight with global firm-ruining facts, and my predictions in the article became particularly prophetic and personal, since Frank had been a partner there for his whole professional career. I contacted the outgoing senior partner and suggested the solution but he had taken the rap and been completely cut out of proceedings by the global office. When I called the Johannesburg building to get the incoming figure head's contact information, it was a shambles, and so, after much consideration, I let it all go, knowing that they would have to come to me for anything worthwhile to work. The healer has to wait for the patient to be ready. One has to do all one can, though, and then leave it.

When Simon was in touch, I sent him the article, mainly to give him a strategic perspective and show the George Michael connection, but it was also part of the deeper story. In the editing stages of this book I was reminded of the piece and, in time, saw its place in the picture. It was inspired by George, as was my life's work, and it was the first form that this writing took, almost a year before the meeting in Pattaya and I started typing back at the hotel. As has been my style since I started out in 1996, when something doesn't slot into the system I make a way on my own. And so the article is getting published at last, in the place it was meant to be all along. Doing what one knows is true can be a rough ride in this world, but one should patiently persist. It's the entrepreneurial way. Here it is:

Be a Hero: Corporate Crisis Defines Your Brand and Our Future

Think of these three people for a moment: George Michael, Tiger Woods and Oscar Pistorius. Then think of your corporate brand, and think long and hard. Prepare yourself for a pivotal point that is probable. Consider it impending and make sure that you are as ready as you can be, within yourself and your organisation. Do the work now so that a rude awakening works in your favour and doesn't leave you an epic failure.

Think first of George Michael. One of the superstars of the eighties and a mega-talent, he bucked the record company machine in the nineties, fuelled by artistic integrity plus the pain of the loss of his lover, taking on Sony legally and publically, losing the case with costs but winning the battle and changing the musical landscape. He put his name on a new level of global recognition, shifting from pop star to timeless champion of the truth. Not everyone understood, but everyone took note.

Eventually, after years of doubt about his future, he staged a comeback with arguably his finest album, *Older*, fortified by hardship and furthering his place as one of the all-time musical greats. Then, a few years later, he was bust for cruising in a public toilet in Los Angeles, and tossed into the tabloids for potentially embarrassing behaviour while being outed for his long-suspected homosexuality, both at once. How did he handle the catastrophe?

First he phoned his father across the Atlantic and talked through the fear and frenzy, processing the personal aspects of the situation. Then he began to see the lighter and serendipitous sides of it, and by that afternoon was speaking live on CNN about the debacle, tackling the problem head-on, coming clean with a sense of humour and perspective, and turning the tide entirely in his favour. This he did with honesty, courage, aplomb and a spin of mischief, showing that he was happy being himself and taking full responsibility for it. There was no covering up or backing down. This made him a hero.

His genius went beyond the music. His valour and confidence brought benefit to the gay community, awareness to the straight mentality, strength to fellow musicians tied to exploitative contracts, and dignity to every individual on earth who felt they had something to hide. It also brought a resurgence in his career, putting him back at the top of the charts when he released a greatest hits album containing the song "Outside" written to comment on and make fun of the situation that could have brought him down. George showed us all how it's done.

Now think of Tiger Woods. At the height of his golfing career and towering status, his behind-the-scenes lifestyle was thrust into the public eye, thereby showing up his persona. From the resulting scandal he did the opposite of emerge as a hero, choosing to kowtow to the sponsorship and cultural pressures and make a pathetic apology in the obvious hope that he would be forgiven and somehow redeemed. What a waste of opportunity! He could have gone from sporting hero to true timeless legend by being real and daring, telling the world that he is who he is and that he would not be twisting that to fit in. He could have shown us how it's done, too, and done his big bit to liberate humanity from falsity.

If sponsors want to leave, let them reveal their fickleness and fabricated values. They will be back when the tide turns and you can negotiate fees on your terms in multiples of the previous parameters. If society wants to frown upon you, who are you to stand in its way? Lying to be liked and accepted shows no dignity. People need to be presented the right way of being in an upside-down world, and given time to adjust to visionary leadership. You will win them over eventually, or not. Either way, you will stand tall and take the global community somewhere new. This is what is required in our twisted times. We need true heroes to exemplify on the global stage what we all face in our day-to-day lives. This will break new ground and take us up.

Look at how abominably Oscar Pistorius fared at his fateful feat. Factual and legal issues aside, he failed as a human being. He could have come clean for what happened on the tragic night and stood by the truth through whatever consequences came and went. This would have helped his case, but more importantly it would have helped his life and career. More significant still, it would have changed the world for the better. Out of the abundant drama that followed that story, what we are all left with most is how it reflected aspects of each of us in our individual lives. It gave us a chance to face our darkness. Oscar could have been a light.

All of us were affected because the events confronted us with our own projections and unresolved resonances, and the man at the eye of the storm could have stood his ground, led the way into a new understanding of being human, and be writing his book now for a future that sets many of us free. He still has time to do that, in fact. Who knows? The human spirit may yet prevail and triumph. He needs the right advisors and support, and to dig deeply enough to find his inner source of strength, but it can be done. Crisis presents this opportunity and responsibility to each of us.

It applies prominently, too, to big business. Global brands have huge social and evolutionary impact. The three human characters above hold mythical positions in the public eye, which shape and inform the way the rest of us proceed individually and collectively. Arguably even more influential are the commercial personalities and communities that we support and follow every day, which are setting a shamefully poor example. Profits may be up but service levels are disputable, employee wellbeing is unfit, environmental health is worse, and the overall message is that exploitation and corruption pay. Success is reduced to crime without getting caught, and clever branding. There is little if any integrity to be seen on the corporate landscape, not to mention sustainable vision and true leadership. Big brands are too much like Tiger and Oscar and not enough like George, and humanity is suffering. And the time bomb is ticking...

What happens when the banks are shown up for price-fixing, bundling debt and selling it offshore, manipulating the market or collapsing the economy? What happens when cellular service providers with abysmal service are hit with colossal fines and then negotiate reductions with so-called authorities? What happens when the insurance industry gets exposed as essentially a scam or political parties become so blasé that they don't even bother to keep up appearances? What happens when the façades wear thin and the cracks in the masks become chasms? What happens when these factors culminate in the waking up of the public to how phenomenally they are being fooled? When people have nothing to lose, they will withdraw their participation in the processes and walk a new path of awareness.

What happens when your brand is thrown into a crisis for your modus operandi and your entire business model is faced with either extinction or sincere reinvention? Even a cursory glance at the market today would suggest that this probability exists for almost every company. Think it won't happen? Think of Enron and the big five auditing firms suddenly amounting to just four. Think of the financial bailouts of the late 2000s and the colossal slippage in the meaning of money. Then look around you.

Do you cover up and cling to your nefarious ways as long as they hold out, and hope to get off scot-free when it comes to the crunch? Are you rearranging deckchairs on the titanic? It's probably not the best bet. Or have you seen the writing on the wall and found a sincere place to come from in yourself and the people you lead? Are you geared for seismic shifts so that you can make the inevitable work for you on a new level of collective consciousness and enlightened progress? Are you prepared to come clean discerningly and demonstrate the new way to fulfil your social and commercial function? If so, you may be poised to become a true hero in a transforming world. Otherwise you might just be one of the run-of-the-mill villains to sink with the changing tide.

We are all complicit with skeletons in the closet. What's telling is how we handle the disguised blessing when these come out.

Robin Wheeler is a business consultant on transformation and global keynote speaker and author on 'being yourself for a living'.

17

Chapter 2:

Edge of Heaven

The sun had just come up. That's how early we were passing through airport security leaving Phuket on Christmas Day for two nights in Kuala Lumpur. I had placed my hand luggage onto the conveyer belt, emptied my pockets into the plastic tray, heard that my watch and belt could stay in place, and stepped through the scanner-frame towards the hijab-wearing security guard with hand-held metal detector. I heard a beep and raised my arms as non-verbally instructed, as I am usually co-operative with a woman in a position of authoritarian woman, at first anyway. She performed her duty, but, as she did, I began to feel a tingle that was, to be frank, not strictly Halal.

Her instrument was aroused by my big buckle and so I raised my T-shirt to explain it, which met with her approval expressed by placing her index finger on the silver steel and holding it there longer than justifiable by any job description. What was that, I wondered, as she made her way around back and examined me from behind. She ran her fingers over my denim-coated buttocks as if they contained some potential crime, and then seemed to appreciate my hamstrings and calves with an unexpected relish. There's no way I had anything concealed in there but she was making sure nonetheless, while I stood like a smiling scarecrow for a suspended moment, wondering if what was going down was actually happening at 6.30am amidst streams of people in front of a duty-free shop. That ultra-conservative woman just felt me up, I thought, before breakfast, on camera, and unashamedly, while my girlfriend was watching!

With official approval to proceed, I turned to Resheka as she crossed the threshold and confirmed by her laughter that she had seen the whole scene. It was far from a figment of my imagination. What a blatant abuse of temporary authority and exploitation of situational vulnerability! What a revelation of covert carnal activity and repressed sexuality. What a suggestive and unexpected injection of revealing sensuality for my writing, and what a laugh. Death lies mischievously and tantalisingly around every corner and so does sexual mischief. Quite a thrill.

I can't wait to pass through the travel gates of transcendence, in case they have a similar threshold guardian half my age. I cannot contain my excitement for the ultimate trip, although I am in no rush to leave this mortal coil. I still love it here and am lingering in this earthly adventure to delay the crossing over as long as possible so as to enhance it. I am letting life make prolonged love to me in the meantime, which is all foreplay for the actual event.

On the plane I asked two Muslim flight attendants, one from Cairo and the other from Mumbai, for a second plastic cup of wine, specifying that it should be Halal. They both giggled and in seconds I was holding two brimming manifestations of exactly what I requested, apart from the official certification, which was fine because that part was a joke. I was already in heaven anyway. The universe is at our service, even thirty six thousand feet above the ground. The most outwardly obedient are often most disposed to assist us with our rebellious pursuits, and the restrained can be cohorts in setting us free. The wine is always involved one way or another. It's Biblical and, in this instance, I am not disputing the timeworn text. Wine and water make the world go round. Amen in every religious language.

Conservative girls from various repressive religions can be wild. Don't quote me on that, because I could end up in trouble, but never forget it. I have been unable to dispute my findings despite relatively extensive research. You might ask the sofa in my lounge, but all I have to do is walk innocently through an airport at sunrise and I have my personal discoveries confirmed. All I have to do is request a plastic cup of red nectar from people who have never let the liquid near their lips and I have two handfuls handed to me in the stratosphere. All I have to do is smile sweetly with an aura of suggestibility and the galaxy hands me more ecstasy. I call it guiltless liberty. Living, mystical reality.

Back in South Africa I received a link from Simon to an article in the UK's Guardian about death becoming cool. The topic is likely to be on his mind a lot at 78, and it's now on both our minds for this book, along with sex, which is always on everyone's mind. Sex and death. What else is there in this world? The two taboos go together and turn each other on. I suggest that they come together, too. "Most people die thinking about sex," I'd said in Pattaya, and he agreed. Death on his mind is partially why he jumped at the title for this book that night in the city of sin, plus he has a manager's eye for a topic to get people talking around the world. It spoke to him on all of his favourite and pressing levels, and it combined them, too. Erotic and liberating. I got straight to work with bringing you this book.

Who the hell would want to live in Pattaya? It's flat, overdeveloped and exceedingly seedy. "You wouldn't want to come here," he had said forcefully in the car that afternoon. I had not been before yet heard all about it, and those two minor reasons, combined with the primary one of meeting him, were my motivators. Something would have to speak to you to keep you there, though. Something would have to grab you by the soul. By the end of our short trip, something had, and I would certainly go back, despite it being for no discernible reason. Sometimes attraction is subliminal. The way I saw Simon stride down Walking Street that night showed he had it deeply. Having not taken in the strip for a year, he said, he had a spring in his step, a glow on his cheeks, and revived vitality in his stiff upper lip. The bohemian was happy to be out to play. Freedom is priceless when you live by the spirit.

I can relate to that radiance, perhaps in Patong before Pattaya, or Phuket as a whole, since so far that is clearly my happiest place on earth. I am still nearly three decades younger than Simon, and less ready to die from that perspective, but I am also as ready as I can be at this age. It's not just a function of time but of understanding, which comes from experience but mainly from spiritual work. As a result, I am ready to die but, like all of us, full of life as long as I can sustain it. I'm ready to come, ready to go, and ready to let it happen, but I have a few things to say and do before the big day.

More sex is one of them, otherwise I'll have to come back again to get my fill and clear my karma, and that would be tiresome. Yes, more sex, and a lot more books to write, although I must say that the former has less of a hold on me these days. In contrast, I have plenty to write and plenty of places to go, both on the planet and in my internal world. This is all still in the domain of foreplay, although penetration has clearly taken place and the climax is on the horizon. I am nearly fifty, after all. We're all fucking beautifully, with death on our shoulder, and the tension is building here in heaven on earth. The ultimate orgasm is coming for each and all of us. We know it and we are discovering it at the same time. We can't wait to remember it fully and we are enjoying the ride.

That article Simon sent is interesting. People are increasingly using their death as a statement, making it part of their life's work. They are seeing and experiencing the benefits of keeping their energies clean, of doing the work of clearing their lives as they age, of facing each moment in the moment and undertaking an incremental awakening as they travel the sacred arc. This is embracing death as a simple practicality while it remains the ultimate mystery. That's where I step in with this book. The practitioners, businesses and books described in the article, and the writer of it, talk about dying well, which is well and good, but they are all still focused on logistics here on earth and leaving out the ultimate issue. They have their backs turned to death and are looking back on life, still contained in the five-sensory dimension and ignorant of and ignoring the nature of death itself. What is it? Look into it!

It's the need that Simon couldn't find satisfaction for, the one he kept asking me about and rejecting the reply to, at least overtly. I know that he heard what I was saying despite his insistence that 'spirituality' is utter bullshit. To him it was an empty word, like the word 'existential'. I jokingly retorted that spirituality is meaningless until it becomes existential, which is true as well as a bit of banter. He stuck to his guns but I could see that it got through to him, not because of my playful wording or even the correctness of what I said, but because I knew what I was saying and needn't have said it. The truth is not in words but beyond it, and we are all searching for the beyond where there are no words.

What is spirituality? One shouldn't be persuaded by anything but one's own experience, having doubted all the way until there is nothing left to doubt. Simon could see that I knew and that I didn't need to say any more, which bugged him as much as the two words that he disliked in the first place. I didn't take offense at his affront, but then began this book to say what he longed to know before his time comes. This book is a continuation of our conversation on that day in Pattaya, for everyone who reads it.

Although it is not my job to convince anyone of the existential nature of spirituality or that death is the ultimate orgasm, I can open up some insight and perhaps then you can see for yourself. At least you can consider the approaching the inevitable in ways that will prepare you. Let's drink to that.

Chapter 3:

Fastlove

The French call the sexual orgasm 'la petite mort', which translates to 'the little death'. It originates from describing a fainting spell, common in the fifteen hundreds, or a temporary weakening of consciousness, not related to sex, but it came to refer to a similar feeling following coitus, perhaps the extreme afterglow or the deeply relaxed state after intense release. There's more to it, though. Spiritually speaking, the sexual orgasm is the closest most people come, if you'll indulge the wording, to tasting ecstasy or enlightenment. Whatever the French reference, there is great wisdom in the terminology.

The little death can mean the temporary exhausted state post orgasm where we pass out as if dead for a few minutes, which is a superficial understanding, or it can mean the sapping of life force in pursuit of sexual pleasure and the wasting of sacred energy for short-term gain, which is a slightly deeper engagement with the meaning. My two interpretations are deeper still and the message of this book. First, when you come, for those few seconds, your mind stops and you exist in a state of pure being, which is what it is like in a state of meditation or enlightenment. In this way, the orgasm is the portal to a fuller experience available to us all as a permanent way of being. It is the gateway to our true selves and higher consciousness, a quick route to the attainment aimed at by meditation or protracted spiritual discipline. As such, if you like, it is the taste of things to come, the sampling of a much more extensive awareness available to us all and lying ahead on the evolutionary timeline of humanity. Can we live in a state of coming all the time? You may not be convinced, but you must certainly find the concept charming.

Second, going through that orgasmic porthole suggests what it will be like one day to die. Life is a build-up of energies, a friction of tensions reaching in incremental waves for an ultimate outcome. It is a long love-making leading to a release, a final burst of abandoning everything to the eternal moment, and so death is the climax at the end of life like orgasm is at the end of having sex. Everything we are experiencing is leading to that and we should understand what we are doing and prepare ourselves. If we combine these two meanings, then we are heading towards the big gush and can live in a state of constant coming along the way. Needless to say, this is a desirable state to be in. Implicit in the mix, too, and contrary to our closed cultural conditioning, is that death is the opposite of something to fear. Instead of avoiding it, we are secretly or subliminally seeking it out, and this should be brought into the light of awareness. We may enjoy the delayed gratification as long as we can, but it's all part of coming to the pursued point. Death is not a problem but the definitive solution, at the end and all along the way.

It is inevitable and approaching, no matter your age. It is the ultimate experience in that it is final, with no return for us, at least in the form that we now occupy. Who knows anything other than that? It is also the culmination of life, despite certain doctrines and many fears to the contrary, and so it has an eventual quality. Everything is leading up to it, including this. Death is contained in birth, as the latter automatically induces the former, and birth is the direct result of sex, which means that birth, death and sex are inseparable. And the sexual orgasm carries at least three tastes of death, in the conception of it, the access to the transcendent self and the premonition of termination. And so the picture here begins to take shape and we begin to realise that we have known it all along.

Perhaps that accounts for our die-hard attitude, obsession with intercourse, confusion about gender identity, twisted entanglement in taboos, inability to get on, ambitious competitiveness and propensity for violence, our loneliness and hypocrisy, and every other inverted explanation for everything. It's all really simple but we mix and muddle it all up. Sex makes the world go round and we are all dealing with death every day on different levels. However, we are we are lost and ambivalent about it, a bundle of drives, desires, resistance, terror and attachment. Sex and death are in everything from a one-night stand to a lifelong marriage, from a new car to an old house, and from a persona to the spiritual secrets behind it.

Sex and death carry the mysteries we run from and that we pursue, and life is how we both avoid and find the answers.

Perhaps, though, we can overcome ourselves and learn to live the truth. It is straightforward and right in front of us everywhere we turn. One place I found it fully was in the islands of Southeast Asia.

I discovered Thailand and its transformative charms in August 2010, quite unexpectedly, when I went there almost on a whim. I was burnt out beyond belief after fifteen years of artistic entrepreneurship and a string of life events that I had handled as they had happened but not recovered from. My devastating divorce in 2005 following the long and ruthless lead-up to it, the almost sudden death of my father in 2008 after an onslaught of leukaemia and two months of terminal treatment, and the sustained financial struggle that had characterised my creative path had all taken their toll, and I was threadbare, knotted and yet still giving generously as a hopeless coping mechanism. That is an artist's way, his strength turned into his weakness. I was so baked, in fact, that I couldn't even discern it, although my body was making it cuttingly clear by not working very well. Being myself for a living had me by the balls.

At the time I was pushing to put out book three in the INSIGHTS series, editing my ass off under duress and, as a matter of course, writing a subsequent title alongside that, which presented a contrast of pursuits that pulled in diverse directions. Whereas writing is free and creative, editing is restrictive and analytical, yet somehow I was managing to do both simultaneously. As a result, I was feeling like the taught vellum on a tin drum. As cosmic timing would have it, I finished the preparations for the printers on the one book and typed the closing lines of the other on the same day, which was an unprecedented climax that I would need to recover from if I wanted to proceed resourcefully or even retain any semblance of sanity. It was a little death that wasn't so little. Plus there were women involved in the scenario, but let's not venture into that irrational factor. I was fucked, let's just say that.

I knew that I needed a holiday but had no idea where to go. I had returned from nearly a month in Europe the previous summer where I stayed with my sister Heather, her husband and three kids in London and moved on to Paris for ten days with a friend, the managing director of a client, who was from there but based in South Africa. In that short time I had seen a string of concerts by some of the finest musical living legends, including AC/DC at Wembley Stadium, Bruce Springsteen and the E Street Band, Neil Young and the Dave Matthews Band in Hyde Park, Crosby Stills & Nash at the Albert Hall, U2 at Stade de France, and Leonard Cohen at Paris Bercy, and, frankly, I was overfed on busy cities and cultural constructs, as sublime as they were. I had even gone off travelling as a result. And so I wanted to go somewhere I hadn't been before, somewhere distinctly restful and possibly exotic, and somewhere with beaches, clear skies, naked bodies and soaking sunshine. I had no idea where, though, and so I handed it over to the universe to show me the way.

The very day I did that I saw a friend at gym, Eugene, of Asian descent, who, upon hearing about my situation asked, "Have you ever thought of Thailand?" I hadn't. I wasn't even sure exactly where Thailand was, but I did remember an old friend mentioning a decade before that he and his family loved Phuket, and that one of Heather's school friends had spent two years in the country after leaving university. Oh, and I had recently eaten at a Thai restaurant in the north of Johannesburg, which suddenly became serendipitous. Although I had never felt drawn to the East, and always felt intimidated by it, I had just asked the big blue for direction, and did want to branch out. Considering, too, that my buddy at gym couldn't stop raving about the Thai experience, I gave it some thought. Just to make sure that I didn't miss the message, though, the crafty old universe then orchestrated an encounter with two other friends that same day, Arthur and Colleen, a couple, who also responded to my story with a similar question. "What about Thailand?"
"Funny you should ask that..." I said.

They were devotees, too, and invited me for tea that evening to tell me all about the best holidays they have ever had, showing me packaged specials that were well priced and, it seemed, quite priceless. Hesitantly convinced I went to the travel agent the next day and booked a ten day trip to Phuket, stopping in Bangkok on my way back. A week later, with my new book at the printers, I found myself on an impressively new plane with multi-coloured seats, enchanting attendants, exhaustion and excitement in my veins, and the doors closing to herald an unexpected adventure that would not only rekindle my love for travel but change my life.

Four months later I was back in Phuket for a six week stint, which gave me a chance to fall in love with the country, the people and the island even more, to get to know the place well, to settle into some proper yet still insufficient rest, and to begin to re-evaluate my life. Following a spree to Bali to get a renewed immigration stamp for more time in Thailand, I had flown back to South Africa in January to do some talks, pick up on my paperwork, and handle my house. In March 2011, I made my third trip there in eight months, for a scheduled three weeks to set in place my new lifestyle that planned to split my time equally between Phuket and Johannesburg. I was still processing my severe burnout and finding direction and so the first two weeks were over in a flash with me feeling nowhere near ready to go home.

I had an old primary school friend visiting Johannesburg from Australia when I was due back, someone I hadn't seen for decades, who was keen to see me again, plus another friend from Portugal had announced at short notice that she, too, would be in town and eager to catch up. I wanted to be there to see them but my body had other ideas and knew better. I wanted to stay in my happy place, but still agonised over what to do, struggling to put myself first when it was clearly the need and actually the only option. Eventually I spoke to the travel agent I had come to know next door to the small residential hotel I was staying in, and she found that I could cancel the flight back with the ticket remaining valid for three months. That was exactly what I needed to hear and so, with it, my decision was made. Thailand it was, as long as required.

Relief and joy ensued, even with the financial pressure I was under, which validated my acquiescence to greater intelligence. The prospect of the continued rest and re-evaluation that I needed was profound, plus, I was in my beloved second home! I couldn't remember ever having felt sustained joy like that, the relationship heartbreak from back home notwithstanding. I caringly let my female friends from Sydney and Lisbon know my decision, explaining my situation but still bearing the brunt of the former's upset and had the latter not speak to me again since. Still, I knew what I was doing. I settled into sleeping solidly for protracted periods, aided by some tablets I was referred to, sometimes dozing off again in the mornings before I rose to get ready for breakfast, whatever time of day that might have been. I hadn't slumbered like that since I was a teenager and my stressed body welcomed a return to one of its great loves in life. Slowly adulthood and the stresses of entrepreneurship had stripped me of wholesome harmony, and I needed the help of some indefinite solitude in paradise, and a touch of medical science, to get me back to nature.

As I slept and slept, my deepest inner resources restored and slowly I got stronger. I ended up staying on the island six more weeks, making it a total of nine, and found a whole new dimension to my being as I lived increasingly in the moment. Day after day became week after week of waking beautifully in my quiet cocoon of coolness, the air-conditioned room where there was no pressure to do anything but obey biology and listen to the whispering mystery. I could really be myself, stay in tune with my body and soul, and read and write. When I was hungry, the appetite lifted me from the bed and carried me through the shower. I wasn't driven by some external schedule or the workings of my mind, but by my whole being, the intelligence of which was becoming more apparent to me. I slipped on shorts, T-shirt and flip-flops and walked out into the humid heat across to the coffee shop over the road where I sat alone with my phone to enjoy my favourite food and, if inspiration struck, write without disturbance until I was satisfied. Without effort or issue, I was most productive, and then I moved on with my day. Being myself for a living was realising itself. Apart from the occasional administrative task, like paying accounts online, I had practically no stress and became an increasingly open channel for flow. This was true happiness.

I would stroll back up to my room through the scorching sunshine to find that, while I was away, three Nepalese women had swept in, done the little cleaning that was needed, and left a fresh scent with zero maintenance for me to attend to. All I had to do was take the shower mat that was folded over the toilet and place it on the bathroom floor, and shift the fresh towels (sometimes crafted into endearing animal structures like swans and elephants) from the king-size bed onto the dressing table so that I could lie down. I was liberated from all the daily demands of being in and running my house, which provided me with the monastic nirvana my spirit needed. What a soaring spirit it turned out to be, and I hadn't even been to the beach yet.

This freedom with no outer agenda to serve meant that I could attend totally to the inner and open to a new awareness. Never before had I been so in tune with my body and attentive to my inspiration. Can you imagine sinking so deeply into your being? I would just lie there savouring the stillness and rich resourcefulness. No thinking was needed and no self existed. Being prevailed. I could follow my feelings uninhibited and go out into the holiday action whenever I felt ready and inspired to, which was usually later in the afternoon when the sun began to soften, and sometimes before that, based on the weather and my spontaneity. I would get onto my rented scooter and ride around town or further afield to bays and beaches north and south on the island. When I found a spot I felt like being in, I would stride the hot sand for a few kilometres, sweating myself further into satori, starting by watching people but drifting in attention more towards the infinite sea. By the end of my walk I was one with the setting sun. This was real wealth as it was intended.

As the sun headed for the horizon, I'd arrive back at my bike, change into swimming trunks street-side wrapped in my hotel towel, lock everything in the compartment under the saddle (although security was unnecessary in the safe environment), stack my sandy sandals on the footrests, tie the ignition key to the drawstring in my shorts, float footloose across the sand, wade into the warm water, and swim out into the vast ocean for an hour or two in sweet and salty solitude. Lying back in the womb-like water I would watch my mind rush around at first, slow down in due course, and then subside, sometimes completely, while the sky turned cinematically to starlit black. It started on the shore side, which became a silhouette of structures and human activity twinkling against a backdrop of deep blue, which then became lighter as you looked higher into the heavenly dome. Some evenings it even turned green at its zenith before shifting into yellow, orange and then deep red on the other horizon out to sea where the roaring orb slipped out of sight at perceptible speed, giving an orgasmic shimmer as it died just so that it could do it all over again the following day. In its afterglow there could be squirts of cloud and galaxies of colour, and sometimes even rain to celebrate the exhilarating hush. When I was ready I would emerge from the water in silence, skipping like an ecstatic child reborn, towel my tingling skin in streetlight delight, get dressed into my dry clothes, coat my exposed limbs in citronella-scented insect repellent, clip my helmet onto my head, ignite the bike, and then spin back into the streaming currents of humanity.

Dinner was pure divinity with my feet in the sand and my gaze into the Andaman Sea with which I still felt an oceanic affinity. Perhaps a stroll around the buzzing city might have felt right after that, or my retirement to my secluded room might have come early. Either way I arrived back feeling fully alive and that, without doing anything specific, I had truly lived that day. Raw and in the elements, heart unwrapped and vision unimpeded, and with another similar odyssey to look forward to in the morning, starting with an English breakfast, custard cream pastry and cappuccino or two, I would sink into those crisp sheets and swim into the folds of the tender night.

Chapter 4:

Outside

"Would you like another beer," she asked.

"I've already had two, Nicole," I replied with a fitting glimmer, "and if I have any more I'll end up staying here all night and seducing the rest your waitresses."

"That's good, I'm sure they'll love that," she laughed over her shoulder as she walked away, towing behind her a slow-motion train of brunette beauty.

I was sitting in the shade on a bench in the gardens of a burger joint in my hometown, Bedfordview, on a sunny summer afternoon in South Africa. The waitresses were all less than half my age and Nicole didn't seem to be kidding, which lifted my spirits even further than their beer-based buoyancy. It was affirming and fun and entirely in keeping with the conduct of the few beautiful women who had been gracing my table, in my head anyway. Like in Phuket, these girls know how to push up their bottom line. The burger joint brings a life-filled feeling tinged with that familiar tingle of Thailand. A middle-aged man needs it. We should all be living this way.

I didn't have another beer but I did justify the two I enjoyed with a soft flood of inspired writing. Alcohol definitely helps that along, although it's not essential. Simon would agree to the point of perhaps disputing the second half, having said with certainty that all cultures that have led civilisation in human history did so with the assistance of 'wine' in one or other form. It is certainly in the spirit of the drug to bring out the less repressed sides of our soul. He's been a keen and outspoken imbiber his whole life and always woven the associated benefits into his professional dealings to notable and reputable effect.

There has never been a distinction between business and pleasure for him, and discerning drinking in more than moderate volumes at all hours of the night has consistently been interwoven with his inventive methods and outcomes. A rare and expensive bottle or two over lunch with journalists has paid for many a cover story that money simply could not buy. A flask of whisky or grappa after dinner has blurred all the barriers needed to think and act laterally when devising and driving through a creative plan. As he describes in his book about the history of the British music industry, *Black Vinyl White Powder (2002)*, in the early days of Swinging London the best ideas came and the best deals were struck in nightclubs at three in the morning. Boardrooms are more than boring in any business.

With that in mind, later in the week, I am having a glass of Sauvignon Blanc with lunch, with no plans to limit myself to that. The young waitresses aren't here today, because I am in another restaurant, but I still feel fine. The souvlakia are sublime, marinated in lemon juice, grilled to Hellenic excellence and further flavoured with a fresh wedge of the healing citrus. The rocket and parmesan salad is a fitting accompaniment, dressed delicately with extra virgin olive oil made in Kalamata, using no biotechnology, according to the angular bottle. The splash of balsamic vinegar made from Greek grapes is also out of an imported flask from the same region. These components are proper, part of living life to the discerning full, which is an acquired taste and fine art.

To die well one must live well, since one dies as one has lived. This is a moment-by-moment enjoyment of all that living has to offer until the final moment when and where it all comes together in what may well not be end. Death is the finest lunch and ultimate last supper defined by every meal along the way to that culminating day, and then we shall see. Savour it all, I say, and then some. Aristotle was no fool when he went to his death with relish.

Another article about dying peacefully crossed my path today, via social media this time, so I read it and then sent it on to Simon. It was clearly part of the picture of this book coming together, sending me into a deeper sense of what I will be writing about and, somewhat disconcertingly, into reflections about my own departure. It precipitated some of the vaporous insights I've had about dying over the years and galvanised my experience into topics to cover as we go. Although I intend to live way past Simon's current age, I am well into the time of life where the considerations are practical and increasingly front of mind. Plus, it's prudent to be prepared for death at any age because it can happen anytime. Death-awareness should be part of any generation's consciousness, wastages of youth notwithstanding. And so I further embraced the task at hand of writing well, and the seized opportunity to face in myself all I can at this stage as part of living a long and fulfilling life.

I must mention at this point that I am happy with the one glass of chilled white wine today as a moderate companion for the clean and crispy food. I shall, however, be rounding things off with a strong, black coffee, an Americano, and an ouzo, possibly a double, to go with the longer after-meal digestive. The coffee and the spirit alcohol both settle the stomach following a meal, the former essentially a long form of a double espresso and the latter expanded to accompany the dark and steaming liquid. Americano is made by forcing hot water under pressure through two servings of finely ground coffee to make a drink with a kick and a crema (the beige foam that you get with a well-made espresso). Purists would have it unsweetened but I like some sugar with mine, as I have a sweet tooth and tend to put (informed) personal taste above purism. I don't mind bending the rules to suit my palate, as long as I am not ignorant, which I almost always am to some degree. There is always more to learn, which is part of the discerning pleasure.

I have taught myself most of these things by paying attention to people in the know and reading up wherever possible. Having an English heritage, I've felt deprived of a taste for food the way it occupies centre stage in, say, Italian, other Mediterranean and Indian culture, and so I have communed with Italians, Greeks, Indians and more, imbibed their traditions and ancient wisdoms, and made those mine while showing them due respect. This is how I have come to live a more refined life and share in such pleasures with someone like Simon, who has done the same in the extreme. It makes life so much richer and death so much more delightful to accept when it comes, which brings me back to sipping on my sweet coffee and aniseed firewater.

The one manager in the restaurant, Chris, who is Greek, like the brand, mentioned earlier, in response to my comments on the origins and quality of the olive oil and balsamic vinegar, that he had read on the ouzo bottles that the right to use the name 'ouzo' is legally reserved for products from one specific region. I reflected that it is the same as champagne coming from that unique area in France, or cognac made from the district-specific grapes. We conferred and laughed at my joke that "cheap shit" from anywhere else has to be labelled as such. Sparkling wine, darling. These are the joys of proper living and fine dying.

Another manager, Vasili, or Basil to the South African palate, clearly also of immediate Greek descent, had passed my table towards the beginning of my meal and I had told him straight-faced that I was doing well while writing another multi-million selling book which would buy me an island in the Mediterranean that he will be welcome to visit. I added that I would send my helicopter to fetch him, and he hurried me humorously to get back to my writing. A little later he checked in again and I notified him in spiralling spirits that we were onto two islands, a few yachts on the horizon, and the renaming of the Aegean Sea after us.

"In other words," I said, "the writing is going well." Clearly, too, the wine was emancipating the Spartan in me.

"Glad to hear it!" he encouraged in the same adolescent vein. Youthful exuberance is usually a refreshing turn-on, whatever your age. Dreaming and playing are good for you, especially when you really mean them (in a detached way, of course).

One of the arguments in that article about being able to die peacefully was that people resist dying when they feel that they have not fully lived. This is a primary point in my view. We do not know how to live and, as a result, we do not know how to die. We avoid life all along, taking it for granted, resenting its challenges, or delaying gratification indefinitely, and get by in a substitute compromise, only to look around one day and find ourselves in a mountain of regret and resistance. How can it be time to go when we have barely begun and have so much still to do? How can we say goodbye when we have hardly said hello? Then we fight and miss out on the biggest opportunity of all, like we have missed out all along. This is a tragically common story.

The antidote is to live rightly every blessed moment, whether pleasurable or painful. The cure is to open to the now with all we have and embrace death every step of the way as part of the trip. There is a taste of the ultimate in every mouthful of food, a tingle of termination in every kiss, and a potent prayer in each sacred

41

breath. In and out, up and down, life and death, all the time. Eternity is transpiring here now and we are living it. Death is not separate from life but integral to it. Enjoy that and you will be exceptionally well, now and always, including on the occasion when you officially snuff it. Kicking the bucket is just another clang on the path of perfection.

Death is in a decent coffee, an appropriate accompaniment, and a suitable serenity. Death is in celebrating the day like it is your last while you intend for the longest run of fine food and drink and abundant book writing known to humankind. Death is in the lifestyle you have created and claimed for yourself and the price you have paid for this freedom. Death is in indulging in the presence of some young waitresses in full awareness of your advancing age and compensatory tendencies. Death is in staying forever young as you age gracefully, in keeping your life simple and soulful while you embrace global fame and fortune, and in remaining wild and playful as you face the responsibilities of adulthood. Death is in ensuring that your worldly affairs are in order so that you can cross into the transcendent anytime, and staying footloose and fancy-free so that you fill the sky while never leaving the ground. Death is in knowing how to really live because, effectively, you are already gone.

I am at home now at dusk with a compilation playing of some choice and sequenced songs I put together a few years ago like I have been doing for myself and friends since I was a teenager. These collections provide for the most satisfying listening I know of and make up most of my sonic pleasures these days. Amanda and Resheka both have their respective and growing collections. In the fridge awaiting my pink lips and tingling tongue is a bottle of local dry rosé, from the same farm in the fairest Cape as the white wine earlier, while a deboned chicken smothered in chili rub is in the oven ahead of the second half of its preparation outside on the open gas grill. There are also some cheap peanuts in the kitchen to snack on and provide a base for the wine while the steaming feast takes shape.

My intention for tonight is to enjoy all of these delights in the still and sweltering heat as I keep writing. Death is in following the inspiration when it makes itself known, and applying one's best effort to making a meal of it, whatever time of day that might occur. Writing is an indescribable joy, a moral duty and the closest you can get to an orgasm without directly involving your genitalia or leaving your physical form. What a way to make a contribution and a living! It beats working in a bank or on a building site, for me anyway.

That article, which is by Karen Wyatt, 'a hospice physician, death awareness advocate and spiritual seeker who loves to help people live fully and fearlessly', entitled "Why Some People Don't Die in Peace" (from Huffington Post online, 8 January 2018) lists that the causes are that people haven't thought about the end of life, haven't put their wishes in writing, haven't talked to their loved ones about their preferences, have been unhappy all of their lives, are holding on to old regrets and resentments, feel entitled to a different outcome, and rely on the medical system to make choices for them. This is classic death-avoidance stuff and an inventory of symptoms of a western culture that has people existing largely in a state of denial and illusion. (How else would you get them to follow religion, vote for a crooked system, work for corporations and go into debt to buy things they don't need?) Karen's corresponding register of recommendations is that we face the reality of impending death, get the related paperwork done, tell loved-ones what we want to happen post mortem, learn to live happily, clear our emotional decks, think about the reality of death more often, take responsibility for our lives and medical decisions, and, in summary, do the inner and outer work, starting immediately.

These are all sound suggestions, some of them more profound and others mundane. They certainly had me thinking, planning and organising, but they didn't change my life. There was still the essential element missing, which is what happens during and after death. That's what further validates the need for this mischievously sincere book. I'm happier than ever to be writing it.

Chapter 5:

An Easier Affair

Death becomes difficult when we are weighed down by stuff, whether it is material or psychological. Possessions, baggage and identifications cushion us from life and leave us surrounded by substitutes, which are difficult to let go or get rid of. They also make us ungrateful. The richer we are materially, the less we tend to appreciate our being, and it often takes the loss of everything or at least something priceless to put us back in touch with who we are and what matters. This in itself is a kind of death that forces us to forfeit what's fake and face what's real. It can feel like the end of the world, which it is in a way, but it brings with it a rebirth and a whole new lease of life. It brings a new world, wiping the slate clean and restoring perspective, which is what physical death does too on a larger scale.

We can cultivate this experience and resulting awareness by being mindful of what matters most, maintaining minimalism in our living, and staying conscious that we are going to die one day soon. In fact, we are dying all the time, as a continuous process of being alive as well as in recursive cycles ranging from going to sleep at night to shifting through formative and developmental stages as we grow and age. We are being born and dying all the time and it's no big thing. We have done it many times on many levels, whether you regard reincarnation as relevant or not. And so we understand it well and know what we are doing, even though we have forgotten and still live in denial and dread. There really is nothing to fear, however. How can there be? This is the way it is! Fear is a fraction of life, far from the overriding factor. Life contains fear and can be trusted, where fear can be surrendered and knowing restored.

Fear is automatically reduced when our affairs are in order and we have less to cling to. Fear subsides when we are grateful for what we have. Fear becomes meaningless when we are in tune with our vitality, living rightly and embracing death consciously. We are a flood of love, a life-long orgasm building steadily for the ultimate experience and, at the same time, steadily slowing and calming down. Yes, we have animal instincts, like to protect ourselves from pain and harm, run from danger or fight with it, procreate and assert the will to live, but purity is more powerful and it is pulling us towards it like a dwell point back where we come from. Most of what manifests is us as fear is psychological and implanted, when deeper down we are heading home with the great gift of life gushing through our sacred veins.

What makes living well more likely is repeatedly shedding the weight that keeps us from clarity, light-heartedness, sure-footedness, spontaneity, playfulness and well-ventilated trust. When we do this as a matter of course as we age, and at particular stages when it becomes obviously needed and pressing, we keep pace with life and its evolving priorities, and find ourselves seldom straying from the core that we should keep close to. We stay in tune with ourselves and able to hear our inner knowing, listen to our hearts, follow our truth, act in flow and understanding, employ our minds to serve our greater intelligence instead of getting lost in them, positively affect others, and be happy.

There's a famous story of Alexander the Great returning home from conquering the known world and having a transformative and telling encounter with Diogenes, a Greek contrary and mystic who lived naked by the river with no possessions. Alexander remembered that along the way on his brutal and bombastic mission he had been advised to gather himself a wise man of this kind, and so he sent his soldiers out to source and apprehend one.

They returned empty handed, though, bearing only stories of their unusual experience trying to talk this well-known, eccentric, highly compelling but uncontainable find into joining them. They had instructed Diogenes that Alexander the Great had called for him but received the irreverent reply that any man who calls himself great cannot be so. When Alexander was told this, and that the defiant deviant had refused to accompany them, he asked the soldiers why they had not just seized the man as instructed, and they explained that a strange sense of peaceful admiration had overcome them in the presence of such magnificent beauty, and that they were unable to exercise their usual violence.

In an unheard-of move, the conqueror himself went to the scene, with sword sheathed and interest more than piqued, to see this strange sight that he was hearing of, and to persuade the mystic through whatever means necessary. When he arrived, though, he too felt the energy and saw the regal authority of this unique being who hadn't a care in the world. Alexander told him that he had come to take him back home and offered anything from his great wealth in return. Diogenes said as he lay naked that all he wanted was for Alexander to step out of the sunshine that he was blocking.

The warlord was shocked to see such insolence and threatened to chop off Diogenes' head right there, to which the mystic laughed saying that he, like the perpetrator, would just watch it roll onto the sand. Overcome with admiration, Alexander realised and declared that you can't control someone who does not fear death. Diogenes used to have just a begging bowl but he had thrown even that away when he had seen a dog bounding down by the water happier than he was with less than he had. He had died to everything worldly while still alive, and had no respect for status or social authority. He was free. Alexander, on the other hand, was quite the opposite.

The not-so-great sword-bearer was amazed by this enlightened and said that in his next life he wanted to be like Diogenes, but the mystic asked him which next life this would be and told him to drop his pursuits and join him right there and then on the sand in the sunshine, and take the only certain opportunity he had. Alexander declined, left the scene, and then died on his way home, never making it back and never taking the step to be like the free spirit he had been gifted to see. His parting gesture was to instruct his aides have his arms hang out on his funeral pyre to show the world that Alexander the Great had died empty-handed. This was his final statement.

He knew what to do but didn't live by it. His ego was too consuming, his attachments were too great, and he thought that he could put things off. How many of us are the same? How much are we forfeiting in our misguided pursuits?

Interlude 2:

I'm Your Man

I've just remembered that there is another piece of writing I did about George, this time about the trip I took to see him live in London. It forms part of HIGHER INSIGHTS, book twenty in the INSIGHTS series, which took form in mid-to-late 2017 between connecting with Simon online and flying to Thailand with Resheka. One of our resistances to dying comes from not having lived, and this INSIGHT shares how to make sure that we don't suffer too much from that affliction. It's amazing how the story of our life's work is always coming together, even before we are aware of it.

Manifestations

In early 2006, the first band I was in fell apart. I had hung on as long as possible, which was much longer than might have been advisable, but that's me. First, I was attached to it, fully invested, heart and soul. Second, I don't give up on spirited things. And, third, when I do have to let go, I need to know that it is absolutely the right thing to do. For that I need impeccability on my part. I may seem like a mad fool, but there is method behind it. I need to give it my all, make sure, and get it all out of my system. So I tried everything to keep that crew of clowns together, but their prima-donna preferences put an end to it. Finally, I was ready to move on. We had done well for a first effort with five notable recordings and the same number of live shows, which gave me a base as a musician, band member and drummer.

Not long after the last straw fell to the studio floor, one of the singer's friends, whom I had met on the live music circuit, a guitarist, invited me to casually "jam with a few people" one Saturday afternoon. I didn't even have my own drums yet, but there was a kit in the practice room, and so I arrived on the day open and mildly enthused, if a little cautious and jaded. The new singer turned out to be a fine songwriter with a handful or two of roughly formed compositions to try out. The bass player, a woman ten years younger than me, had a striking backing voice and a talent for song writing too. Unexpectedly, I was part of a strong mix.

Settled behind our instruments, we listened to one piece on vocal and guitar and began to pick up our respective parts. Two or three runs-through and we were already sounding like something, something notable and exciting. By the end of the day, I knew that magic had happened in that room and that I was into a new surge of creative and productive energy with a talented and committed bunch of collaborators. The bass player had to have her scheduled wedding and go on honeymoon, but she would be back, and so the other three of us played with two sit-in musicians for a couple of months fleshing out the songs and developing the sound. When our fourth element returned, she slotted straight in and we took right off, playing our first show in the middle of that year and getting signed after our third gig just two months later.

Immediately we were opening for some of the country's biggest bands, doing short and thrilling sets in front of significant crowds and working hard behind the scenes to be our best. My drumming leapt forward with my application of self to the challenging opportunity and fuelled by my love of the music and the thrill of a dream coming true. I was thirty eight years old going on nineteen, a grown up entrepreneur of ten years, an author for six of those, and a kid all over again. Being myself for a living had a new lease of life. Being in a band took me to the next level, and manifestation had me in its rhythmic grip.

The rise of our yet-to-be-named four-piece phenomenon happened heartily from a strong communal base of friends loving the music and supporting the shows, and it quickly reached the broader public too. The end of the year rushed up in a heady haze of late nights in a range of venues across town and a soaring, melodic indie-rock sound, festive in its sincerity and rapturous reception. Along for the ride but taking a bit of a back seat was my writing, which was in swing again after my divorce, plus my corporate speaking and training, which had more of a rock 'n' roll feel to them than ever.

Outside of these activities was my personal enjoyment of music, wall-to-wall in the unfolding of my ideal life. Woven into that, with the twenty fifth anniversary of the release of Wham!'s first single, George Michael had surprised the world with the announcement of a tour starting in Spain in September, covering Europe for three months, and climaxing with four closing shows at Wembley Arena in London the week before Christmas. He had not toured for eighteen years amidst alternating doubt and confidence about his future typified by outspoken withdrawal from the industry and then comebacks that surpassed his previous peaks. Here he was, playing live again, like never before. I simply had to see him despite my frustrating isolation on the southern tip of Africa.

My sister and her family were living in London and so I looked into visiting them while I attempted to buy tickets online for at least one of the special shows. That pursuit proved seemingly futile as prized positions in the venue were snapped up in no time while flights in peak season were prohibitively expensive, plus my brother-in-law's parents were scheduled to stay in the guest bedroom for the holiday season. I had been to see Bruce Springsteen four years before, flying to London without a concert ticket, haggling at the door on the night to buy one from a tout, ultimately getting in to the show, and writing my book *Hunting Power (2003)* about the life-affirming jaunt. And so, doing something similar for George Michael did occur to me, but I was so absorbed in making music of my own that the longing hovered on the outskirts of my rich consciousness that was welling from within. I did track the tour dates, though, watching the set lists as they arose, but only from the distance of resignation to my mixed fortunes. It seemed that the price to pay form my fulfilment behind the drum kit was to sit out the George Michael experience, for the time being anyway. Maybe he would tour again.

My dear friend and musical brother, Paul, also living in London, had secured tickets for the first of the four nights at Wembley, on the day that they went on sale, much to my envy, but this too had faded in my mind as the summer months down south wore on and the band and I beat our way around our gold mining metropolis at breakneck speed. On the Monday night of 11 December, though, I was sitting quietly at home in my apartment, a long way away in thought from Wembley Arena, when a text-message ping on my phone raised no suspicion at first but tugged at my intuition as I made my way across the room to read it. It was from London and, in Paul's customary style, had a huge impact through minimal wording. 'Here we go...' it simply said.

In that instant I was electrified into full engagement. My spirit was suddenly in the cavernous room as the lights went down and the legend took the stage in the city where both he and I were born. The possibility of my body being there too burst out of the deep blue into my remote location, and I scrambled to see what was happening online. Unbelievably, tickets had become available for the following night's show, seemingly held back and then released for sale at the last minute. And they were at the original price! Luckily I hadn't paid three times that on unofficial sites during my investigation phase months before. Flights were also suddenly available, those too at bottom-of-the-range fares. This was incredible. A gap was opening up in the week of the events...

I spoke to Heather, who said that her au pair was scheduled to go home to Poland for Christmas, which freed up a room in the house form me. "Come!" she said in excitement. "We'll make it work."
I slotted straight into gear. Concert tickets were not on sale for the later shows in the week but I figured that they might be made available closer to the time. I was right. As the days passed, they came up. Also, an extra date had been added on the Sunday night, which was feasible for me since my final commitment for the year with the band was on the Friday. I could fly on Saturday and land just in time to make it. It was tight but attainable.

With George's recent album *Patience* playing on repeat and the framed poster of the cover watching me from my wall, I monitored the online sales and tried repeatedly to buy three tickets as soon as they went up, with no luck. In the song "Flawless", he kept singing that maybe he would see me that night, repeating that it I had to go to the city. Maybe? Hopefully! There was no point waiting and I was working on it.

I dropped my online application to a single seat on the Sunday and one became available. I made my move and secured it. I was in! Ten minutes later I slotted a second for Heather, a couple of rows back, and twenty minutes after that I wrapped up a third for her husband, Jason. *We* were in. Next was my flight, which, without issue, joined the list of confirmation emails. With that, my wind-down week took off in the most thrilling direction.

Adrenaline and sleep deprivation had me on a high, enhanced by a year-end show that blew the roof off the local venue where we had played our first gig six months before. The next day I packed my winter clothes for a month away, locked my apartment, tied up a phenomenal year with the tail of a comet, and was taken to the airport by my loving and patient father (for whom, it would turn out, it was the second last festive season on earth). As I checked in with him by my side, I noticed that the departure time was three hours later than scheduled. Once I was through customs, I established that both the flights on my airline that night were delayed, which meant a stretching of my anticipation before getting off the ground and on my way.

While I waited, the delay was extended and the later flight even cancelled. If I had been on that one, I would have been shunted to the next night and not have made it to London for the concert. This was turning out to be most intense. Tired beyond belief, I eventually boarded the plane in the early hours of the morning and sat upright for half a day until we landed at lunchtime instead of before breakfast. I took the tube from Heathrow to Wimbledon, met Heather at the station, saw the kids quickly, put my bags in my new room, showered and dressed, and set out for the show.

We drove through the city streets, found parking at the venue and queued to convert the email print-outs of tickets to the real thing.

As we received those, I looked at the seating plan, which suggested that they were some of the finest in the house. Could they actually be that good? I didn't give it much thought but we would soon see. The three of us made our way up the stairs and into the buzzing arena, finding our respective spots not next to each other but close enough to communicate. I was right on the railing of the first tier straight up from the phenomenal and by now famous stage, with Heather beaming behind me and Jason smiling a few rows back. And, yes, the seats were in prime position, clearly kept for VIPs and released at the last minute. What a place to find myself. What a moment to be in. What a culmination of effort, opportunity and seized good fortune. What a manifestation.

I had been a fan of George Michael since I was thirteen, if not of all the music then certainly of his genius and career. I had travelled all the way through it with him from the first song to the quarter century celebration. I had seen and shared the ups and downs, been inspired and mentored, and felt concerned and supportive through the twists and turns, as had millions around the world and thousands in the room that night. I had made it all the way from my bedroom in early high school through my climactic week with the band to the city of my birth, and there I was looking at the big black cloth draped like a velvet void in the sizzling crowd over the soon-to-be well-let centre spot. I was encrusted by exhaustion, cresting on cumulative experience, and liberated by pure presence. It was tough to tell pleasure from pain.

Immune to my state but speaking straight to it, the lights went down and the stage lit up. The people went crazy, my heart pounded, and the show began with an acoustic song from George's second solo record, *Listen Without Prejudice Vol 1*, from 1990. It was the album's closer, now opening the historic evening, "Waiting (Reprise)", sung from backstage. There was still no sign of the star but as the song ended the door in the middle of the stunning stage opened and George Michael walked out into the frenzy of love. "Good evening, London!" a most familiar voice said to us all as the next song started, the one I had heard on repeat in my lounge only days before telling me to go to the city. This time I was there, in the room, not maybe tonight, but definitely, and about to hit an all-time high.

Song by magical song I disappeared into that mystical night. My tensions fell off me like dry mud, helped along by plastic cups of strong beer and increasingly uninhibited and ecstatic dancing until I was clapping like carefree toddler under a Christmas tree. Poignant moments punctuated the timeless proceedings leading into colourful flares of escalating festivity with out-of-this-world visuals and sublime sound increasing in volume and vitality until there was nothing left but the totality of the occasion.

One of the musical highlights ever for me, the break into the last verse of "Fastlove", came to pass and took me over the top. Two hours and a lifetime of music later, just before the end of the show, George apologised self-deprecatingly for playing it, adding that he simply had to, and then launched into the only performance on the tour of "Last Christmas" with snowy scenes on stage one week ahead of that particular Christmas in the singular city.

By then I was a bundle of bliss. I had never known such joy, love and communion. My whole life had led me to transcendence.

Manifestations exceed all expectations.

Chapter 6:

To Be Forgiven

The two biggest social taboos today still are sex and death. There they are together again! Even though sexual liberation has swept the planet in the last few decades, the sense of sinfulness instilled by church and religion across all persuasions over the centuries runs deep in all of us, wherever we are from geographically and culturally. While we may be making love with all our hearts, and enjoying the pleasure, intimacy and health benefits, we still feel somewhere that we are doing something wrong. And, thus, we love with guilt, ambivalence and repressed rage.

This is the real sin! Who the hell implanted this rot? Who separated us from ourselves and severed us from nature, and why? Corrupt people with nefarious intent, that's who. With our consent, I might add. And so sex and sin are seen as synonymous, overtly and on an insidious subliminal level, death is out of bounds, and we cannot safely discuss or relish the most natural and spiritual experiences in the world. Equally, or perhaps more so, we cannot embrace death as the primary agent of enlightenment. Awakening is kept away.

People in political, economic and structural power do not want individual or broad-based enlightenment. Anything that allows or promotes it will be condemned and, as much as possible, crushed by the system. Far more important to the politicians of all kinds is that we are distracted to devote all of our inner and outer resources to discussing their distorted agendas so that they can continue with their power mongering and profitable pursuits. They want us severed from our roots and absorbed by their deceptive deeds. Awakened and empowered people will see through the charade and have nothing to do with it, enjoying a life of freedom and co-creating a world of wellness and enhanced wonder. Those hungry for position will be put into mental health institutions to be rehabilitated, not voted into states of tyranny.

Taboos indicate covert control. Rules benefit rulers. Freedom is in the hearts and hands of individuals, not the collective. There is actually no such thing as society. It is an assumed structure but one unidentifiable when searched for. The harder you scrutinise, the less you will find it. Individuality, on the other hand, or subjectivity, is real, and it's the only reference point we all actually have. True power is in this understanding. With it comes liberty from conditioning, corruption and control. With it there is an almost total release from the clutches of fear and the return in all of us to the ability to live fully and in the moment. This is our true nature. It means freedom from the mind, and residence in the whole being, thriving in peaceful, co-creative harmony with all existence. In it there can be no taboos. Sex and death live happily together, in the individual and the resulting collective.

Karma, despite popular belief, is instantaneous. It is not carried over time, as is assumed or corruptly presented, nor does it accumulate. In the mind, maybe, but that is memory not reality. There is no time. Everything is existential. Karma is about consciousness and that is entirely in the present. If the notion brings of it anxiety, it is not genuine. The real deal is self-contained. You do something wrong, you know it and suffer there and then. That's what makes it 'wrong' and that is your guide to go right. You do something right and the same confirmation applies. Do more of this. Wrong and right are simply synonyms for unconscious and conscious. Karma makes you conscious by showing you how to live rightly, in alignment and harmony with yourself and the whole. Presence is the door unlocked and opened and the fully conscious moment alive and well. This is death and life combined into an organic wellness, not turned into abstract linearity. This is completeness and joy, love and the absence of fear. This is the new humanity into which we are currently transforming.

Sin is a scam. How can we sin? It's absurd. We can go against God, if we consider the premise of there being one, but that returns us to the idea of separation, of asserting a self independently of the whole and, thus, by our own hand, being cast from the Garden of Eden. This again is just karma in action, the immediate induction of suffering and the instantaneous realisation that it is a sign for us to return to harmony. Sin, therefore, is simply a loss of awareness and alignment, a leaving of the moment into the hell of illusion, or going from rooted being to dominant thinking. We need simply to shift back. 'Entering the Kingdom of God' means restoring our consciousness to an integrated presence, and rediscovering 'eternal life' in the only time there is, the now, having sampled the relative experience of leaving it, albeit only in illusory form. Enlightenment is a return to the natural and the now and being ourselves.

Freedom, then, is a relative experience of our true nature in contrast with our false sense of who we thought we were. It's a homecoming, an orgasmic restoration and, in that, of course, a death.

When I was in Grade 1 in 1975 my new school held a fete for which the classrooms were turned into stalls and mini entertainment areas featuring largely handmade products like paper puppets, painted dolls, wool crochet toilet-roll holders, and garagey toys for boys. On the one little desk (more or less where I normally sat facing the blackboard with a chair bag full of books hung over the back of my seat) was a contraption that caught my attention. Functioning as a competition with a small prize, it was someone's homemade test of concentration comprising a flat plank of wood as a base with a piece of coat hanger wire moulded into a rollercoaster-like shape and mounted on it, beginning on one side and ending on the other. This was connected up to a battery and a buzzer and linked, which lined it into a circuit with a loose handle that had a wire loop at the tip that encircled the twisted strip of modified coat hanger. The result was an electric challenge of getting the little loop from the source to the destination without touching the wire and setting off that pesky alarm.

Boys and men were beguiled but no-one could complete task. Some made it respectably far down the snaking way, with an invested audience looking on, but that brutal buzzer broke them eventually. One lad, a year my senior, took on the challenge and made it, not without serious sweat beads forming on his forehead and a few intensely shaky moments on the ruthless twists. He went on to be Head Boy five years later, which might have been related. The image of him concentrating, and the insight from the exercise have stayed with me, with the latter making for a meaningful metaphor dozens of years later.

Staying in the moment is similar to navigating that simple obstacle course, except that it's about presence and not concentration. The two are contrasting existential spaces. Whereas that kid focused himself to victory, the knack of being here now is not to concentrate but be alert, relaxed and expansive. Instead of narrowing down attention to a single spot, you let go and open up to being boundless. Instead of making concerted effort, you make none at all. Rather than forcing, you surrender, and rather than becoming pointed, you disappear. You float so freely that there is no you left to float. Any 'buzzing' shows you that a self has started to form and that you are drifting off course, which then brings you back to being. Karma is the guide and presence is the method and the prize. No perspiration required.

Chapter 7:

Amazing

Most people die unaware. Most of us avoid being conscious throughout life, which includes staying in denial of death, and so when the day comes we are not ready for it. Also, society conditions us into oblivion and seems to distract us every way it can. And so the tendency and massive momentum are towards missing reality and dying in ignorance. The fearful preference, then, is perhaps to slip away in our sleep so as not to be here when it happens. Naturally this relates to averting any suffering at the time leading up to it, which makes sense, but it is more a function of the meandering mind, and it shows a lack of understanding of the opportunity that the occasion presents us. Would you like to sleep through your whole life too? That's effectively what humanity has been choosing and doing. I would like to experience life and death consciously and feel that living in a way that promotes it is what our species and the planet need. Have you considered dying in full awareness with the utmost acceptance, trust and interest? Not with a belief in heaven or any other hopeful utopia, but lucidly and responsibly? Have you tasted what it is to be fully awake in life?

Science would describe consciousness as arising from evolving organisms. It would say that, at one stage in earthly progression, organisms formed and consciousness of a rudimentary kind came with them, advancing over time into complex creatures with increased awareness related to their contextual functioning and survival. Humanity is an advanced form of organism that contains advanced consciousness, unlike, say, a rock, which has none. Seemingly a plant has some form of it measurable by ever-advancing instruments. The origin and essential nature of it, however, remain unknown to science. The language and method are based on using the physical to explain the physical, though, like the mind uses thoughts to think, and so it cannot see past itself. Science is a reflection of the mind. But what about the mystery beyond the bounds that? Reality does not confine itself to the limits of our conceptualisation. Far from it, in fact.

Science's ability to explain is expanding into the quantum realm, however, and increasingly able to accept if not articulate dimensions beyond the bounds of the five senses and linguistic lexicon, which is a turning point in our modern understanding. It seems, though, to be voicing in one language what the mystics have been saying for millennia using another. Science is beginning to see and say what poetry has been expressing along, and in that point to the beyond and voice the truth rather than just state the facts. The two languages are coming together and humanity is becoming whole again. The simple oneness from which we strayed into complex thinking is restoring with holistic awareness.

The mystics have been saying that physical form arises within consciousness rather than the other way round. Consciousness comes first, or exists timelessly and boundlessly, as a universal quality and beyond, and physicality and all manifestation come and go within it. We are effectively awareness becoming aware of itself, with birth into human form involving a degree of forgetting of one's oneness with the big picture to live the journey of remembering it to advance existential understanding. Death is a return and a remembering, and can be accessed and encountered fully before leaving this physical form, which brings this physical form to fruition. It is a triumphant coming home with greater relative awareness, which makes life into what it is meant to be. Physical death becomes the climax of the journey, which makes it quite a rush at the time and all the way up to it. Wouldn't you want to face that with full and lucid awareness? It could be amazing.

Chapter 8:

Faith

"I must warn you," I wrote in reply to her message seemingly sent in error, "that many Indian women have tried to seduce me and not all of them have failed."
Her note was about me to a friend, she explained to me afterwards, in discussion about why she can't find a boyfriend or, more precisely, she then clarified, why relationships don't work for her.

Yeah, right. It made me think of what George sang in his late-eighties single about knowing the games someone plays because he plays them too. Hmmm. His assessment in the song was so stay strong and show the person the door, but then games are largely unavoidable in life, and he certainly wasn't giving up on them. It's perhaps preferable to embrace and participate in them with consciousness, which caters for clarity and authenticity as a base, and then with fun and meaningful mischief adding spice to the modus operandi. It's best not to take life too seriously, even though it is an ongoing do-or-die situation. George knew that as well as anybody.

His famous song was using the notion of faith in a strongly sexual context rather than an overtly religious one, although the track does open with a church organ, which points again to our discussions here about sex, death and spirituality being essentially the same stuff. What he was actually referring to, though, behind the smouldering and best-selling experience, is better described as trust, which would have made for a wiser statement but a less compelling album title without the same, erm, market penetration. Still, I like it. Maybe I'll use it as a book title one day.

Trust happens when you know, while faith is needed when you don't. Trust shows that you are wise while faith shows that you're a bit of an idiot by your own admission, and since George had a song on the same album called "Kissing a Fool", the picture seems to hang together quite soundly. Truth stated in jest aside, George was a genius, which meant that he could laugh at himself. A wise person knows their oneness with existence, existentially, and can have fun with life's absurdity. It's central to spirituality. This intelligence is not a function of thought, theory or belief but of experience and knowing, expressed creatively. It is not speculation or the following of some doctrine, and it is not clung to out of fear but seen with one's trusting totality. The wise are not cooped up in a sense of separation but feel with their entirety that they are unified with everything and can never be any other way.

A sense of distinction is delusional and a function of a corrupted consciousness, although still something we can work and play with. A separate self is the phantom we call ego, the biggest problem in human history, which is based on something that does not actually exist but that forms part of how we participate in the pantomime. The key is to stay aware. Someone lost in that illusion and unaware state, though, which we all know well, through ignorance or political cunning, needs religion and faith like a drug to fake feeling connected again, when there was no disconnect to begin with bar the erroneous assumption of one. A conscious person is connected and able to dance in the drama while detached.

Faith is like belief in that you need it in lieu of knowing and trust. Rather than claim to have either, it is incomparably better to admit that you don't know, and then to endeavour from there with the utmost rigour to find out. This will increase consciousness. What better quest could there be in life? What is life with anything less? People who claim to believe are not making themselves or the rest of the species look good. People who proudly proclaim their faith actually defy comment and haven't even begun the journey of authenticity yet. Death will make that all clear in due course. Best we bring it forward and face it first and proceed with the arising awareness. Because you've got to have trust and sing the song of life from here.

Life is a journey to compassion, which is also a function of consciousness. Whatever abrasiveness we bring or gather gets cleared by ongoing death experiences along the way and when the big death comes we are filled with light and understanding. At this point we are completely cleansed and we see and feel fully and clearly. We return to love. Life is a journey back to love. Awareness and love go together.

Life is a series of highs and lows that together can take you all the way to the top and then beyond it. Life can give you all you came for, all you seek and more. To do so, it must strip you of everything you think you are, and all you are not. This brings you back to love. Life has a lot of deep troughs without which none of it would work. The deeper the better because the ability to live is defined by the limits we set, of which there should be none. All suffering is worth it because life is a journey to compassion. Lows make us soft and insightful and lead us to compassion. When you are high you are too happy to be humble and soon you lose touch with tenderness. Something needs to sober you up and put you back in the earth where your roots can grow. Love is your roots and compassion is earthy.

Compassion comes when you have lost it all and, in that, found it all for real. You cannot lose what's real. Compassion comes with death and nothing less will do to wake us up. Compassion comes when it all lines up, and when what is beyond all bounds can channel through you clearly. Compassion is a reunion with our ancestry, a realisation of our relative individuality, and a reconciliation with beauty. Compassion is love at its highest level. When you get it all right, in life and death and love, compassion and consciousness are what remain. Fall in love with that.

(

Chapter 9:

Flawless (Go to the City)

Some of Steve Jobs' most famous quotes talk openly about expiry. He seemed aware of the ancient wisdom that keeping a sense of your death close to you is the best way to live your life. He spoke of keeping in mind that you are going to die when making decisions or needing perspective. He recounted the early round of experience he had with life-threatening illness and how it helped him stay on creative course in his career and life's work. He had a Buddhist persuasion, which, in its truer form, cultivates lucid awareness of death as a reality and constant presence. Hinduism, too, brings death in as essential to awakened living. Meditations in cemeteries make it nice and tactile, removing all tendencies to avoid reality or float around in dreamland. The body gets burned in an ashy furnace in front of everyone's eyes. This takes hours, as I found out with Frank. This is our worldly fate. How refreshing!

The answer is not in a bigger house or faster car but the detachment from all things material, while enjoying them to the full. Your house is crumbling around you as you sit in it and your car is costing you no matter how you look after it. Your best work is washing away like a sandcastle on the beach and your regal words are mere writing on water. Death is the overriding truth. Dig it. Celebrate it! Rejoice in it every moment.

Of course, a festive feeling is not the only one we will find in the presence of death. Certainly there will be melancholy and grief. The great sadness shall surely overcome us at times and, when we are aware, run alongside all other sentiments and sensibilities. These emotions are all part of the picture, the richness of life, and the wholeness and completeness. But the bottom line is profound gratitude and uncontainable ebullience, tempered by supreme sobriety. What a blessing and amazingly fantastic experience. Thank you, dear life and death.

Carlos Castaneda started as a Hispanic American academic, an anthropologist, studying psychotropic plants in Mexico, but that turned into a phenomenal foray into being trained as a sorcerer and man of knowledge or spiritual wisdom by his mentor, Don Juan Matus. This resulted in a classic series of a dozen dazzling books written and released from the late sixties into to the late nineties, which take us through vivid accounts of Castaneda's (perhaps fictional but certainly compelling and deeply resonant) experiences via the masterful and mischievous (character or real shaman) Don Juan. The teachings are transformative for living on earth and encountering the beyond.

One of the early lessons of the sorcerers of their lineage and keys to anyone drawn to attaining knowledge is to use death as an advisor.

Your death is seen as an actual presence, not an occurrence at the end of a linear timespan but something that stalks you at all times waiting for the moment when your guard drops and it taps you. We can perceive it presiding patiently but persistently over our petty affairs until the inevitable gap opens in our ongoing efforts to keep it at bay, at which point we succumb. Best we be ready! The work of a worthwhile life is a relentless effort to extract as much as possible from the unfathomable mystery of our being here until death happens, and then making the most of that, using the knowing all along that death will happen and is happening all the time to leverage optimal essence from the great gift. This is the way of the truly wise. They call it impeccability. Anything less is a deluded waste, the way of the average human. Well, times have changed. The way of the wise is becoming the way of every human. The species is awakening. Death is central.

Death is the crowbar with which we keep the window of being alive open so that we can see as much as humanly possible and feast our inner knowing on the whirling wonder of it all. Death is the perfect perception-cleaner, the wiper of our otherwise hazy screens, the cloud-clearer in our consciousness and the exposer of the boundless sky. Death is the bringer of magic by its presence and by promising ruthlessly and infinitely compassionately to take it all away one fine day. Death does the trick. Make death your friend, because it is the best one you can have. Be death's friend because it will welcome you accordingly. All of life is a celebration and a preparation.

At times when life seems too much, consult with your best friend death. What does it tell you? If it is time to go, embrace it and make the most of it. If it isn't, make the most of that too. Embrace everything through awareness and ultimate understanding. Death makes it clear. You can carry on and let go. You can laugh. Drama is an indulgence and a dance. Truth prevails behind the veil. You can love. Life is love and death is the door to it.

At times when a decision is draining you with its endless oscillation from left to right, and its alternating pros and cons on each side, see what your death has to say. If this were a matter of life and death, a deciding factor, how would you proceed? That will give you the insight, traction and crystallised core with which to act with wisdom. Death will give you guts and clarity, and make you calm. The best moves are often made when the stakes are the highest and you haven't room for confusion. Realise that you are always on the very edge and facing the definitive moment at the ultimate level. Revel in the glory of death and your living relationship with it. It's nothing short of orgasmic, and avoiding it isn't going to help.

Mortality will make itself known to you with or without your willing participation. Last year I had my appendix removed, unexpectedly, of course, which brought about a little rendezvous with reality. It took two months of recovery and rest to reflect most surgically on all accumulated baggage as I cut it loose. I made the most of this acute encounter with vulnerability and the avalanche of associated insight, ranging from the need to keep re-evaluating my perspective and position as I age, to appreciating friendship and affection from people who genuinely care for me. I can manage my awareness with death as a trusted advisor, I realised, but I will be taught what I need to learn whether I do that or not. Last year, too, Resheka went through a bout of chemotherapy to treat a strand of life-threatening lymphoma, taking me with her on an extreme trip of pain and awakening. Her brush with mortality made for great growth, more than we felt we could handle at times, but we found out that we could not only handle it. We could emerge more enlightened, and healthy in a new and priceless way. Vitality and freedom are more our middle names than ever. Today, as I write in the New Year following a celebratory holiday together, she has had a maintenance treatment, which has been another opportunity to value what matters most and grow in love. Death and wellness are inseparable. They feel completely on the edge and alive. Sexiness and wellness are also one thing that feels supremely good.

Riding around Patong on a fuel-injected scooter is another way of staying ultra-aware. On the island, if you don't get on your bike and ride, you succumb to fear, miss the freeing experience, and cannot make the most of the island and its transformational treats on sale. But if you have the courage and wherewithal (or in many people's cases just the sheer stupidity), you gather your wits, mount the motorbike and, make your way around town and the coastline. You risk your life but, therein, find and live it. Other two-wheelers whizz past you wildly like Asian beach cowboys while cement mixers, double-decker coaches racked with air-conditioned Chinese tourists, mad minibus taxis, and every imaginable form of local and transitory fellow rider swarms around you. You are unguarded and alive!

Static concrete and moving steel make soft flesh and brittle bone feel far more immediate as you balance on the three or four square inches of rubber rolling on the undulating roads. Deep ditches beckon along the way to outlying beaches, ensuring you keep your composure and your steady grip. There is not one second where you can afford to drift out of the moment. Thinking is kept in check by the commanding power of presence. Death does its thing and full vitality arises in your piece of paradise. At night, having really lived, you go to bed satisfied, and charged with the anticipation of doing it all again the following day.

Another way that we can encounter death most vividly and regularly is through eating. If you haven't ridden a bike around an island, or if you are still manifesting your trip to Thailand, the experience may feel a step removed right now. Or when I say that breathing in is like being born and breathing out is like dying, it could feel metaphorical and abstract. When there is a carcass on your plate, however, there's nothing ethereal about it. Somebody slaughtered, skinned and sliced up that once-living creature, someone else grilled its sizzling skin and flesh to perfection, and yet another human being delivered it to your table with a side of your choice. Some animal no different from you gave up its life so that you can continue to have yours, and a string of complicit others conspired to help it happen. You may not see the blood on your own hands or around your mouth but it's there. You may have worked on a spread sheet at the office that day but the client who paid you did the killing and packaging, and the financial proceeds made their way up the production line into your bank account. The subsequent swipe of your credit card at the supermarket was not as clean-cut as it seemed. As unsoiled as you want to feel, you are feasting in cold blood. Make no mistake about it.

We may be consumed by customer service and cushioned by abstractions but we are lethal beasts. And this is not meat-eating specific. Death is directly involved in every bite we take. Veganism does not eliminate the killing factor. Nothing can. The soil in which the plants grow carries the bodies of beings reintegrated into the earth. In no uncertain way we are feeding on our ancestors, perhaps only a couple of degrees of separation away. Inhaling a lung full terminates countless organisms, as does exhaling, and neither can be stopped, unless you kill yourself. There is no escaping death in every moment, no matter how unconscious we are or how karmically clean we attempt to be. The only wise and realistic option is to turn the other way and face and embrace it fully. Our lives are infused with destroying life. Life and death are one.

What intellectual approach do we use to justify this to ourselves? Christians might feel that God gave us His lesser creatures to serve our higher status. Hindus might find the whole idea of killing for food abominable but do it anyway, despite the perceived karmic consequences. Muslims may have no problem with it as long as the food is prepared to scriptural instruction. Somewhere, though, a huge piece of the picture has to be obscured so that we can eat in peace, unless we admit that we are ultimately eating ourselves. The basis for this understanding comes from Don Juan in Castaneda's books. Kill and eat as you must but know lucidly that the same will happen to you. The same is happening all the time. Accept and live in awareness of it. Wake up!

People in parts of Tibet, China, Mongolia and India feel it fitting to leave their corpses out on the mountainside or edge of town for scavengers to consume. It's called sky burial. This demonstrates understanding and serves as a token of respect. There is no euphemism involved in dealing with reality, no 'passing away' or 'kicking the bucket'. Just as we lived, showing no shame, so we die. The compassion with which we were allowed by the world to survive and thrive is shown in return when our time comes to be the food. I resonate with this rawness. Eat but be eaten too. This makes you aware and makes your eating true.

Chapter 10:

White Light

If our physical form arises mysteriously and inexplicably from the formless realm, precipitates somehow out of the ether, has material and measurable manifestation for a time, runs its genetically-determined and environmentally-influenced course, and then disappears again, getting absorbed again into the ancient stardust from which it took shape, then there is distinctly an element of the beyond running alongside if not containing our temporal and temporary being. It is where we came from and where we must be going, unless we aren't coming or going at all but continuously being. You could argue that we simply cease to exist when we die, in which case we will just have to wait and see what happens when we do. Obviously we will have to wait and see anyway, but, while we wait, what do we do and pursue? Do we linger lost or wander in wonder? Do we avoid, deny or believe? Do we postpone in fear, faith or hope? Or do we devote our time to finding out? Sooner or later we will find out. Do we leave it all until then or do we endeavour to discover death and its secrets while we are still alive?

Do we make the most of life not just as a hedonistic bender but as a meaningful exploration of who we truly are? Do we do justice to our mysterious existence? When I asked Simon in the car through Pattaya how he viewed the future of humanity, whether we would just carry on travelling this unsustainable trajectory, extinguish ourselves or shift into a new awareness and world, he said that he didn't care. The exact phrasing he used was, "I don't give a fuck," which he repeated a few more times in different contexts over the time together, in jest but sincerely too. Interesting choice of terminology, don't you think?

Who does actually care? Can we afford to in a world hell-bent, it seems, on travelling one way fast? Do any of us see past immediate survival and occasional pleasure? Caring can seem too costly or out of our individual reach, yet can we sincerely not be bothered by our untenable state of overpopulation, rampant consumerism, prolific pollution, sprawling city madness, ongoing war, climate change and all the rest? And is this human mess likely to continue unfathomably in a linear fashion ending in the death of the species and planet, or are we shifting through a tipping point and taking an evolutionary leap? It didn't matter to Simon, first, perhaps, because he was speaking as a seventy eight year old who has lived well, and second because it was not his paradigm to consider such stuff. If spirituality is meaningless, as he insisted, then caring what happens to humanity might be equally empty.

Challenging me to show otherwise and asserting more strongly still afterwards that his points stood, he seemed to be asserting himself more than seeking an answer, and I had no problem with that or his jibe that I didn't know what I was talking about. He knew that I knew, and I did get through to him, not so much by what I said but by how I handled him. There was no pressure to change his view but I knew he wanted to know for real and deep inside, like we all do, not by adopting someone else's views but by our own keen insight and awareness. In his case, he is processing his impending death, as we all are, and it would naturally be one of his pressing questions, as it should be for everyone. He had done pretty much everything else in life, bar having a family, which he did say that he would like to have done, and would do if he had his life over again (which sounded reminiscent of Alexander the Great's situation). That partially explained his loving, generous and fatherly way with me. The bigger picture, too, though, was that he was asking questions that he had not been interested in before, or felt pushed towards until then. Our meeting was no coincidence.

He was frank with Resheka and me that he could no longer perform sexually, and explained how, as a result, he had to find a new source of energy from which to work in his creative and business life. He still delighted in seeing everything as sexual, from the extravaganza down Walking Street at night to the motivations of every individual to generate, fight, sell, or succeed, but he was forced by biology to explore another place in his being that had been quietly waiting in the wings while sex had taken centre stage all these years. With sexual thrust practically out of the picture, he was pushed to truly consider his spirituality for the first time, and he was having a few new glimpses into it from our encounter. This book follows in part from those questions. It precipitated on the night of our day together with my energies ripe for a new level of expression and engagement, and all of the strands are flowing together in this writing. What is the nature of the beyond and how do we come to know it? What is life and how do we live it rightly? Who are we and what are we creating together here on earth? As they say in Thailand when you walk past the massage parlours, "Where you come from? Where you go? I go with you?"

After Simon and I had developed a trusting rapport, and he said once again that he does not give a fuck, I pointed out that he can't fuck anymore anyway and, thus, that things fit together and make sense. He looked at me with a certain charged intensity but took my point. He might be in a place of realisation. His stage in life is one of dealing with such matters falling into meaningful place, and this relative youngster had a go at saying so.

When you are seven, you have no sense of sexuality, but at fourteen your hormones kick in and suddenly you know all about it. At that point, a third seven-year cycle, one we call adolescence, grabs you by the balls or the ovaries and sends your body and brain into a frenzy of urges, obsessions and explorative expressions. At twenty one you are a ripe adult but your charge has already begun its gradual decline and, at thirty five, two cycles later, your life orientation is reprioritised again, with your motivation engaged in holding together a home, family and heavy-going career, and your sexual gearing evolving on. Two more seven-year spins and you are forty nine like me, still sexual but distinctly less powered by the push in your pants (and sometimes out of them). I can feel where I am in relation to my youth, on the one hand, and Simon's situation on the other. I am still grateful for my carnal facility, still troubled by it too (as we all are when we admit it), and well on my way to letting it all go (which is death right there and me fucking for my life while I still can.)

It is as normal to have wet dreams as a teenager as it is to be physically asexual at seventy eight. Later in life the mind may still be that of a juvenile, which is a problem we all live with because we are absorbed in our heads. We don't live each stage of life properly, since we are squashed and repressed, and so we don't evolve in alignment with the rest of our being. It's proper to go through all the developmental stages, and process the deeper lessons that come with each of them, and when we do we can move on without unresolved stuff holding us back. It is healthy to be asking the big life-and-death questions when we are older, and being open to the answers. The answers are here all along and we are simply finding our way to them by living out the complexities of remembering ourselves.

What does being ourselves entail? It is certainly a remembrance as much as it is a discovery, and a surrender as much as a creation. Being ourselves means balancing both. Also, the realisation along the way is that, more than anything else, the consciousness with which we enquire needs to change. It must expand. The answer we seek is not in the objective truth conforming to our scrutiny but the arising of proper awareness of our subjectivity. To understand the truth means to know yourself with absolute clarity. There is nothing but subjectivity and so it must be our primary area of interest and understanding. The journey is solitary and introspective, although it is reflected in communion and external experience. The inner and outer go together, they come together, too, and they begin and end within.

And so the self that has not looked inwards with sincerity to see its own nature has not even begun the journey of knowing reality. It may exist physically and psychologically, but it has not been born yet spiritually. As such, it will believe in some explanation, be that religious or scientific, but it is still totally lost, lying to itself and pretending to others. The same self who instead admits to not knowing has stopped the charade and can begin the journey. The same self who then seeks with uncompromising rigour and a playful spirit while enjoying life in the moment will expand to find the truth where the seeking stops. Here the illusion becomes apparent and the truth takes over.

The answer is where there are no more questions. There is no more questioner, just total presence. Understanding is where acceptance meets love and inspiration. We remember where we stop forgetting, but first we must stop believing so that we can see with clean eyes. This process of elimination will ultimately take us to where all that remains is the truth. Our physical and psychological form, our bodies and personalities, and our overactive minds, are all characterised by forgetting our essential nature. When these constructs dissolve through awareness and presence, we recall it.

This surrender comes with nothing less than death, which can be physical or psychological. Letting go of form releases limitation and welcomes us home to who we are, which can happen at the moment of dying and while we are still alive. We can release the tension of identity, and let go into oneness, stillness, purity and knowing. This is coming home, the ultimate orgasm.

Instead of your stubborn little self insisting on answers and, thus, upholding ignorance, let yourself lose your limits. See it as an expanding of your awareness and an alchemic shift in your sense of who you are. Allow your awakening. That is all it takes. The ego can interrogate existence for verifiable evidence but that will simply validate the confines of the ego's perceptive ability. The conclusion might then be that you were right all along not to give a fuck. What to do, though, about that hole inside, that domineering doubt, that gaping need, and that approaching death? Ascribe them cynically to some jaundiced joke? You might be clever but you could be missing out on what it's all about.

Face death while you are alive. Make it your friend, because it is already the best one you will ever have. Death is not the problem, your perception is. Drop the distinctions and barriers, open your being, and don't give up until you know with your totality. If your dick doesn't do the deed anymore, thank nature for its wise ways. Now you are free to make decisions without the interference of your little head. Even the one on your shoulders is small and a big distraction from the truth. Free yourself from the lot. Life has blessed you with the chance to find out who you are before crossing into who-knows-where. Settle into your sexless centre and come from somewhere serene. Watch sex swarm around but not disturb you. Enjoy it but do not lose your awareness to it. This is awakening. One taste of consciousness and you will thank nature for everything, especially your death.

If the idea of remembering upsets or puzzles you, consider your recollections of being one year old. Can you testify to having any? Your first conscious memory is likely to be from around two or three, which is when cognitive functioning takes over from a more holistic and less structured awareness. Before then we perceive organically, more like an adult on strong LSD, with a flood of intense and unstructured experiences, with a sense of inner perspective behind that. Remembering before this age will not be a function of cognition and, therefore, not seem accessible to our adult mind. We do remember well, but we don't recognise the memories because they don't conform to our current, limited awareness. The recollections are there but we have lost our ability to recognise them and access that level of awareness. We have forgotten ourselves.

Thinking is a social construct conditioned into us, which kicks in as we become linguistic and fully takes hold and over when we are two or three years old. At this point our broader more mystical ability is largely lost to us. Society considers it constructive, but that magical blob that we can feel and taste as much as see turns into a 'light', a solid object and conceptual entity with boundaries and an accompanying name. We have been repeatedly told that it is a "light, light, light..." by the innocent and conditioned parents until one day the world of wonder disappears and we come to agree. "Yes, Daddy, light. Look at how clever I am." Sadly, the opposite is true. Real intelligence is lost.

When we look back as limited adults to our preverbal life as infants, we claim that we cannot remember them clearly, but we do have a primal and feeling-based sense of them, which is simply non-conceptual experience. It's just that the self that is looking back does not identify the memory because it is using cognition as a base and reference point. It is our current limitations we are seeing reflected to us, not the truth, although we can be forgiven for not knowing any better.

Perhaps a regressive therapeutic encounter puts us back in touch with a palpable memory one day, or a body massage triggers a primal pain that brings a repressed trauma flooding back, or the death of a parent resets our awareness and we remember all that we have known. Wow, where did that come from? Well, it was there all along, held away by the mind we use to manage our little reality. What else might be lurking in those vast and mysterious tunnels of the unconscious? Plenty, for sure. We need to find out if we sincerely want to know ourselves and live wholeheartedly. We must do the work if we want to die in freedom instead of clinging to some phantom of a life.

Best we realise that we remember. Best we wake up now. The world certainly needs it and may not survive if we don't. Unconscious behaviour is killing us and our precious planet, whether you give a fuck or not. In 1975, when I was seven years old, the population was four billion people, and now, in 2018, when I am just forty nine, it is racing towards double that. Madness is running rampant. When you have sex, do it not to spawn more kids, or even for the pleasure and escape, but to encounter the beyond so that you can bring higher awareness to bear in the world. Fuck for fun but come for enlightenment and the survival of the species, for fuck's sake.

Similar to the loss of our memory of being an infant, the process of being born in physical form and emerging from the ether brings with it a forgetting of awareness more subtle than the mechanisms of the physical world. And so we forget ourselves and our bigger picture, identify with a little self and, frankly, become a big problem. We head down a tunnel of narrow, five-sensory consciousness and attach ourselves to it, and only later in life and closer to death, with a bit of luck, do we begin to sincerely question who we are within it and long for who we are outside of it. The memories and faculties are still here awaiting our remembrance.

The glimpses we have had along the way - like those youthful years as a small child, all those orgasms and moments of mind-free clarity, those few hours a night of deep and ego-suspended sleep, and some experiences of meditation, shock or bliss - invite us to a fuller reawakening. As we go with this return, all those years locked in the matrix lose their grip and we become available to the workings behind the screen. Our inner mirrors become clean again, our reflections become true, and our nature becomes crystal clear once more.

We should be encouraged to interrogate our reality with rigour because a wise mentor would know that persisting with this will bring us back to awareness outside of the confines of conditioning. And so he may tell us to keep seeking the truth until we release the assumed boundaries of the seeker, at which point we will truly see. Then our questions and answers will disappear together and we will remain in our true form, which is formless, boundless and brimming with knowing. A new humanity will be born bringing a new earth with it.

It is not only the truth that we find but ourselves, and it is a remembrance. It is a state of simultaneous death to the false and awakening to the real, which is timeless and orgasmic. It's the evolutionary impulse of the universe, the future for us all, and a cosmic wave cresting as we speak.

Don't die without finding out for yourself. No God, heaven, faith or hope required.

Chapter 11:

Older

Getting older may make you wiser in some ways, but wisdom is not necessarily a function of age. It comes from knowing yourself, which means facing and accepting who you are, your darkness and your light, and your physical and your spiritual, which involves coming to terms with sex and death. On a worldly level wisdom amounts to experience but that may make you closed and crusty rather than open and trusting, which is certain to keep you from yourself and the great mystery. True wisdom means being sage-like and innocent despite all that might have made you jaded. Are you lost to voluminous knowledge or steeped in seen-it-all cynicism? True wisdom means retaining or returning to childlike wonder, staying spontaneous, being patient and receptive, feeling your feelings without repression, living in the moment, brimming with innate and boundless joy for no external reason, being playful, retaining perspective, trusting life, and being willing to grow.

Aging runs the grave danger of convincing you against life when it should deepen your love for it. You should soften as you mature. Sometimes we need towering effort to stay ahead of time nipping at our heels, though, and any neglect we show this issue is increasingly difficult to catch up on. And so we need to feel alive as much as possible as we live, otherwise the slippage can swallow us while we aren't looking. To do this we need to live rightly, to realise and materialise who we are meant to be, to thrive in harmony with our nature, and to be of service to the world. This is the opposite of what school and society teach us, and so we need to follow our inner knowing despite all pressure and coercion to the contrary. Wholesome living is pure rebellion and the ongoing exercising of innate intelligence.

We need to do what we love, whether it's George Michael-style, who hit his high in his teens and then fought for his stand through the rest of his career, or Simon Napier-Bell-style, who has consistently created and taken opportunities with tenacious panache, or Robin Wheeler-style, who followed an inner knowing in his twenties and stuck to being himself for a living no matter what. What it means is doing it your-style, which carries universal themes and archetypes as well as individual singularities. How can you die in peace or with dignity and relish if you have not lived on your terms? The power to assert our uniqueness, no matter the circumstance, is our enduring and most valuable one. You've got to have soul, guts, flair, creative enthusiasm, smouldering sexiness, righteous rage, uncompromising trust in the truth, and an insatiable willingness to let go, all balanced by an intrinsic sense of satisfaction and bottomless love.

You need to be a mystic, in your unique way. A theist believes when he knows he is ignorant, an atheist claims to seek evidence when he knows he still has issues, and a mystic lives the mystery. These can be seen as three levels of spiritual awakening. A theist is yet to be born, an atheist is yet to grow up, and a mystic has come home. He is a contrary, a bold yet bashful rebel, and a change agent who doesn't mind whether he has an effect or not yet has a transformative function. She is an artist who has transcended her art yet keeps practicing it for the intrinsic joy and inspiriting others to do the same. He is an entrepreneur who doesn't care how much money he makes because it's always enough and he is always grateful, all of which makes him ever-richer. She knows that her work is meaningless but continues with it as if it can make the world of difference. This, of course, it does. Life is a contradiction and the mystic is a master of such unsolvable ambiguities. You can call it alchemy.

A mystic is not a philosopher and not a thinker or thought-leader, but a present-moment being exemplifying the living answer for those with eyes to see and ears to hear. A mystic is not a scientist and not a researcher or academic, with no loyalty to a method or a scholastic structure. A mystic is not a preacher or a teacher and not an adherent to an organisation, although everything she does will educate in the true sense and have a structural effect. A mystic is not necessarily older and not bound by age, but is someone who makes optimal use of whatever time may share on the enigmatic ride.

93

A mystic is an old soul in a young body and a young soul in an old one. A mystic is a paradox and a poet because life is paradoxical and poetry is the closest you can come to stating some of the unspeakable. A mystic is usually quiet, absorbed in the sweetness of silence, spreading it wherever he goes or stays, and saying everything without speaking. A mystic is a musician with whatever literal of metaphorical instrument works well for her. He knows himself and, therefore, understands others, and in that introduces them to themselves. She may be bohemian or deceptively mainstream, disruptively deviant or cleverly conformist. He is a magic-maker who brings crisp consciousness to bear in every encounter, spreading transformation without doing anything. She is optimally creative, bringing awareness into form via simple presence or complex collaboration. He is always growing and always staying the same, evolving in a state of dynamic stillness. A mystic is of the moment and timeless.

A mystic is mature and playful, a contradiction and a reconciliation. A mystic is innocent and experienced, a child and a grown-up, and an intriguing integration. A mystic is a uniqueness who has reconciled specialness with ordinariness.

A mystic is wise and the way.

Interlude 3:

Last Christmas

George Michael had died on Christmas Day the year before our meeting with Simon, and there was a feeling that somehow he had a hand in the connection. His life ended in a sad way, with heart and liver problems following years of decline, hardly the climax of his career, but he still went out with a bang. In the closing days of an annum that had taken a dozen of the world's finest musical stars, he topped the tree with a tragic twinkle that, frankly, we should have seen coming and probably did.

Not long after that Amanda had reread and then sent me her copy of Simon's book about his Wham! days. Reading about his inspiring aptitude and daring attitude had me excited in a way I hadn't felt for a long time, and the musical memories brought back a youthful enthusiasm that had long been buried in the weight of midlife pressures. My sense was that George might have put me in touch with Simon had he been alive and visiting for tea. The book led to connecting on Facebook, which steered Resheka and me to Pattaya, which brought on this book, which resulted in you reading it. Who knows who or what is behind this all? The sense is strong, though, that converging currents are taking us downstream and all the way to the ocean.

I always admired George's musical and production talent (right out of the remarkable starting blocks), his instinctive sense of confidence and knowing about his place in the pop landscape, his courage to stand his ground in testing circumstances (many of which he brought on himself), his supreme standards to the point of perfectionism, his hard work showing as exceptional quality and seeming effortlessness, his crossover sensibility that bridged styles and united fans, and his visionary way that changed music and the world. I always felt for him intensely, partly because of his openness and living out loud in public, and partly because it so represented the silent plight of anyone creative, wounded and struggling to find an individual voice and place in the collective. He was a true superstar.

Simon had known George since just after the beginning and so saw him in a different light, and so it was delightfully insightful for me to speak to the one man about the other who still carried a mythical quality for me in spite of my advancing age and relative sobriety. He kept a presence and came up in conversation between the three of us a few times on that day in Pattaya. While we were walking through the gay quarter towards having dinner that night, Simon said, like he had done recently in the press, that there was surely some sort of sexual abuse from the singer's youth that explained his drive, pain, anger and life story. I asked if he knew this for a fact, and he clarified that he didn't but that a few psychology experts had described the symptoms as classic indicators.

"Someone had sex with him when he was seven or eight," Simon stated in his matter-of-fact way, as if it's an everyday occurrence in the world, which it is, and old hat to him, which, to someone with his experience, it must be. He has also just released a film he was finishing making at the time about the strong link between childhood trauma, art, fame, business exploitation of musicians, and their often tragic collapse or death in the public eye. It made me wonder if I have some such repressed memory driving me. The mix of factors told to you here is all I am aware of, but I can relate to the syndrome. Perhaps it was the lack of emotional support from both my parents as a child, my feeling invisible at home and out in the world, and being isolated and bullied at school. Powerful pain is mixed into the spirited fuel.

George was, to my mind, a modern-day mystic and social change agent, through his particular talent and overall voice, and without overt recognition as such but with massive impact. His music and work will stand the test of time. In a way I am carrying on where he left off, since for the thirty four years that our lives overlapped, he had an inspiring and fortifying influence on me, and his spirit lives on in my work now more than ever. Society needs challenging, people need liberating, and I am as driven as ever to do all I can with my life to stimulate the proliferation of essence in an awakening species. Most of what I do comes from within and has been here all along, but much of it I learned from mentors like

George. In the possible role as such an influence myself, I hand the heroism on to other souls to run with. It's not just in these words or this book, but in the package deal of being myself for a living, in the marketing and publicity, in my voice in the media and, as you will see, in my playfully provocative way on topics of the most fundamental import. Sounds like someone we know, doesn't it?

Amanda loves music generally and George Michael particularly, and grew up a few suburbs east of me, two years older and as obsessed with the pop scene as I was. Yet we were unaware of each other until about ten years ago when she was marketing manager for a mall across town and I did a promotional appearance there with the band I was in. She admired my writing and other work, and so one day not long after that, when I was in the area again, I dropped in to the management office to surprise her. We had a magical chat and I gave her a copy of *Hunting Power (2003)*, my third book, which tells the story of flying to London without a concert ticket to see Bruce Springsteen at Wembley Arena in 2002. That inspired her and her husband Alessandro to take a trip a few years later to see Pet Shop Boys live in Paris, and the two of us gradually got to know each other. We worked together for a few years following her departure from employment, with her doing publicity for BEntrepreneurING and my personal brand, and then we took a break for a few more years to reconnect as friends not long before she sent me Simon's book. And so Amanda has had a hand in all this journey and writing, and she will tell you that George Michael has, too. She's in tune with those things, intuitive and powerful in her quiet and behind-the-scenes way.

For my birthday last year she gave me two more of Simon's books, *Ta-Ra-Ra-Boom-De-Ay (2015)*, which is about the history of the global popular music business, and *Black Vinyl, White Powder (2002)*, which recounts the story of the British music scene that he has lived through since the nineteen sixties. I was reading *Ta-Ra-Ra-Boom-De*-Ay on the Thailand trip, had it with me in Pattaya, and had Simon sign it for Amanda in the hotel foyer just before we headed out for lunch. In the inscription he chose to thank her for putting him in touch with me, which credits her for her pivotal role in everything happening here today. She is being herself for a living, doing what comes naturally and having a huge impact.

She has been along for the ride all the way, running parallel back in South Africa while Resheka and I were away, getting updates as we went along, and supporting me feverishly since then with the writing. As a result she has been party to a few insider secrets as I've felt ready to release them, as has Sheke. Between my two co-travellers and confidantes (and George producing from the ether) I have had the resonance and reflection I've needed to do the big work. They will be the first two to read it when the author has done all he can to get it ready. Then it will probably head to Pattaya.

Another book in the mix is a biography called *George Michael: The Life 1963-2016 (2017, John Blake Publishing Ltd)* by Emily Herbert. Amanda saw a single copy at her local book store last year and snapped it up to send to me. Strikingly and almost unnervingly the book's cover looks like it inspired by those of the first three titles in my INSIGHTS series. Friends who saw in my home assumed before a second glance that it was once of mine, so similar is the design, the font and even the gold embossed text. When it arrived from Amanda, I took a photograph of it beside mine and sent the picture to Simon. It's hardly his style to leap at such strands of synchronicity but that did not diminish the uncanny connection, perhaps only emphasised it. If George were up to something celestial, that book cover design factor would certainly be a strong sign.

Something significant that I gleaned from that biography as I made my way through his life story was how, as much as his pain had taken him up, it had eventually taken him down. Myself suffering from a strong dose of sustained desolation at the time or reading it, I found out from George's example how not to succumb to sorrow. Like Springsteen learned the lesson from his hero Elvis of how to keep it real and not get lost in celebrity, I learned from one of mine to be grateful for my good fortune, and to keep going up.

Chapter 12:

Round Here

I was born in Wimbledon in November 1968 when Simon was chasing thirty a few tube stops away in Swinging London. My parents were South African newlyweds living overseas for what became two years, and I was conceived (probably on Valentine's Day) in 35 Alwyne Road (I assume), where they rented a semi-detached house, and then born a few blocks away in St Teresa's Maternity Hospital in a street named The Downs just off the roundabout up the hill in Wimbledon Village. This was all while The Beatles were working on their last recording, *Abbey Road*, and setting it in sonic stone in the famous studios with that name not far from where I was adjusting to being in my little body. Our London suburb looked very much like the cover photo on that 1969 album.

My mom, Beth, was a secretary in the city, Frank wore a suit to work in an office on the Thames, and the man almost exactly his age, who is now my new pal in Pattaya, was surely donning flashier attire, socialising in Kings Road, and doing music-industry deals in the early hours of the morning in clubs in Soho. At the same time

George Michael was starting school in north London, with us, the three Wheelers, in our home in the south west.

When I was six months we went back to South Africa by boat, the Pendennis Castle, and I grew up as a South African in the eastern suburbs of Johannesburg. Owing to my birth in London, though, and my parents' loving memories of living there, as well five or six of my great grandparents having been born in England, effectively making me a third generation immigrant, the motherland held a mythical quality for me. I first put adult foot on British soil at the age of twenty three in 1992, when two decades of unspoken undercurrents eventually became full-blown life experiences.

Walking around Wimbledon then evoked a painful memory that had me crying in the streets, a sense of things never vocalised but carried with me for decades, alongside a deep joy of feeling at home. Was it an ancient melancholy in the soil in that city, the history of humanity there, or was it personal? Was it sad or happy, or simply intensely whole? It felt like the anxiety and trauma of surgical birth, the isolation from my mother at the time along with her emotional issues and my father's unexpressed feelings and history. It was also beautiful. It didn't have words and pictures attached, just energetic elements, like a dream you can taste but not articulate. I remembered London the way I had experienced it then, as preverbal and primal. Perhaps our recollections from before we were born as humans are the same, palpable but misperceived because we don't know what to look for. Perhaps we go way back on levels just outside of what we remember clearly and call reality, and these inform our lives.

The three Wheelers docked in Cape Town, made our way up-country, and then stayed with Frank's parents in their home in Irene for a few months, which, following Wimbledon, put that spirited abode in place for my lifetime. Situated between Pretoria and Johannesburg, not quite in the countryside but with that feel, its red-rocky earth and fervent birdlife, Irene gave me a sense of connection to my ancestry and my inner calling. My grandfather, Richard, had built the family home on an acre of land in the early fifties, when there were sand roads, no streetlights, and the house needed an anthracite-fuelled ESSE stove to keep the water hot and the family fed. It formed a solid reference point for us all wherever we roamed, starting, for me, before I could speak.

Then we moved to a flat in Hillbrow, which was a hip suburb of inner-city Johannesburg back then, characterised by European architecture and culture, and rich with a mix of continental immigrants. That was a transitional home for us, too, soon to be replaced by the first house bought for the young family, on the outskirts of Kempton Park, made complete with the arrival in 1971 of my sister, Heather. Five years in that remote spot, and five in the following one nearby, a slight upgrade, gave us our first decade on the East Rand, right between the suburb my mom grew up in called Kensington, just outside of central Johannesburg, and Irene. A move in 1980, when I was eleven years old, to Bedfordview, which is right next to Kensington, brought me to the defining place and community where I have lived most of my adult life so far, itself bridged by a three month stint in Irene on that seminal soil while the new Bedfordview house was being finished.

The grand old home where Frank and his brothers, Peter and Denis, grew up speaks to my soul still, and the property remains in the family and Peter's care awaiting possible revival if, as planned, I take it over and restore it to past glories and beyond. That has always been a calling for me, perhaps since I was first there but certainly since I can remember waking on school holidays to the symphony of natural sounds, listening to music on the B&O sound system, hearing the dependable chime of the clock on the mantelpiece, and walking around the garden as an inspired child.

Somehow the writer-to-be was already hearing the words whispering in the tall trees. Something there also echoes our English spirit and sensibilities and speaks for my grandfather's unexercised creative voice which I came to live out in later years. On my desk I have a copy of the house plans, drawn up by him and ratified in 1954, stating at the bottom in bold text: "New Residence for R. Wheeler", which applies as much now as it did back then. My grandmother Fan's vocation as a teacher is in my DNA, too, and in the Wheeler history in that leafy suburb, where she taught Grade 1 at the local primary school for twenty five years.

More even than those factors, though, there has always been a feeling in me of how I should live, an intuitive guide for the existential space in which I should centre myself. When I was seven and walking those grounds, I knew how I would feel when I grew up and thrived on my own terms. When I used to service my first car there in my late teens and university days, guided by my uncle Peter, I felt that inner knowing stronger than ever. In the ensuing decades I have returned there in body, mind and spirit to feed on what has nourished me all of my life. An author living at home in himself on a writer's estate, with a majestic garden, a music studio out back, and a fine sound system in the front room. Vast and terraced lawns with red-rock walls, regal trees, a wealth of birdlife and a family history as a base for global travel. The vision will manifest, like everything else has. It's been coming together all this time, and time is what it takes. When I set out to be myself for a living in 1996, it was essentially my acquiescence to that spirited call. Soon afterwards I gave words to the experience, which became my global brand.

Wimbledon, Irene and Bedfordview are integral to my sense of soulful purpose, and, in the last seven years, Thailand has also taken its place in my ideal life and my dreams coming true. Although I am identifiably not from Southeast Asia, it feels anciently resident in my cells somehow. Could this literally be the case? Only death would know, but I feel happy and at home there. All of these places reflect aspects of my story, of how it has been taking form and where it is heading. Strands like these weave together over time and help us make sense of our journeys. What is your evolving story? What secrets does your death whisper to your secret self? George sang on his last studio album, *Patience (2004)*, about his parents' meeting, his youth in bustling London, his success starting there, his reaching deeply desired global renown, and his return to the special city that brought out the best in him. That is the place where he wanted to put his hands in the earth again and where, ultimately, he chose to die (just outside in Goring on Thames). Where we are from and where we live are woven into who we are, what we create and how we die. I am sure that a sense of my formative places will be with me when I go. Perhaps I will even do it in one of them.

When I was twenty three and backpacking around Europe, London had a central role in my travels, and the suburb where I was born was a base to work from. I was living in a commune in West Kensington and would take the tube out further to the end of the District Line when I needed to walk alone and tune in to myself, or phone South Africa and speak to my family, which I did from the booths around Wimbledon station. When Heather and her young family were transferred to London for Jason's job about fifteen years ago, they put in an offer on a house in the area, but the deal fell through at the last minute and they had to stay in a company apartment in the city until they secured somewhere else in their suburb of choice. The house they eventually found was in The Downs, the exact street I was born in, and the school their boys went to is on the corner of Alwyne Road where the three Wheeler's lived in the late sixties. These amazing co-incidences are the coming together of the weave of life. Surely your story is different in detail but strikingly similar.

After my backpacking pilgrimage in my early twenties I returned to South Africa to take up a position in the Personnel Assessment Department in the Human Resources Division of a large commercial bank with its head office in downtown Johannesburg. I had found what I had been looking for on the road and happy to be home and was ready to move on to a formal and stimulating career. The academically rich work environment and my intelligent and educated new peer group, plus my exposure to all aspects of Human Resources and corporate financial services, provided for rapid growth and a base from which to buy my first apartment down the road from where I grew up.

Soon I had two properties in my budding portfolio, and a set of Frank-inspired mutual funds that were growing steadily in value, like any decent banker and accountant's son. However, what still spoke to me most was listening to music at home in the evenings, often after smoking a joint and sometimes with fine friends who shared my true love for the creative and spiritual life. Money didn't mean that much after all and employment was for the (willing jail) birds. Nonetheless, my three years of corporate exposure were educational and essential to my impending awakening.

Two years into my stint there, and after one application at university for the sought-after Masters in Clinical Psychology programme, I went through a fatigue-induced epiphany about my career and calling that changed my direction. My head was telling me to keep climbing the organisational ladder and growing my investments but my body had other plans. In fact, it was the whole of me that my body spoke for when it made me lie down on the floor at the office one day and would not let me get up again. Eventually I was wheeled to the sickbay downstairs in a chair, which put my youthful philandering into perspective. I was actually unhappy in that environment and going against myself increasingly to stay there, just unsure of what to do instead. What I needed was a sense of direction and a push out of inertia, and I was about to get one. First, though, I needed to be utterly immobilised until I listened to what my heart and soul were saying.

Medically, it turned out, I was in perfect health but I would sleep for twelve hours, get up and shower, and then sleep some more before I could contemplate food. My body simply forced me to rest and so I stayed at home and did so, listening to the music I so loved and being myself instead of some suit-wearing strategist in a cesspool of meaningless meetings and competitive colleagues. At first I had some leeway to work with but soon I became seriously concerned that my psychologically trained co-workers were diagnosing me in my absence and that I might not get better at the rate I was going. What the hell was wrong? If I stayed with myself I felt fine but when I pushed to return to old ways, the debilitating symptoms returned mercilessly. I was stuck and, frankly, terrified. On some level, though, I knew that all was happening as it should and that the fear was part of the process. What I needed was to access and follow the lessons on that deeper and truer level. In this, though, I was alone. No boss, commercial brotherhood, parent or president could help me. Even the doctors had validated my good health. And so it was, I saw, a spiritual issue.

I took on some writing work that I could do at home using a company laptop, to feel like I was in circulation again while I did whatever soul-searching was required to figure out how to proceed with my life. One thing was already clear, though: get the message or stay immobile. Days and weeks passed until one morning, in a fit of desperation I shook off some of the static energy and then said to the universe in a fit of frustration and sincerity, "I've had enough of this! What is the message I need to get? I'm listening!" I was finally total in my enquiry, not conflicted in my head, and open to the answer, whatever it might be.

All I had been working through in the preceding months and years, and, in fact, my whole life, suddenly gave me a clear picture, right there and then. I needed to do what I really wanted to, and had always wanted to do. I needed to be that man I knew intuitively in my youth when I was walking around Irene, the one my grandfather wanted to be too but sacrificed to common sense and circumstance. I needed to be me! Not a psychologist or corporate climber, or anything else the world prescribed, but what my heart felt and my soul knew. Not what others expected but what I longed for and loved. And not some compromise but the real deal all the way. It was that simple and had been there all along waiting for me to return to it. What had changed is that I was ready.

With that, a burning vision revealed itself, a white light of clarity and compelling attraction filling the horizon in front of my inner eye like someone had set magnesium on fire before me. The psychology studies and my understanding of people, the analysis of work and performance and the future for humanity, a call to entrepreneurship and freedom, and the sale of my empowered insights back to the business world, which I could gain only by living it, integrated with the reconciliation of my ancestry and the courage to take on the shared mythology... all of these were resolved in this revelation.

I took the step into the light, symbolically and literally, right there on my lounge carpet, agreeing wholeheartedly to what lay before me. The Irene and Wimbledon feelings were there, as was Richard's spirit and his legacy, and Frank's unlived destiny, with my talents and dreams to assist me, and a knowing like none before it. My grandfather had been creative and expressive, too, but had shelved that side of him to be an engineer in the railways. He had paid off his house and put his sons through school but then spent his retired years seething in an unsatisfied state to eventually die of brain rot. As well as he did in life, he didn't live his truth or realise his potential, and I could do it now for him as well as for myself and everyone else.

His son, one generation younger, had done similarly and admirably, qualifying as an accountant, paying for an education for his kids, and putting away a little nest egg, but he still suffered from the same syndrome. At fifty seven he had to keep going on his trajectory, but, at twenty seven with nowhere else to turn and my hard-won insight enlightening me, I was able to set out to be myself for a living, for me personally, for all of us in the family, and, while I was at it, for the whole of humanity.

This was my rebirth in the realm of spirituality. I died to my old self that day, to everything set up in place of sincerity, and was born into who I was meant to be. The false burned up in a furnace of ruthless truth. I knew what I had to do and knew that I had always known, and I underwent an explosion of joy, like an orgasm of destiny. Isn't that what death is meant to be?

Chapter 13:

A Different Corner

"So you're a drummer," she said, sitting up straight on her side of the bench at the burger joint, perky and interested.

"Yes..." I answered slowly as I processed the topic... "I'm more of a musician, but drums are the instrument I use. So, yes, I'm a drummer."

"And are you, like, a good drummer?" she asked, not quite finding the right words for what she was trying to say but still conveying it in her tone.

"That's a matter if opinion," I laughed. "I'm not the technical type of drummer and I don't know all the tricks and the licks. I play in a relatively simple way, focusing on groove and feel. That's my thing. But, if I'm playing music I feel for and like, especially if I have written my part of it while working with other musicians, I can hold it together and give it something."

"That's great," she smiled, still erect and intrigued.

"It *is* great," I agreed and reflected on that, looking into the near distance and seeing a patch of shadows under the umbrella at the table across the seating area, like it was a living thing.

I wondered if she wanted to get her hands on my sticks, knowing that she probably did. Who wouldn't? Drums are sexy, particularly when played simply with groove and feel. They speak to primal places where no words can go, and all of us want to get past the limited world of words. Subtle innuendo mixed with unspoken sexual tension is the best way to handle situations like the one I was in on the bench outside the burger joint. That and patience. Best to take it slowly. Not that I was doing any of that in this instance, I just thought of it at the time. I was sitting with Nokwethemba, head of a hospital in a neighbouring town, and we were talking business, with me helping her with being herself for a living.

"Time is money," a professional drummer and teacher buddy had said to me earlier in the afternoon, in the mall, when we passed each other and stopped for a quick check in. He was overworked from the festive season and still stale from having forfeited his holiday for what turned out to be an unfulfilling project.
"Timing is money," I'd bantered back with meta-reference to our mutual predilection, and taking a shot at lifting his spirits and tightening his groove. Drums, like in the game of life, are about playing. Sometimes, in life anyway, that involves having your clothes off, but I've got used to that over the years. I've got into a healthy rhythm. Music is like sex, and sex is like death, and death is life, and life is music.

Drumming brings you into the present. There is no time to think behind the kit, particularly on stage. Everything happens in the now and you need to occupy that fully. This, along with its primal nature, makes drumming spiritual. Like sexual orgasm, it is a portal to timeless awareness. Drumming is, thus, a kind of death. That's one of the reasons we are drawn to it, as musicians or music enthusiasts. It's like riding a superbike at twice the speed limit on the highway at night, tearing through the membrane of illusion and living utterly on the edge where we feel most alive. Add to that the magic of collaborative harmony and a few hundred fans and you are in a kind of individual and collective heaven.

Drumming is also distinctly non-verbal, speaking without words, singing with your whole body and driving with your outer extremities held together by your beating heart. For someone as cerebral as I am, it provides a healthy balance, to the point of redemption. No-mind and a fully inhabited body buzzing with meditation through rhythmic movement while on a throne of steady stillness. It's otherworldly indeed, and, at the same time, as earthy as you can get, with sticks and steel and sweat. And when you hit that high of integration, it's something else. All that dedicated preparation, repetitive rehearsal, rising to it while relaxing into it, making it second nature, corralling the nervousness, clutching the courage to take your singular seat in the spotlight, cracking through the barrier of the first songs, finding the pocket, riding the rocket, staying calm as your spirit soars, building momentum throughout the set, feeling with your totality, giving it your all, making sweet sexiness to the world, breaking open with unbridled love, and riding the thundering stallion home...

Chapter 14:

Freedom

Death is the ultimate release. We all long for it. As beautiful and blessed as life can be, it's also too much sometimes, and eventually we get tired. The body wears out and the insistent stupidity of society grinds us down. The cycles keep coming around and we get bored with them, and we begin to feel drawn to be elsewhere. The wheel turns once again and we find that we want to get off it. Death becomes welcome in that way, whether we admit it or not, and, notwithstanding the ever-fierce will to live, we start to feel ready to finally let go and move on. Our kids are grown up, our grandkids are beautiful, our books are all born and proliferated, our work is done, and our struggles are over. We've seen and soaked in the wonders of the world, and it's the same everywhere. Our limbs are lame, our bones are brittle, our teeth are gone, our will is waning, our time is borrowed, our peace has come, and our lives are gone. We are free at last.

Death is also a discharge of all the built-up tension. It is a culmination but also a gentle relief. Everything we have applied ourselves to mounts mercifully into a concluding crossing into the gracious void. It's a subtle explosion, a quiet quickening, and a lingering shudder in the membrane of space-time. It's our whole stand that, if we've lived properly, becomes a beautiful bowing out that caps the entire trip. It's the last lunge during which time stands aside in due respect. You have earned one concluding chance to look with vivid vision at every step you have stridden with dignity.

This freedom comes with responsibility. We have to own our awareness. You can't be liberated if you just give up. You have a myth to live out and your death to face. Chucking in the towel will cost you more in the long term than it seems to save you in the short. Conversely there is the choice to die consciously. Is it not our ultimate duty? Do we not owe it to existence as a debt of gratitude? Certainly we can be forgiven for times of despair and defeat, but are we not obliged to stand tall to the end, and be bullish whenever possible? Humbly, of course. This is the universal leveller we are talking about.

Resheka's shattering brush with mortality showed her up for the game she had been playing with her life for her whole life. I could feel that dynamic when we first met, although I couldn't put my finger on it or express it verbally, but it took a leg-swelling lump in her right hip, a piercing biopsy, a shocking diagnosis, a total swing in approach to the idea of dreaded treatment, and six devastating bouts of intravenous chemotherapy for her to see that she had been calling the bluff of her blessed presence here. Her subsequent insight and testimony to me was that she had been daring life to relieve her of her repressed misery, choosing the idea of death as a way out from her victim mentality. The problem came, however, when death obeyed her instruction and she then saw that she didn't want that either! She hadn't budgeted on the reality of dying, just the drama of avoiding responsibility, and in the face of immense self-induced suffering, she changed her tune. She did not want to die and very much wanted to live. Consequently she had to face what she had been violently avoiding, which was far from easy.

Being the brave and fiery soul that she is, and with significant support from her family and me, she tackled her baggage via the therapy and her own inner work. Healers helped transformatively, with a top oncologist and an Ayurvedic expert applying their respective expertise, but Resheka did the work and continues to do so as her journey unfolds and her life lifts. There is no easy way out, she might tell you today. Suicide, whether a gun shot in the night, a leap off a roof, or a slow self-torture, is no solution. It absolves you of absolutely nothing. Yeah, have another cigarette. How hellish must be the build-up to such a swift or drawn-out act? Is it not easier just to face life head on and to grow, however agonising it may be at times? Having been born means that we have chosen this whole ride with death as part of the package. The only option is to live rightly and embrace destiny.

Freedom is in taking responsibility. It's too late for anything but total integrity.

Chapter 15:

Heal the Pain

George died alone in bed on Christmas morning in 2016. He couldn't take the pain anymore. He couldn't turn it around and into redemptive art any longer. He didn't have another comeback in him. I'd hoped that he did but I'd become doubtful. The drugs and health scares got too much, too.

"I could have helped him," I said to Simon in the car.

"We all could," he shot back, "but sometimes people don't want to be helped. Think of yourself when you are miserable. You just want to be left alone."

I suppose so, but deep down we still want to pull through. We need a reason to live, though, in order to do that. Without that we are on the back foot and falling fast into being fucked. We need to go through periods like that, especially as creative people, but we need to bottom out and emerge with a new lease of life for another round of cumulative brilliance, for fuck's sake. George didn't have a reason to live anymore and was weighed down by media attention and public pressure. His money might have worked against him too. He knew that his career had come full circle, and so he wrapped it up and let go. There could have been more to the story, though. This here is more.

I would have helped George dig deeply and find a new energy source to come from, and then align its expression with what the world needs and what he was still passionate about. I would have been his friend. Others might have helped him in other ways but I would have got him back in touch with his truth and inspiration and let it take him to a new level of creativity and serenity. That's what I felt about him over the years, but it was not to be. His life had its course to run and he slipped away before we could meet.

He rounded it off with the essentially-finished documentary of his story, called *Freedom,* which screened a year after his death and helped take the re-release of *Listen Without Prejudice Vol. 1* to number one in the UK, which the album did when it came out the first time in 1990. George was thus speaking from the grave, still having fun in the charts, and smiling that white-toothed beam like he did when his work did well. When you look back on his body of creative contribution - on the talent, craft, courage, confidence, pain, struggle, grief, music, visuals, vision, extravagance and class - and see it as a whole gesture on his part, you know that it went exactly as it needed to. He was being himself for a living from the beginning all the way to the end, and the sadness was as much part of it as the genius and the joy. Take heed and do the same in your way.

Artists heal pain for a living, their own (if all goes well) and the world's (when we are ready). Artists wouldn't be in the public eye if we weren't propelled into it to compensate for our suffering. Healing is our calling and we wouldn't be artists were it not for some enduring agony. Our alchemy is in turning that melancholy into some form of redemption, whether it's in musical or written form. We strive to share a transcendent experience to propel us into salvation and speak to the souls of others everywhere in return for fame and fortune. Pain makes our world go round, fuels our work, medicates our audience and makes us rich. We give away and, where possible, sell inspiration. Sex also drives it, and George was famously big on that. And then there is good old death, which sent him back up the charts one more time. Wham!

The sexual stuff got a bit much towards the end, when the wheels came off generally. His raunchy side shocked and set us free in 1987 with "I Want Your Sex", which squirted him into solo stardom. A decade later it was still there and strategically clever with "Outside" in 1998, following his bust in LA. But it became gratuitous and unsettling with "Freeek!" in 2004 and eventually turned concerning with the smell of general excess and creative bankruptcy as the years wore on. Yet we loved him all the same and respected his point. He brought gay wisdom into heterosexual culture, which was transformative for both, in my view, anyway. But it all seemed increasingly desperate in the Hampstead-Heath years, despite the self-parodies. Word was that he'd confessed to sex with more than five hundred men by then, which were hardly Gene Simmons or Julio Iglesias numbers, but still. They were not a sign of wellness. It seemed that the pain was taking over, compensations were becoming more exaggerated, and cries for help were getting increasingly disturbing, until sex and death were both uncomfortably dominant in the man we saw in the news. Having said that, I might go past the burger joint this afternoon to surround myself with women half my age, have a few glasses of wine, and do some writing, without paparazzi, thankfully.

George had the courage to die alone, which I admire. And he died in bed, which is a fine and popular place to come and go. Where else would he choose? In the shed with a shotgun? Not very gay, is it? What about in some form of accident? Well, he came close in one strange incident on the highway towards the end, and that would have been suitably dramatic, but it was too messy. In the nineties he was spared the fate of his first love Anselmo when HIV was still a killer, and towards the end Class A chemicals certainly contributed to his decline and weak organs, but he managed to maintain enough grace to escape an overdose. Surrounded by family and friends would have been a loving and nurturing departure but more fitting if he were thirty years older and less of a solitary soul. The bottom line is that he was alone in his deepest talents, insights and pain. Despite his communal warmth, he was a singular and peerless presence.

He may even have been awake when he slipped away that religious holiday, conscious of death as it approached and possibly orchestrating it with his usual perfectionism, which is the way to go. It was his last orgasm and poignant way of capping a year of epic departures. Trust George to bow out with composure. With it came closure, freedom from pain, release from the responsibility of fame, relief from the weight of the public eye, and escape from the money that can so easily turn against you. Maybe, as Emily Herbert's biography said, he hadn't been truly happy since the Wham! days when he had that supportive bond with Andrew Ridgeley. Back then he had to break loose and go large with his solo career, but that was equally the onset of his misery, which relentlessly consumed him for the rest of his life. It's not an uncommon narrative for the exceptionally talented. The fate, however, needn't be. We can all be ourselves for a living and develop a community of understanding and support. We can turn the tragedy around and make it healthy and profound.

What George sought out in order to fulfil his potential and compensate for his pain, like artistic recognition, global renown and sizable fortune, did not heal him in the end, although they made for some of the finest pop music ever created and gave us all a hero's story of note. Both will stand the test of time. He gave us all a great gift through his generous life and, in return, enjoyed a bountifully blessed one. In a way his success made his suffering more severe, though, with the glare of glory amplifying his issues and forcing him to chew more than he should perhaps have bitten off. That can be the plight of those possessed by such virtuosity. Maybe all he needed was a friend and a collaborator like me. Maybe the two of us are getting to work together after all.

Chapter 16:

John and Elvis are Dead

Lennon and Presley barely made it past forty, one dying by a bullet and the other bloated on the crapper. George reached fifty three and Frank was gone at sixty eight. Simon's heading heartily for eighty and I'm turning fifty at the end of this year, for what it's worth. Time is probably less important than intensity of presence, but I'll take a long life brimming and building with intensity, thank you. A sustained combination of quality and duration takes wherewithal, though, plus a dose of good fortune.

Bruce Springsteen watched Elvis go down early and used the chilling insight to avert suffering the same fate in his superstardom. I've done the same since I was a teenager, watching my mentor-mirrors like Bruce, and did so strongly with reading the recent biography about George. The book came at a pivotal time last year, filled in some missing pieces in his picture, and helped me process my pain via accessing his in a way I hadn't done before, despite my closeness to his story. I saw how suffering and celebrity took him out, and felt the blessings of his overall gift to me, which includes the wisdom to circumvent the ditches along the path.

I was also grateful for how long it has taken me to reach where I am, for the graceful journey that existence has given me, and for my freedom from financial opulence at first, which would have made it much more difficult, as it did for George. He was very rich very young and it certainly brought troubles then and all the way after it. Staying real is the prize and worldly wealth is a saccharine toxin if not sipped in perspective. My path has been patient and perfect, and money has its rightful place. John, Elvis, Marvin and George are dead but my death is still stalking me steadily and giving me the best chance I can muster to live to the full. It's a fine Friday as I do so here on my leather couch.

Your dreams coming true can be the worst thing that can happen to you unless you have done the work in yourself to understand their origin and handle them wisely, and then the work only beginning. The work is always beginning. There is no shortcut or way out, and it's no joke being rich and famous. It's no small feat to face your talent and fear, and to navigate the tightrope tempered by your impending termination. This is being yourself for a living. Only the best of the best attain to it. We all have an equal chance and we are all the best of the best in our respective ways.

"Only the good die young, John," I said with a comforting but cheeky grin to the malcontent Greek man I see in the Bedfordview mall in the afternoons, "so you've got nothing to worry about."

He tries not to smile but fails, because that misery is just a mask. It's tiresome to deal with but educational to see. He's always draped in black, snowed on by flaky skin, with a big belly, white beard and permanent scowl, unless I see him and coerce some kefi from his hidden core. I like to spread exuberance and mischievous humour.

"One day at a time," he says to me with an expression like the weight of Ancient Greece is on his shoulders. "One step at a time," he updates himself convinced by some of my energy. "At my age, you have no choice," he adds cynically. "I'm seventy two, you know?" He's been saying that since I've known him and probably much longer. It seems to serve him, getting him a free coffee here and there and roping in naïve participants to give him sympathy. He says the same thing every time, I hear him, and then I make uplifting jokes and move on swiftly.

I also reflect on how he represents many people, particularly a side to me and maybe us all. I am grateful for his reflection and the insights it gives into my drama and indulgence and the human condition. I know that his drama is his identity but I know what I give him does much good and maybe even keeps him younger for a moment, one day at a time.

"Why are you always happy and smiling when I see you?" he often asks, not waiting for any answer, as he is complaining and not enquiring. I laugh and listen, sometimes reflecting his feelings and telling him that I understand. I certainly do. I have my own string of miseries and gripes too, and so I empathise, but I don't get roped into his.

"For me it's a combination of being free, doing what I love, and sex with women half my age," I've said in the past with a deadpan expression, which makes him pause and then chuckle before he bursts into another rerun of his problems.

Usually he's to be seen alone but occasionally with a crew of other pensioners who sit together in the afternoons. Vincent, who's the same age as John, and still with a heavy Czech accent despite decades in South Africa, tells me, "He always speak like this, ne." Turning to John, he asks, "Why you always talk about your age, huh? I live at the retirement village with old people all around me and they are happy!" Turning back to me he elaborates, "The one vooman she is like this," making a right-angle shape with his hand. "She cannot stand straight but she walks from the home to the shops with a trolley every day. And she is smiling. Why? Because she doesn't think about age. She lives for now and only thinks about today." John just grumbles. Vincent is always beaming under his white moustache and sprouting insights from his latest reading of classic and underground literature. He has the power in his apartment switched off, takes cold showers, and always wears shorts, summer and winter.

John and Vincent are alive but in different ways. They meet at the mall most days with their little community of other immigrants to stroll and sit around, and tolerate each other's quirks in exchange for the companionship. They know where the coffee's cheapest, what eatery has specials on, and how to shop-crawl to get an optimal experience over a few late afternoon hours. They are all younger than Simon, but none of them seems to have nearly as much to live for or give.

George ran out of life, saw it coming, wrapped it up responsibility, and then went out with poise and a splash of tinsel, leaving us the gift of waking up on Christmas Day 2016 to the tragic news. Erm, thanks, old friend. A memorable move with quite a sting. We'll carry on here. I'll see what I can do with what you left us.

Frank also ran out of convincing reasons to stick around. His career as chartered accountant had been cut short by company politics, which compromised his last few pension-building years and crushed his self-confidence. That sort of slippage can hit a numbers man hard at that age. The late-in-life divorce from my mother broke him, too, especially since he never handled his emotions properly, and the combination of these factors with the directionless feeling of retirement left him with little if any wind in his sails, even though he was still young. A few years later, after his new companion in life died of cancer, he too succumbed quickly to a strain of the dreaded disease. His life seemed to have come full circle, although he had no intention of checking out yet and fought hard to survive the chemotherapy. That's what often happens when death comes sooner than we expect. We realise that we haven't fully lived and can't let go in acceptance and peace.

We need something deep and driving to keep us happily here, but even that doesn't fully explain it. John the Greek tells me every time I see him that he's had enough and ready to go, but there he sits week after week shrouded in gloom and willing a death that doesn't take him Why? He lost the family fortune, he claims, his siblings don't care about him, and all the retirees are fake friends. Whatever our respective narratives and vibrations, we must have a reason to be here, just like we have a perfect reason and time to go. Whatever I have forfeited on my path and struggled through to live my way, I am grateful to have plenty to live for as I approach fifty. I'm only warming up here. Staying true to myself has kept me on course and it gives me more growth and fulfilment now than ever. Neither John nor Elvis had that. Simon has it still and I am inviting if not seducing him into it more. Resheka discovered it in herself anew last year, which brought her through the trying treatment, and has her happier and healthier than in her previous incarnation.

Death puts everything into perspective. New life ensues.

Chapter 17:

Fantasy

In Thailand, all you have dreamed of can come true. Whatever you want, you can have. That changes your life. Any repressed fantasies can be lived out, which sets you free from them. Everyone is accepted as they are, too, and there is no social stratification. Shorts, T-shirts, sarongs and flip-flops, day and night, all year round. Whatever you are, you can be and find more of there, and whatever you want to try is presented to you before you can think of it. This is the opposite of a thwarted humanity. In that, and other ways, Thailand is transformational. No wonder everyone wants to live there and writers work it into their script.

Have you exercised and exorcised all of your desires? Can you lie on your deathbed and sincerely say, "Right, there's not a single threesome with women who between them add up to my age and my weight left in me. I'm ready to go."? Or do you feel that, even if you have not reached all your realisations in physical form yet, you are giving them a go impeccably each moment of the way? If not, your unlived dreams and desires may be directing you from behind the scenes. Unlived lives are the biggest regrets for good reason.

You can't die rightly if you haven't done what you came here for. And all the while, death is approaching, which makes your crisis more critical and your defeat or suffering more intense. How you deal with it all is in your hands now. Anything you have brewing or bubbling in your churning urn of compelling imaginings is best brought off the boil and onto your plate, and tasted with a discerning palate. Gay culture is good at that. Artists, too, tend to live more liberally. All of us, though, are in line for a thorough unleashing, whatever our predilection. It's part of humanity coming into our own and realigning with nature and cosmic intelligence, and going to a new level. It's happening now.

That may mean more than a jaunt or two down Walking Street in Pattaya, or a boogaloo down Bangla Road and back in Patong. A healthy dose of those trips should restore the system and clear the pipes, making you psychologically lighter and spiritually clearer. There are also bigger fish to fry. What about living the simple life on an island as long as you like? There's a dream come true for you. Or crafting a writer's residence on your ancestral land? Or both, flying between them on repeated round-the-world trips? Are you going to go for it? What about visiting new and exotic places as a matter of course while you help people self-actualise? Absorbing that richness will do you immense good, keeping you stimulated, happy, fulfilled, wise, fully-lived and, thus, able to let go with trust and relish when the time comes. Simply being yourself wherever you are in acceptance and relish is as important, and available.

Being the biggest pop star on the planet might be your deep, driving desire and dream. If George hadn't gone for and lived it, he might have died much sooner as a conflict-ridden wreck or some kind of deviant delinquent. Worse still, he might have run his father's fish & chip shop for fifty years. With the help of his talent, courage, crew and good fortune, though, and against his father Jack's wishes and judgement, he stepped into the manifestation of his inner myth and walked the rich and rocky road, on which he could be bohemian for a living, live out some wounds, and pull off a whole life performance finishing with the *Freedom* film and a number one record post mortem. He could be the delinquent but as a successful personal brand, and straighten society out a bit while he was at it, doing his community service for his sins.

And then, as tragic as it was, he could bow out in his bed to wrap up his package the way he wanted. He exploded onto the scene, created a compelling arc, shared an inspiring and unsettling message, and left with an affecting completeness. Fame and fortune are no answer in themselves, and they can make the presenting problem more pressing, but sometimes you have to ride them if you want to wrestle those demons and save the world.

Like Jack did with George, my father had difficulty accepting his son's ambitions. He was conservative, logical and methodical by disposition, training and practice, but underneath the surface, like Richard and Robin, he was creative. And so ultimately he related to, admired and supported the risks and steps I took, especially as time passed and I proved myself. I reckon everyone wants to take

131

these strides and wishes they had the balls, and the help. With their help, I'm doing it for him, his father, my unborn children, you reading this, and the whole fest of human form ever to roam this earth.

My dear dad paid for my degrees in my teens and early twenties, seeing law as a suited career but backing psychology as a profession and my passion. He helped me take my backpacking pilgrimage in the early nineties and was happy when I returned to work in the corporate world in a big bank in the city. Those traditional values were the ones he lived by and instilled, but times were changing and he knew better, despite not having the strong enough inclination to act on it himself. That was my job.

When I set out on my own at twenty seven, leaping without a plan into the great unknown with some experience behind me but going on intuitive vision and total trust, he surely saw it as a temporary soul-searching deviation or re-evaluation phase. Then I kept going. Then I went through tough times and stuck at it still. Then I stuck at it no matter what. I put out a book and made a name for myself in the media. I voiced the vision and lived by it. I sold a service and sent in a dose of transformation in a Trojan horse. I sometimes sounded radical but my ideas became less disputable as the world evolved and his personal experiences in his pre-retirement years proved my points. The 'big five' accounting firms became the 'big four' overnight six years after I set out, when Arthur Andersen went down with the Enron scandal, and now, sixteen years later, his lifelong employer is in big shit. His son had a point and by the time he died he held me in the highest regard. The ten years since have been the collaborative experience between us that I always longed for. Death brought down barriers and we could work together without the constraints of physical form and father-son relationship dynamics. Do what you know is true and stick to it.

Jack Panayiotou was openly against George's pop star aspirations and actions in the beginning, but he soon swung around with the band's global success, especially being a businessman himself. Artistic integrity came with the vast wealth generated by his brave and bold boy, which also flicked some switches on the mythic family level. The singer paid the price, though, and we are all left with the legacy to ponder over and from which to extract wisdom. That was part of what George gave overall, as if he had come here specifically to do it. His body of work is a heroic story lived out in the public eye for the community to be inspired by and learn from. This is shamanic success and true community work. All of us are living our myth in this way, even if it seems less spotlighted by celebrity. Through George, we live better lives, and through us, so should everyone.

It's wisest to do what you long for so that your soul can be set free and move on and your global tribe can shift forward. You should be particularly mindful along the way not to be too swept by the dark side that comes with your perceived salvation. Face your talents, fears and challenges with artistic tenacity rather than conservative caution, while still being careful, and stay close to the ground and rooted in your realness as the bounty and bumpiness beguile and inspire you forward. It's judicious not to expect any external elements to fill the hole inside but to encounter that in solitude, resourced with self-love. No bar girl or best seller is going to hit that spot, although they may each have their place in the story. The work is the same for all of us, no matter the metaphor. Death levels all playing fields all the time. It's pure joy with no regrets.

Every moment you are preparing for your death, whether you are aware of it or not. Every moment you should be letting go and dying to the present.

Chapter 18:

Waiting for that Day

My friend of thirty years, Paul Christelis, a psychotherapist, mindfulness teacher and author, who lives in London but travels extensively, wrote a chapter about his initial experiences with ayahuasca for a book called *The Wisdom of Not-Knowing* (edited by Bob Chisholm, Triarchy Press, 2016). The chapter is called "Ally in the Jungle - Everything I Ever Wanted to Not Know About Ayahuasca" and it describes various explorations he made in his life into the lesser-known realms of human consciousness, starting with trying to black out as a kid to see what death was like, through a vast array of drug experiences and spiritual teachings in his thirties, to the towering insight he found in the Amazon on a guided retreat taking the increasingly well-known power plant. He is working on more writing, as he has experienced more insight since.

What the chapter describes, once he is in the forests of Peru and on his second ingestion of the brew, is an encounter with death. It's an accelerated experience but something I can relate to in somewhat tamer terms as a general way of being in recent years.

The acute ayahuasca trip pushed Paul through such barriers of psychological pain that he wanted to die. He testifies to not being able to handle the intensity but somehow surviving, and being stripped to a new level of rawness and emotional realness. He saw, all at once, the blinding truth that we shield ourselves from, or nature does for us, because it is simply too overwhelming. Also, perhaps similar to the notion of your life flashing before your eyes when you die, he saw all of his 'stuff' condensed into one brutally revealing elucidation, and felt it with areas of his being he didn't know existed. He was uncontained by boundaries of self or methods of mind. That's not somewhere just any of us can go, I tell you, but it's somewhere we all need to, one way or another. To learn to live, we need to die to the illusion and awaken to the real.

I have no plans to take the plant because I relate to what it gave Paul, just spread out over my day-to-day living. The last two or three years particularly have been like dying each day, with intense emotions of rage and grief, explosions of cutting insight, waves of clearing baggage, washes of growing tenderness and empathy, and dawns of emerging joy. With this is a liberating understanding of how it all works under the obvious workings and surface-level dynamics. What happened for Paul on those few days in the jungle has been happening for me steadily over months, losing the illusions and finding out the truer truth. Could this be the waking up of humanity? Are we stripping down to who we really are? Is the past dying and falling away and leaving us alive on a new level of compassion and sincere living? Death is a central to it. What's on the other side is worth it. Paul keeps heading into the jungle for more.

Although the account in the chapter hardly describes the trips as overtly orgasmic, it certainly shows how they leave the traveller cleansed and healed. Perhaps the transcendental orgasm is simply more intense than those more familiar to us, and just needs us to trust and go with it. In keeping with the title of the book in which it appears, *The Wisdom of Not-Knowing*, the piece of writing opens the way for the awareness of living beyond the mind. We are wise but it is not through knowledge. Conversely, it is through the suspending of what we know that we begin to see. It is in stripping away the layers of illusion that we find the truth of who we are and how the world works.

This is the spiritual awakening, the second birth that we give to ourselves, the cleansing of the third eye, the passing through the doors of perception, the dying while we are still alive and, thus, the learning to truly live. This is the shedding of the fear of death by facing it. The initial terror Paul talks about reminds me of taking LSD, only much stronger. Perhaps it is this resistance and release that happen with death. If we have gone through it consciously beforehand, we are able to understand and embrace the shift. If we are weighed down, though, we may be preoccupied or petrified at the pivotal time and miss out. And so, the great teachers say, die while you are still alive so that you may be reborn. I know what they mean.

This is the work of the shaman, the spiritual traveller, and the social change agent. This is someone being themselves for a living. He dissolves the boundaries of normal, contained awareness and ventures into the unknown, possibly even the unknowable. Here he encounters the wonders of awareness both terrifying and transcendent, tastes truth and bliss at the risk of annihilation, survives intact, finds out who he really is, and returns to the tribe to transfer his insight as teaching to the community in the form of art, writing or therapy of some kind.

The loner ventures into the mystery and brings back redemptive rays of power to take the crowd and collective consciousness forward. The true teacher is a dealer in death and an alchemist with the basic elements of life. She goes past the finishing posts and comes back with a magical message the world longs to hear. The day will come for each of us when we see with our totality too. We do not really die, and what we think we do is nothing to worry about. We may even laugh at how we ran from it unnecessarily fearfully for so long.

Chapter 19

I Want Your Sex

Sex is perhaps the quickest route to the taste of enlightenment, to awareness outside of ego. The urge to merge with the other is the same intense inclination to reunite with all of existence and the beyond. What's required is consciousness to take sex out of its animalistic associations, past the corruption of taboo, and into awakening.

Simon laughed at his own statement that sex is a complete waste of time during which you achieve nothing at all, but this is not necessarily the case. If you pursue just pleasure, which is the lowest level of experience, then sex is at least that, along with avoidance (in the short term) of pain, unpleasantness or the mundaneness of life. It is an escape into mindless activity and feverish behaviour steeped in good feeling (but the induction, too, of its opposite). This can be therapeutic in its own right and certainly not without value in the whole picture, and in that sense it is not strictly a waste of time, but it can become mundane too. The problem with pleasure, beyond inducing a balancing experience and avoiding life, is that it keeps you superficially engaged, plus it is addictive. Sex for fun is a bit like a feel-good drug. It may come back to bite you and force you to face shifting onto a deeper level of awareness, which you should have done in the first place. What it gave you to start with may turn into the trouble it causes and, thus, the unpleasant opportunity to find another level of meaning to it.

The urge to merge is more than a sexual drive. It's a death wish! We all want to go home to where bliss is basic and we are free from friction, as pleasurable as friction can be sometimes. Some of us are aware of this inclination and able to suspend action towards it while we savour living and its blessings. Death is inevitable anyway, so why not hold it off as long as possible? Many of us, however, can't contain our compulsion towards suicide and act on it in small steps that add up to one big assisted euthanasia. We smoke a cigarette every fifteen minutes, seeking sick relief in every suck on the next toxic stick. Forty a day amounts to fourteen thousand six hundred a year or seven thousand three hundred packs in a decade. Stack that up on your kitchen table if you want a good look at self-destruction.

We behave recklessly for no apparent reason, barely holding together a semblance of a healthy lifestyle. Our inner need to be free shows strongly through the cracks. We can't take it here on earth and want to go back. Maybe our suicidal shots at reprieve are too strong to conceal in our shirt pocket. We find ourselves putting on a false front and then backlashing with actual attempts on our own lives, like out-of-control drink and drug binges, risky sexual behaviour, high-speed bike or boat thrills, unconscious flings with attention-seeking, and more of the like. Even riding a scooter around an island paradise has that strange pull into the ditch running alongside you all the way. With just a flick of the wrist...

Jim Morrison was fascinated with death and gone at twenty seven. Janis Joplin, Brian Jones, Jimi Hendrix, Kurt Cobain, Amy Winehouse, and other less famous names died at the same age and seemed to have a fixation with self-destruction amplified by excessive hedonism, blinding talent, emotional anguish, chemical dependence, inescapable pain, and a palpable sense of a pull towards death. The 27 Club may have no sound statistical evidence to prove itself a phenomenon, but the type of people who succumb to the syndrome do seem to have an overdose of something seeded in us all. (At the time of editing, Simon announced the release of his latest movie *27: Gone Too Soon* which looks at exactly this syndrome – How's that for synchronicity?)

We long for the realm outside of this mortal coil. George made it to fifty three but the signs were there already twenty six years before. The artistic types tend to hide it less as they skirt up against the limits of wellbeing more openly and often than the average conformist. Sex and pleasure are part of it but the fixation with the dark doorway and the vast mystery beyond it is woven into the fabric of their music, voices and legacies. It speaks to us all and for us all.

The urge to merge can mean the need to re-integrate with the rest of physical form to alleviate the pain of polarity. I am a man and you are a woman and we want to be one. Or it can arise from the pull to transcend material existence and return to our truer and timeless nature. I am spirit and you are spirit and we are torn asunder by this temporary torture of being bodily. Or death could simply be a state of peace that is inherently appealing since we are in one of intrinsic tension. Having life is innately unresolved and we pine for resolution. Sex gives us that sense in short doses, and orgasm is the most intense taste we get, albeit momentary with burdensome gaps in between. Death is the ultimate realisation, the one we resist with our physical instincts, psychological constructs, religious doctrines and persistent ignorance, yet seek with our deeper selves. However we relate to it, death is coming.

Best we wake up and embrace and understand it before then, lest we get taken by surprise or caught on the back foot. Best we distinguish between what we leave behind and what we take with us, and be ready for what we head into. Best we live in full awareness and appreciation while we are here.

Chapter 20:

Free

Until you can face death you will live in fear and come from the wrong position in life. That's pretty much all of us at this stage, but it's changing. An awareness and comfort with death must accompany an awakening of consciousness, and we are awakening, no matter how jaundiced you are or how little of a fuck you claim to give. We can encourage this emerging in ourselves and others by coming to terms with death, or, conversely, we can awaken our consciousness and we will find ourselves coming to terms with death. Either way will work because these go hand in hand with each other and with freedom. The system cannot control us anymore and falls away, and a real, responsible and emancipated humanity enjoys the earth on a new plane of wellness. Awakening, death and freedom equal living in a state of orgasm.

We can avoid this shift but that will simply serve to accelerate it. We can deny it and, thus, be its biggest advocate. We can insist on evidence that we will never get and, therein, stubbornly bring it all about. Whatever angle we take, we are it happening unavoidably. Believe it or not, buy it or not, be it or be whatever you want, but we are free and will always find our freedom, no matter what twists or turns we take. There is one inevitability alone and it is evolutionary and immense. Freedom is our true nature. The best way to it is through willingly sinking into ourselves and finding our source.

Are you quiet inside? Can you sit in stillness with no need to go anywhere, do anything or avoid yourself? Can you extend this inner silence to someone else, be peacefully in their presence and simply listen without resistance or the urge to speak? Can you hear them and reflect back what they say with respect and resonance?

Are you ready to retire with relish or are you terrified by the prospect of stopping decades of distracting activity? Are you running from that wall that is rushing up to hit you? Can you come from a creative rather than an evasive space? Are you at home in yourself?

To be still inside you need to die to all that is diverting you. You need to allow the compounded discord of a dreamy life to move through so that you can wake up to who remains on the other side. Possibly you need to suffer immense discomfort so that you can settle into eternal easiness. Perhaps you have been doing the required work all along, in which case you will have no problem. Perhaps, though, you have been putting it off, against your better judgement and growing indications from circumstance that you are increasingly off course. Then there will be a price to pay, one well worth it, and one that you cannot afford not to part with. The time has come in your life and human history.

Once you have laid your money down, surrendered all insanity, and nestled into infinity, people will start to pick up on your inner serenity and, without you promoting it, approach you when they are ready to face the false and find themselves. Twinkling equanimity will be your unspoken brand and you will be the effortless guru, the portal to peace, and the high priest or priestess of sizzling humility. You will be title-free royalty, a towering sovereign of sincerity. It's a position that cannot be inherited, bought, stolen or simulated convincingly. It cannot be taken away.

Tranquillity transcends all tensions. The richest and roughest cannot touch it and, in good time, will bow down to it, having gone to the ends of the earth to find it and possibly perished on the way. Ask Alexander when he comes around again.

When you die, you will take it with you. Make no mistake: there is only one prize and it is priceless. It is here now. Are you?

Chapter 21:

Hard Day

When you are down, you want to die. Artistic people in particular can go through the pits of depression. The fight to live feels like too much and the interest in doing so becomes lacking. The momentum simply isn't there and doesn't seem to respond to any effort to induce it. It's as if you need to be where you are, but all you want is to be out of it. The world is tinted by a dark filter. This state would be the wrong time to die but it is often the chosen one, or the one where it happens against your will, or by surprise. The psychological death you are going through can be so severe that it snaps across to the physical. It comes with the territory. Suffering has a lot to teach us.

Fear is depressing. When you feel afraid it doesn't take long for pessimism to take over. Your sense of inner power is missing and your direction isn't clear. Your spiritual roots seem severed and things are not working at almost every turn. Something heavy inside seems to keep pulling you down, vitality is hard to come by, and a grief hangs in the air. Sometimes it can go on for years, or most of a lifetime.

Death from depression or in a depressed pole of life must take that flavour with it. Whatever relief it may bring, it still tastes wrong. No matter how bad it gets, I still don't want to die that way. I want to go on the up and in a state of understanding and full acceptance, or even more preferably, perfect calmly, with enthusiastic peace. I want to be excited and intrigued, or absolutely centred, or both. I want to know what I am doing and be open to adventure. I don't want to feel dejected, although that's always a possibility.

Death is an explosion of energy, not a defeat. Even in a down-swing or at advanced and brittle age, death needs a surge to transpire. It's like getting a car over a speed hump: there is inertia to overcome. An old friend of mine, Stephen, now retired in the Karoo, was into reflexology years ago and had his frail mother living in the cottage at the back of his home. She had been ready to go for months and barely conscious for days, but still hanging on, when he went into her room one afternoon and massaged her body and feet. Then he left briefly and returned to find that she had gone. She needed that mobilisation of energy to make the shift. He helped her over the hump.

Some of us die after protracted suffering, finally letting go following a fierce fight, and some snap away like a twig in some seeming accident. Many need to be made unconscious by nature before they can face it, in their sleep or a coma, but what if we encounter death with willing awareness? What if we live and love rightly, understand ourselves and our crossing over, prepare for the physical reality as well as the possibilities for consciousness, and go into it with loving awareness? What if we enter death with coherence, friendliness and intense curiosity? I feel that this will have a transformative effect.

Aristotle drank the poison that was his punishment for being intelligent and speaking the truth in a society resistant to reality. He relished the opportunity to explore the new having lived fully while in his physical form. His followers were flabbergasted by his excitement and watched him as he took the trip. First he lost the feeling in his feet and exclaimed that he was still there and, therefore, not his feet. Then his legs went numb and he could attest to still being there and not his legs either. As the death of his body progressed, his consciousness continued to awaken. He went into it aware and in wonder, showing us the way.

Frank died holding my hand in hospital after two months of treatment for what was initially a chronic form of leukaemia that turned into an acute and more threatening one, especially at his age of sixty eight. The initial oral chemo seemed to be working and he went home for a few weeks, but then took a turn for the worse and, back in hospital, needed intravenous treatment for the more aggressive strand, which then took him out. During his second stint in the oncology ward, I'd been in to see him three or four times a day, taken care of his daily affairs, given him as much help, love and life force as I could, and been through the dramatic ups and downs with him in constant touch with Heather overseas.

One Friday morning, at my wit's end, I stopped in to see him on my way to a meeting I needed to attend more for the distraction value and downtime than any other reason. He didn't look right, having turned a dark red colour overnight, almost a purple. He was out of it, too, just not fully there, but the medical staff didn't seem concerned, so I wasn't too troubled either. Besides, I was pretty out of it myself. While I was at his bedside, the man with whom I had the meeting scheduled texted to cancel, less than an hour before the time, which was typical of him, but I drove through to his building anyway to leave him the parcel I had brought along. It was really just to clear my head. On the way back I spoke to Heather in London for forty five minutes, venting my pent up emotions into the car's speaker phone and getting heard by her. It helped immensely and I felt much lighter and more resourceful when I returned to the hospital's parking area, ready to see my dad. It was a sunny afternoon with a golden light filling the green gardens and beaming through the big windows into the wards.

As I walked towards the reception area, an old friend Mike from my corporate days called me having read a chapter in my new book INSIGHTS and decided spontaneously to act on what had just happened for him. He'd opened it on a chapter called 'Fishing' and been reading when his young son had come over to show him a picture he had just drawn. It was of a fish. The synchronicity had struck him as an affirmation of our deeper knowing, my work, and our connection, and inspired him to call and share the moment. It was exactly what I needed then and there, and gave me a lift and the strength to head inside the hospital.

My dad looked like he had earlier, only much worse. His upper body was blue and he was struggling to draw breath, gasping deeply with big gaps in between. I called the head nurse and she did a quick assessment and ran off to get the oncologist on duty, a kind soul who wasn't the main man treating Frank. He arrived in no time and told me in seconds that my dad was septicaemic and on his way out. "Say your goodbyes now," he told me. I asked him and the nurse to leave the two of us alone and shut the door behind them. I was ready. I came close to my father's side and held his left hand firmly, clasping the familiar fingers that so resembled mine. He was heaving and slumping alternately now, and I tuned in totally to him and the moment, knowing instinctively what to do. I heard in the unspoken that he was hanging on, detected why, and voiced to him that it was fine to go. "Don't worry, Dad, Heather and I will take care of things here. Just go. Do what's right for you. We all love you."

I called my sister on the cell phone and she answered instantly, at swimming lessons with her two boys. "Daddy's dying," I said, "and it's time to say goodbye." I turned on the speaker and placed the handset on his breastbone so that he could hear her and we all could connect through the heart. He couldn't speak or show acknowledgement but I knew he was right there listening while his body grabbed desperately at the air. Tears streamed down my cheeks and dripped onto the hospital sheets. Heather told him that she loved him and called the kids to speak to him too.

"Hello, Grandpa," the one shouted youthfully. "We love you. Goodbye."

We could let him go, and we so did with such love, and he went with his two kids by his side. With the phone line live and our hands clasped, his desperate drawing of breath stopped. His body lay slumped to the side with his mouth open, then, quite some time later, gave a last gasp, leaving him lifeless and already a yellow colour. I finished talking to my sister for the time being and stood back in the single ward to look over the scene before me, seeing the whole setting where it had taken place with just his corpse for company and an illumination in the air. That was reality right there.

There was such intensity in the room and I was properly present. Where was he, though? His dead body had been shed but what else was happening? As he had died I had felt a jolt, as if all of his worldliness was transferred over to me, bequeathed instantly in a clunk. With that I felt suddenly stronger, like his physicality had joined my energy. Whatever he had to leave behind he gave to me, and what he took with him was keen to depart. I felt it go, like a little boy of about six with a nineteen forties haircut and wearing school uniform shorts, someone who had been waiting patiently to run off and do something he had been wanting eagerly to do for some time. He had something with him, too, which seemed like a bundle tools or toys wrapped in a cloth, or a little bag of special belongings he held close to his chest. This was the spirit of Frank, someone I knew inherently and intimately in a way that only a father and son can. He was finally free and where he wanted to be. I was liberated too.

It was a remarkable experience for me in my own right and to share with him. I was enlightened by it and the bond between us came full circle and resolved, thanks largely to the work we had done by talking openly over the eight weeks or so, but driven by timeless love. We didn't cover everything in that time but we covered what we needed to. We had clearing conversations and sat together for protracted periods of silence, speaking without saying anything, letting the past go, facing the emotions, and feeling the shadows and cobwebs clear. We did the work that our souls had always wanted to and it paid. And so, when he went, we were both at peace, which was the most intense peace I had ever felt. Driving home that Friday night, after handling the logistics with the ward staff and setting off away from the sunset, I was still deeply sad and raw with other emotion, but I felt something I hadn't for a long time, perhaps ever in my life. In the presence of purity, life, death and love, I felt satisfied. This, I realised, is what we seek. We need the full experience of being alive.

Death is profoundly powerful and I would recommend being near it when you can, particularly with people you love. In addition to the personal side of my experience with and through my father, it was simply phenomenal to be in that sacred space when someone died. It awakened me to the nature of death and the gift of life, and it blessed me beyond bounds. It was like I was standing in shower of jasmine petals, a bountiful benediction.

Chapter 22:

One More Try

One of the most difficult things in life is to say goodbye. Do you know how to say goodbye?

We will avoid it, soften it, cling to consolations, hide behind pleasantries, glibly spew euphemisms, and usually do whatever it takes to keep goodbye at bay, because facing the finality of the big one is too much, and staying sincere throughout every little one takes mindfulness and a riveting relationship with reality. And so we slip past it and keep going in the dream, postponing true living one more time. Usually, too, by the time we are greeting in temporary farewell, we are happy to be rid of the person for the time being, so we don't mind doing the deed in haste. "Cheers, bud!" Every time we utter whatever understatement we choose, though, we have that potentially terminal element to deal with, the knowing inside that this could be the last time. And then one day it is, and we may well have rushed through it. "See you soon," we might have said out of habit, and then been left with it forever. Worse still, it might have been a feisty and foolish, "Fuck you!" Well, hey, that's no way to say goodbye.

Sometimes that's what you have to live with, though, when the other fucks off in fury and leaves you with the scenario and no recourse. Even managing yourself through the strain and hurt and staying in a state of love doesn't quite quench the lingering sting. Imagine the person might feel if never given the chance to redeem themselves? The pain might promote further imprudence on their part. We are all walking wounds rubbing salt into ourselves. Sad doesn't begin to describe it. Trust does sooth it, though. Everything is precisely as it is meant to be and all experience can be integrated and ultimately understood. The longer it takes to come around, the greater the relief, revelation and resolution, and the stronger the love.

The big terminations are tough to navigate but sincerity will see us through. They require our best attention and then leave us redeemed rather than regretful. They are the indisputable real deal where life reveals itself, like the loss of a lifelong loved one in their presence. "Goodbye, Dad," I said, and meant it with all I knew and had in me. That was a moment of truth. I was fully present there and his life as we knew it was over. Death was in the room and winning the day, whatever was happening outside. This was the time to live and love totally with no room for games. Every moment ought to be that way. That is awakening. That is enlightenment. That is orgasm.

If you can say goodbye properly, every moment and in the big moments, you are getting life right. In my view, a purely pragmatic approach will betray you at the transformational times. A matter-of-fact attitude about the practicalities of death on this side of the threshold will not hold up in the face of the imminent loss, the beckoning beyond and the overwhelming of love. There will be too much emotion, too much intensity, and too much realness for an ounce of cynicism to survive in you. Everything will come to the fore and you will be faced with facing it. If you are facing it all along, you can really rise to the occasion. Let's be in the business of facing it all the way. Let's live on this new level. There's more to life than getting your affairs in order, although that is part of it.

"Goodbye, Simon," Resheka and I said through the soft rain in the street an hour after midnight as we jumped into the backseat of the Thai taxi. It meant, 'What a great evening, thanks so much for the connection, see you again soon to pick up where we left off, and take care and have fun in the meantime...', but still it contained a lightning flash of 'this could be the last time.' There's always an element of, 'we'll have to wait and see,' a streak of mystery and of the beyond built into the seemingly ordinary. That's what makes it magical. We never know, yet somehow we do. We cannot know, yet we are knowing itself. We need to live in this paradoxical and profound awareness. This is presence, and presence is packed with hellos and goodbyes.

One of the saddest feelings for me around the illness that Resheka went through last year was the image I kept having of saying goodbye to her. It was based on the possibility of her dying, and in us not knowing what was going to happen, and I wept for weeks over that alone. We hadn't even been together for that long, so it wasn't time-based. Somehow it was in her energy field, too, and that still stalks me sometimes. It was as if the dying thing was in her template or karma, and that was what I was grieving for. I was feeling her repressed grief. The dynamic of death was in her karma or story, to deal with like that, and her game of tempting death was soaked in such sorrow that she acted it out but never faced it or felt it congruently. She didn't know how. Consequently I felt it on her behalf. The reminder of my dad was also in there, as he had died of a very similar disease. I was stricken with that grief too.

It brought back the memory of the movie *Blade Runner* from the early eighties, which made an impression on me then and has been one of those enduring artistic statements in my mind since. The main character, Deckhard, played by Harrison Ford, is a retired Replicant hunter brought back into his old role to terminate four escaped artificial humans who are powerful, dangerous and on the loose. Bred for productiveness and kept off earth, these products of artificial intelligence have discovered that they have an expiry date programmed into them, but they don't know when it is. All they want to do is live and get to know who they are, because as they become aware of it, they realise that they don't know. They can't trust their implanted memories, they know that they are dying, and life is too precious to let go of.

Resentfully and under duress, Deckhard takes on the task of finding and killing these living robots, and returns to work. But he discovers along the way that there is another Replicant involved, one not identified as from the escaped and feared four. She is

Rachel, and she has figured out her predicament too. In the end, the two of them elope to solve their problems, and he reflects that he has no idea how long she has left, but that none of us know anyway. They are left flying off into the unknown, living in the moment, hovering, as we all are.

Chapter 23:

Like a Baby

"No-one talks about death and how to deal with the grief, isolation and change," Bev told us with tears in her eyes. Resheka, Nokwethemba and I had been sitting having breakfast at the nearby golf club on a Sunday morning when a seeming stranger had approached and asked if I was an author. This took us into a quick conversation about a book her husband had wanted to write and had spoken to me about in the mall. "He died last year," she told the three of us when I asked about him, "of a heart attack. He was at his favourite coffee shop in the shopping centre."

"I heard about that and actually walked past the scene," I said, "but hadn't put two and two together. OK, so it was Dan that day..."

"There were paramedics there and they spent an hour trying to revive him, but I knew he was gone," Bev said. "His time had come. He'd already had one heart attack a few weeks before and this was his first proper outing since then."

Resheka and I saw Bev again on our way out, which is when she told us about the experience for her of dealing with the consequences of his death. "No-one recognises me," she shared teary-eyed, still in the fragments of shock that have accompanied the last seven months. "Everyone knew *him* and spoke to *him,* but no-one ever saw me," she added, explaining how she was discovering her identity for the first time at sixty two. Dan was a charismatic character and fairly well-known golfer. Bev had very few understanding and insightful people to talk to, and I related to that, and gave encouragement for her transformative time. When Frank had died I was left largely on my own to make sense of it and work through it. Death is not in the language of society but it needs to be. Usually it takes a death to drive this home. You need a real encounter to wake you up. Death is the real deal.

Grief. So vast, like a glacier, slow moving. So deep, soaked in rain. What grace it gives. It needs to be felt, respected, savoured, shared and understood. I am who I am because of grief. I owe it so much. A stiff upper lip may work in some situations but it is not the way on the whole, and certainly not with with grief. It is vital to the language of love and wholeness.

Isolation. Have you ever felt so alone that company amplifies it? Have you ever been thrown into the deep end and had to swim with wisdom you never knew existed? Have you ever been thrust into change beyond your comprehension? Death will do that to you. Death will set things straight. I am who I am because of isolation. I am steeped in the unspeakable and I am sharing it with you. Seclusion is helping me along and connecting us.

Change. Everything changes with death. The person is gone for good. Their presence has transformed into something subjective, something only you can sense in your private awareness. Is this life outside of the five senses? You might not be able to show or prove it, but you'll know. Is the person still around? Perhaps more so than ever, boundlessly, present and palpable. Everything has changed, particularly your awareness. Something has opened up inside you that you might never explain, and your day-to-day doing carries a whole new element of being. Emotions have never been this intense and somehow the ether is more available. You can sense eternity in the air.

Where would you like to die? Have you considered it? Your favourite coffee shop at the local mall surrounded by surprised friends and a couple of red overalls? In bed alone on Christmas morning? In a ward in a nearby hospital with your son by your side and your daughter on the phone from overseas? In an assisted-suicide facility in Switzerland? Romping around naked? Would you like to be fully aware when it happens? If you can get past the anticipation of potential pain and discomfort, then the crossing seems to be worth embracing openly.

I had a friend in Phuket, named Peter, a South African journalist who lived on the island for fifteen years. Like me, but ten years earlier, he discovered the unexpectedly crazy place on a first trip, wondered what the hell he had stumbled upon, and then fell in love with it and couldn't get enough from then onwards. He made it his new home straight away and arranged to keep his writing job with the South African newspaper from there. And so he worked from paradise and appeared in print every weekend on the other side of the globe. When we met I was on my third trip there and considering it as a place to stay, and he gave me a blunt and balanced perspective. He talked about South Africa still as somewhere to keep a base and connection. "I don't know if I want to die in Thailand," he said tellingly. Your roots run deep and death is a return to them. He died a few years after that, I'm not sure where, but he had been unwell and spending time back in his birthplace. Perhaps it was on African rather than Asian soil, where he felt most at home and ready to go. It's significant where we choose to die.

Spiritual teachers and great masters make their final statement with their death. It is the ultimate way to have your ultimate say. Lao-Tzu wanted to merge with the mystical Himalayas but was famously (and perhaps mythically) apprehended by a guard on the Chinese border who forced him to write a book as a condition for letting him pass. And so the Tao Te Ching was born and the old sage could disappear into the ancient power of the mountains. Zen master from Japan, Roshi Taji, was dying when one of his disciples dashed around Tokyo to find him his favourite confection, bringing it back to where he lay surrounded by many who loved him. Steady-handed and fearless, he ate it with delight. His disciples asked what last words he may have to leave them and leaned closer to listen. "This cake is delicious," he famously declared, and then died. What better statement could anyone make? Live in the moment. Enjoy every bite of life.

Alexander was not nearly as great but he made a gesture of departure as worth reflecting on when he let his hands hang openly from his funeral procession showing that, after all of his brutal pursuits and accomplishments, he died empty handed. George Michael perhaps pointed to the pointlessness of a public persona at the expense of a more settled life, or showed how pain can create a bitter-sweet arc of significance and sadness. His death certainly presented his career wrapped up into a contained statement.

Following a late-in-life revival taking him and his work to a new level, plus a fresh cycle of recorded genius, Leonard Cohen released a stark last album called *You Want it Darker* and then bowed out with his renowned charm. David Bowie, too, died with the release of his last record and left behind a cryptic set of artistic messages to crown his epic body of work.

What gesture or burst of words can be your perfect parting shot? What are you actually saying with your life? Be conscious and deliberate about it all along as well as at the end. Give your gift with your presence and ultimately with your death and eternal absence. Let it echo boldly and silently through the valleys of time.

Interlude 4:

Something to Save

Is it all too much at the moment? Are you unsure whether you can handle life? What does your death tell you? Maybe it says, "I have not taken you yet. Be open, you can handle it." Death is ever-expansive yet immediate with its clarity. Maybe it also says, "Hold on. Never let go, even in the face of your perceived demise. Keep your dignity against all odds." Keep your death close and go to it with your hard-won impeccability, plus a flash of audacity and plenty of tranquillity. Death will tell you to have fun! This is the ultimate ride and coming to an end. There is the perfect amount of time when you live to the full and stay in the present.

What knits you to infinity? The heart, of course. The heart should always come before business and show the way in all walks of life. If business and worldliness can catch up, all well and good. Surely there can be an overlap, but the heart will be out in front, leading the way. Death speaks the language of the heart. Be open to hearing it.

You can float along in your head but your heart will never leave you be. You can gear your investments for compound gain across decades and even the boundaries of lifespans, setting up legal structures to cater for your gene pool, and build absurd resources with a cunning glint in your eye, but that cannot come close to hearing your heart and catering properly for death. The more you manage your money, the more the money owns you, and the more of life you miss. The shrewder you become, the more you risk betraying yourself. The heart is childlike and wise. There is only one truth and it is staring you down, despite your diverse portfolio and clever devices.

One human's love is stronger than a planet of business. The financially shrewd might be left clinging to their empty currency when the chips are down. It's all a huge gamble and money will leave you short. Life is a bet on one thing alone and that is the heart. Gamble all you have on love. It will be there for you in the end. Not attachment and fantasy, but the real deal. Find it and bet your life on it. It is the essence of everything.

I wrote my first book in 1998, two years into being myself for a living and quite unexpectedly. I had defined my brand by then, given it the BEntrepreneurING name and developed its identity in the small community in touch with me personally, through an emerging online presence, and in the local press. I had begun writing for the employment section of the big daily newspaper in the Johannesburg area and was enjoying that creative outlet, publishing thrill and growing reach. Without planning it or being too aware of its primary role in my life and work, I had slotted into being a writer, which was starting to take centre stage in my creativity and productivity.

I had also been seeing people individually, in a counselling cum coaching capacity, which was to burst into bloom in due course. I was doing talks on my new topic to make my way onto the speaking circuit, and running training courses themed by it but still positioned in traditional corporate terms. One of those public programmes, on awakened recruitment practices, which was my area of expertise from my employment years, led to my connection with the newspaper and grew into a long-term relationship with the editor. As much as that was all happening, however, and quickly, I was feeling frustrated with my plans seeming to progress too slowly. I needed to make more money, but was not driven by it, and my vision was so clear to me but barely cared for by anyone else, especially close friends. The effort required to build it seemed monumental.

After a two-hour long coffee with a freelancing friend one weekday during which I demonstrated all my alchemy at great energetic expense to me, I felt rewarded but depleted, with a building sense of inner turmoil about my efficacy. Two weeks later, when we reconvened to keep up our networking and mutual support, he had gone back to square one, as if the last session had meant nothing, and I walked away pissed off and resolute never to put myself through that again. With that decision to stop wasting time talking to people who want to stay the same, I shut up for a few days and let the internal energies stew under pressure. That precipitated a seismic shift in gear from the verbal to the written, and suddenly, spurred by a cash shortage at month end, I had the idea of my first book. Instead of struggling over a few grand to cover expenses, I transmuted my tensions into producing something of strategic significance. This is the entrepreneurial way: go bigger to solve the little issues. The idea of a book had always been there but not felt vaguely imminent, and then it dropped from the astral plane and took over my life.

I was so inspired that I wrote with every waking moment, scribbling notes by hand and pouring insight into the computer. Friends would arrive for dinner and find me at the keyboard, and I would return to it throughout the evening unable to stem the flow for even a few hours. Not that I wanted to, as I had never been that enthralled in my life. My vision, voice and vehicle were coming together in a great gush of goodness, and they flowed richly like that for about three months, when suddenly the work was done, for the moment anyway.

Naïvely I printed out a few copies gave them to people to read, expecting rapturous responses but receiving silence or constructive criticism instead, tinged with more than a little ambivalence. It was tough stuff to digest and, mixed with the vast prospect of approaching the publishing process, meant that the book was shelved for months while I worked out what to do with it next. While it incubated, I carried on with my overall endeavour.

As 1999 rushed towards the turbulent turn of the century, with all of the speculative madness and energetic discomfort that went with it, I started to see that the book needed to come out without delay, firstly because it so captured the zeitgeist of the time, and second to open the way for my writing and publications to come. I brought the piece of work out from the back of my mind, and took the manuscript down from the shelf. Following some investigations into more formal routes, I had decided to publish it myself and learn as I went, which was in keeping with my mission and the freedom of my creative voice. No compromise, just artistic integrity and entrepreneurial ingenuity.

And so, with vastly evolved insight in mind and refreshed determination at hand, I disappeared into my den and emerged with a dramatically developed and improved body of writing that was formatted and ready to go to print. To usher it into production and celebrate my achievement, I took a quick trip to Cape Town, and then returned to Bedfordview to tackle the distribution to South African stores. By then I was also presenting a weekly business coaching show on the main community radio station in town, and writing for the press regularly, and so I had the platform to promote the pending arrival, which I did passionately.

Stock arrived like a first child, surprising me with the love and emotion it awakened in me, and soon afterwards, book shops received their stock. I held a signing at my local branch and then went to London for a month to see in the new millennium and present my weekly slot on the radio from there.

After the transformational year-end and an underwhelming trip, I went to visit my uncle Peter in Irene, just to see him and spend some time there. I drifted into the bedroom where I used to sleep on school holiday visits to my grandparents, the one where my gran used to keep her diaries. On the shelves where they still stood just as she had left them, I came across another black exercise book, this one inscribed by my grandfather back in 1934, five years before Frank was born. Richard was then in his early twenties, freshly qualified as an engineer, probably working on the national railways, and yet to marry and settle up-country where his firstborn grandson from his firstborn son was now reading his handwritten words sixty six years later. In typical attempted-diary-fashion, the first entry was longer, stretching to a page and a half, neat and calligraphic in blue fountain pen ink, and the second, a day or two later in a different shade of ink, filled only half a page. And then nothing more. It was enough, though, to give me what I needed to see.

As my eyes made their way through the words, I became mesmerised by their motion, sentiment and style. Aside from a few turns of phrase contextual to their time, they could have been penned by me. What I had just begun and then seen through with my book the year before, my good grandfather had had dabbled in decades before. What he had started and then left, like so many of us do, I had run with and taken to completion. The theme that ran silently in the family and been passed down paternally had born fruit through me, and it was all revealed in Irene, where it had first been revealed to my youthful soul in the seventies. Being myself for a living was meant to be, for everybody.

Richard died of Alzheimer's Disease in the late eighties, which may or may not have been related to his lack of self-expression and fulfilment in life but was certainly a symbol of it. The man I remember in his retirement years was characterised by frustration, blocked creativity, and a resulting sense of defeat. When I had searched my soul and followed my calling in the mid-nineties, I had found confirmation of my direction in considering his incomplete legacy. I did what he wanted to do. My decision to leap was supported by his son Peter, who in that represented Richard and the rest of the Wheeler family.

A few years after that, the rite of passage of producing my first book broke new ground, became a firm foundation for the future, and formed a fine piece of history, all steeped in my ancestry. Going with your inner knowing and doing your bravest and best work sets the scene for the rest of your mythology to unfold optimally. This backbone of your worldly journey holds together your being yourself for a living. There's a story running through your veins. Hear its whisper, feel its roar, and live it out in world. It will give you all the meaning you need, and help you die happy.

Chapter 24:

Please Send Me Someone (Anselmo's Song)

To write a new book you need to find a new voice. After finishing the twentieth title in the INSIGHTS series last year, I went looking for one. I didn't drop that way of writing but I took a deliberate break from it so that something different could arise after a period of distinction. The collection wasn't necessarily complete but the number was nice and round and certainly substantial. More important, I was overdue for a big shift onto new levels of work and engagement. I had been productive but felt stuck and was in search of something that would make the difference I needed.

This morning at gym, on my first day back after five weeks in Asia, I chatted to the boxing coach, Jono, who wished me a good year and asked how Thailand had been. "Did you get the inspiration you were looking for?" I'd forgotten discussing it with him before, and when I paused, he continued, "Remember you said you go there to get inspired?"

"Yes, I did," I confirmed, thinking of this book and the general sense of enthusiasm I have about me from the trip. "Lots of inspiration," I added, filled with gratitude. Jono put me in touch.

To write a new book you need one to precipitate, and you need to act on the accompanying inspiration, which means that you need to be ready and disposed. You need to find the thread and then run with it, and then you need to keep going all the way until it is done and you are transformed. It takes more than commitment, it means devotion. You need something big and worthwhile enough to work on for you to give the best of yourself to it, and then you need to be taken along for the ride, wherever it goes. It is a creative and a receptive act, which informs your new voice.

To write a new book you need to grow onto a new level. You need to take opportunities and see them through with trust and loving attention. You need to be done with what was, and sincere on a higher stratum. Then, when the tome drops out of the ether, say one Saturday night in Pattaya, you spot it and go with it. You give it due respect. You came all this way for it and, showing you due respect, it whisks you with it. You go along unreservedly, opening your heart and using your best judgement. This gives you and the book what both of you need.

This means dying to the old you. Even if you were down to nothing before you took the leap, some of your ties will come with you wanting attention. Even after you have shifted you will be unstrapping yourself. Dying is a fulltime job. There have been times while writing this where I have felt like I was dying, which became daily when I reached the editing phase. Every morning was the beginning of a ride of emotion that swept me up and down and had me head over heels at high speed. Tears of grief and release, and tears of exceptional joy and relief, day after dedicated day. Struggles through tough patches and bursts into fields of green. An acute climb in a short time and a new me emerging all the way. Birth-canal blues, growing pains, letting go and taking hold. Being a servant and becoming a master. Finding what I was looking for and turning into who I was born to be.

I went to Thailand overdue for this discovery, knowing what some of it was, staying intuitively in tune as we went, and waiting for whatever it was to drop. Having actively not written in the INSIGHTS voice for a few months, I had eventually secretly gone back to it just to get writing again, and to processing the usual flow of inspiration coming through. I had a quarter of book twenty one saved when we flew up to Pattaya. That's when *Death is the Ultimate Orgasm* stepped in and took over. I have added some chapters to the other book during the gaps in this one, and it will be born sometime, too. That voice, it seems, is a staple, and this one the main meal at the moment. Surely there will be others like it, as I can feel them brewing already in the bustling queue for my attention.

After lunch and our afternoon together, Simon went home for a while, and Resheka and I put on our swimwear, walked down through the hotel pool area to the private beach, used the gym, lay still for a bit, showered and then took a tuk-tuk into town to meet up again at a hotel in the heart of the action. Guided by the eye-opening characters sitting around us on the back of the open vehicle, we made our way down the beachfront road packed with neon-lit bars, found our stop, and jumped off into the swarms of people at the top of Walking Street. Looking for the specified location in disbelief that we would find something classy in that seedy environment, we asked as we walked and, sure enough, eventually came upon the place Simon had said that he would have recommended for us, the Siam Bayshore Hotel. We were a little late for our rendezvous, having not budgeted for the enchanting stroll, and we found Simon waiting patiently in a high-back chair in the reception lounge. He was glowing with renewed energy and a taste of the copy of SEXIER INSIGHTS I'd given him earlier, some of which he'd read during our break. He likened it to the beat poets of the sixties as we stepped back out into the night.

He'd wanted to show us Walking Street so we did a second trip down it, up to where we started, tripping even more on the energy and scenery, with Simon buzzing on his first time there in over a year. It was as good for him to have some youthful energy around with some solid conversation as it was for us to have met and got to know him. That's what you miss living in Thailand as an expat - intelligent and sophisticated conversation in your own vernacular. Stimulating resonance is scarce among the opulence of other pleasures. I've missed it myself on long stays, and seen people who live there leap at it when we've met.

The three new friends proceeded past the top of the throbbing pedestrian trip, over the teeming intersection where the tuk-tuk had dropped Resheka and me, and into the gay section, settling spontaneously for supper in an authentic-looking Italian restaurant with five or six tables in it. Simon and I sat next to each other and, from across the table, Resheka watched in amazement as two similar souls consolidated an inspired connection, and proceeded with mutual seduction. We shifted roles, dancing between mentorship, brotherhood and creative collaboration, and then he told me what he thought my writing needed, in order to go where it needs to go. Like I have done for people over the years, he knew the title when it dropped out of the sky, and then sketched how he felt I should address the writing style and structure.

It was mixed up with his feelings spoken boldly but I was able to filter the essence and see past rough edges and discern exactly what I needed to gain from the universe's orchestration. My ego took a backseat as my spirit seized what I had travelled far to find. With the book on the table, he bantered about his commission and I bantered back about doubling it when he brought me the right deal, saying that I would have it written in three months. It was a daring statement, but I knew that I could do it and have since held up my side of the deal.

In this first meeting, we tested parameters, checked out styles and enjoyed being playful. They were early steps, but we took them quickly. I sat there feeling the book take shape as the moments lingered and we spoke on about other related stuff. I had begun writing it in my head. Resheka and I made it to sleep really late, exhausted and wired, but I was drawn forward by a sense of inspired direction already in place. I typed out some ideas before bed and wrote at the airport as we waited for our early flight.

Ahead of leaving home a month before, I had sorted out my affairs, cleared all my admin, left an empty fridge in the kitchen, and let go of everything to head into whatever the universe had in store for me. Along the way, as we explored and enjoyed the island together and took trips from it, I shook off the past even more until, on the first day of the New Year, we followed instinct and opportunity up to Pattaya.

A new voice began speaking and we came back to South Africa with these words streaming from my thumbs.

Chapter 25:

Jesus to a Child

We are all so scared. We want someone to save and look after us. We are terrified to face life and death alone. I was fearful even going to the dermatologist this week. It's brave work. Fear stalks us. We are still children inside and struggle to grow up. Coming to terms with your death realistically and mystically must be the most grown up you can be, don't you think? Is it not the full coming of age, whatever age you may be?

Death forces maturity upon us, and once we ripen through it we are grateful for it, not only despite but because of the struggle and pain along the way. The wisdom is worth it, although not a natural consequence of suffering. We have to do the work and claim the wisdom as power. Death is a ruthless teacher and, in that, infinitely compassionate. As much as some people can perform the parental function for us for some of our time on earth, we have no true parental figure. We long for a transcendent God-father and earth-mother, but we have to find these roles within ourselves and our subjective relationship with life. This coming of age is wisdom. Death is always there with the key and a loving hand.

Living in love is an antidote to drowning in conditioned fear. On the level of duality it is the affirmative pole, but pure love is the overriding nature and intent of existence. Love is the fundamental choice in life, the finding of the higher and the ability to observe the lower. Love is the way, and we know it, but fear creeps in cleverly and through corrupt and nefarious means, which are promoted by social constructs that benefit from our frailty. Love is the truth and fear is fake, taught to us from the moment we are born. But it's crafty and convincing and carries the payoff of appealing to our propensity for renouncing responsibility. We are vulnerable as babies and need parental care to survive, but then we are exploited out of our authentic power and kept dependent on the system as a surrogate guardian. We even fight to defend our oppressors, such is the insidious nature of fear and the calculating persistence of its promoters.

Love is real and fear is a construct, but we are drawn away from the authentic and towards the fictitious in this Disneyworld we call home. That's part of the process of bringing us back to ourselves, and part of the playful pantomime. We are sold a reasonable facsimile with special effects, in lieu of strong roots in the real thing. Love is the source and the destination while fear is a distraction along the way, albeit a convincing one with valuable lessons. Love is the parent we always need, and the way to love is through knowing and loving ourselves. Love is both mother and father, and who we are, too, and so we're sorted. We can relax. We can relax and love.

Sitting. Just sitting. Hollow inside, like a flute. Empty, and full of purity. Coming from and going nowhere. Being here. Dissolved without distinction. Simply one, infinitely vast. Pure and present, perfect for music to play through. Humming in harmony. There's a word for it somewhere...

A draft beer after a coffee in late-afternoon early-autumn. Cakes in the palate-pulling fridge, crooner jazz coming out of the overhead speakers, a jaunt to the burger joint imminent, a book before me next to the beer, a thick grey sky outside and an empty sky within. There's a word for it approaching...

The word for it is neither here nor there, neither good nor bad, both up and down, and everything integrated. The word means life and death, coming and going, eternity and timelessness, all and nothing. It is enlightenment, but 'enlightenment' is not the word. It is poetry and silence, and mystery and clarity, like a fan hanging motionless from the ceiling, chocolate-coloured and arching against a smooth and earthy roof scene. The word is on the tip of my tongue...

The word is on my mind, in my mouth, between my legs...on my fingertips, in my heart, between the lines...on the horizon, in the moment, between you and me...on point, in tune, between islands...on board, in transit, between lifetimes...on my deathbed, incarnation, and betwixt and between. The word is one you probably already know but need to rediscover...

The word, like me, is back at the burger joint, a second draft down and well underway with a happy-hour fest from the gods. The word is a quiet Tuesday in the Easter week, half-price appetisers at sunset, spirituality thriving in the mundane, the rich life with a book to write, and true wealth to spread. It is a heap of deep-fried delights with garlic mayo, someone my age's daughter delivering them on a platter and staying to chat to me, more of that mayo, and more of these waitresses...

The word is a divine breath blown beautifully through a fine reed, an inspired life expressed through a bold and brassy sax, a sad song with a happy tune, a backbeat on the front foot, a poem in prose-form, a white head on a new gold beer, a sexual subtext to every scene, a razor-sharp attendant and a subtle innuendo, a trip to my car with a young beauty to give her a book, an exchange so sublimely delightful I wouldn't know how to tell you about it but to write you a whole new fucking book, a moment in the moonlight that makes my youth look like it's long gone yet only just begun, a joy so sweet and innocent, and a longing that goes on forever...

The word is an orgasm, a little death, a big deal, a small token, a huge heart, a short squirt, a long story and a bottomless cup. The word is the one you are looking for...

The word is Tantra. Do you know it? The word doesn't matter but the experience does. The experience is everything. Use the word and then forget it. Take the boat to the other shore and then live on the new land. Cross the river and then thrive in an awakened life.

Tantra is a state of total awakening, both spiritual and physical with no distinction between the two. It is the personification of integration with a great living thrown in for the existential fun of it. It accepts opposites without preference, embraces all of life without restraint or hesitation, and, thus, it attains transcendence with a big bank balance to boot. It is the highest form of being.

Chapter 26:

Praying for Time

I read an interview that GQ did with musician, producer and multi-active man Quincy Jones, having been drawn to it by someone on social media calling it the 'the greatest interview there has ever been'. In it the eighty four year old says that he has heaps of girlfriends around the world, none older than half his age. He goes annually for advanced medical maintenance in Scandinavia, and expects to reach one hundred and ten, based on expert projections. He's busier than ever with dozens of projects on the boil, having lived through all sorts of extremes from poverty, hardcore gangsterism, wild living, extensive creative collaboration and flippancy with knowing practically every celebrity. He says he lost sixty six friends last year to death. He knows how to live, it seems, which is inseparable from knowing how to die, although he showed little awareness in the interview of some of what we've been discussing in this book. That's a pity, elder-man with a lot to say.

Quincy knows how to be mega-worldly but has he seen beyond that? How deeply has he been into his being? This is the key question of our age. Do you know yourself? If not, now is the time to find out. Death is the great teacher. Can you sit in an inner stillness and silent knowing that makes men twice your age envious? Can you make the mightiest power monger put does his sword in admiration? Do you have what money cannot buy? Have you done the inner work? There's no other way, no shortcut and no substitute. You can't procure it, seize it violently, fake it, or hide not having it. You have to live it. It is time for us all to live it.

If we subsist in denial of death, not only do we miss out on most of what life is really about but we become callous protagonists of a society cruel towards aging and the depths of human experience central to wholeness. We are full of information and opinion but devoid of essence and substance, empty shells with big mouths and no centre or presence. We are soldiers on the surface but cowards to the core. All the outer wealth in the world can't help with that, but only make it worse. Life on earth is a sojourn through paradise but also not far from hell. It is so much more than seeking pleasure and avoiding pain. The depths of our own delving determine our degree of resonance with that and with others. The heart of being human is yet to be discovered on the whole, but we are breaking through the dark clouds. We are learning to love. The illusion of ego is shuddering in the new light and fading from prominence in our emerging consciousness.

Resheka stayed at work late yesterday afternoon, a Friday, to do some writing. She finished her meetings for the week and stuck around the office to get down what had come to her in the form of strong insights the day before and since. She wrote eleven hundred words, which is a solid chunk and my average for a day here, and later we talked about it over dinner. I heard her for her own experience and also for how her words should make their way into my book here. I am on the lookout and took note so that I could convey them to you, but now I have forgotten them for the moment. This red wine, ice water and Saturday-afternoon-with-discerning music combination at the burger joint might help, or take me down another path entirely. We'll have to see. I have to follow the writing. I am a servant to the inspiration and the art. I made my commitment long ago and can only follow it further, wherever that leads me. I do my best to navigate the humble service prudently and in line with my sense of self-love.

My devotion to divinity and serving humanity has just led to a twenty one year old waitress, Shannon, talking to me for ten minutes about creativity, growing into adulthood, being true to yourself while you work out who that is, and expressing yourself in a raw and real way. She made me think of many things (some of them distinctly sexual) and one of those was something Simon drew my attention to a few times and that I have been meaning to mention here. Perhaps this is the time. I'll get to it. The writing and the moment show the way. We have to go with them and get it all down.

"Then you have an end product," Shannon said about drawing and writing.
"Yes," I reflected remembering how satisfying it is to not only to write but to produce a book, the end product. It's an enormous

endeavour but it's always worth it, intrinsically and ultimately, because then, after the journey, it stands as a testament. You have been transformed by the process and have a tangible outcome that was created through you. A friend of mine, Ewen, who is an advocate I often see at the mall, has a few times noted to me that he finds the lack of such satisfaction a characteristic of his work. When the case is done, he is left hanging, whereas my efforts have staying power. He is also a musician, which probably plugs that hole in his life, among others.

Standing here next to me, Shannon also talked about expressing herself through unbridled art and believing in not editing it too much to preserve that initial energy. Then she shared the existential struggle within her to reconcile that sense of self with putting on a certain face for her waitressing job and other roles in her life. Pretty profound. I could see this beautiful woman and the great love and wisdom given to her by her father, whom she mentioned a few times. I commended him silently and then vocally to her while I felt myself in that role for a moment, resonating with how Simon must have felt seeing me and wanting to support and feed my work. Everything he saw and felt was mirrored to me with Shannon, the attraction, admiration and parental pull. Life is a circle and it's a magnificent experience to have a book in which to watch it come together.

The first thing Simon wrote to me last year was, "Hi Robin. Your concept appeals to me greatly. The problem being, as you obviously know all too well, that people have to find out who they are before they can make money from being it. Presumably your seminar helps them with all that." Not long after we met a few months later in Pattaya, still in the foyer of the hotel, he recounted a decision he'd made that week about what to post on social media and whether or not to state his opinion in the comments, knowing that it would cause an outcry, which would mean unnecessary response-work for him. His question was: who was he? The instinct to just say it or the prudence to pull back? His point was that we are constantly questioning, assessing and deciding who we are, or at least who to be socially. That's what Shannon has just shared from her experience. The day with Simon left that initial question still hanging in the air: who are we and what does it mean to be yourself? Another way to put it would be: what happens when we die? All of these questions are woven into every question we face at any age in life, whether it's twenty one, forty eight, forty nine, seventy eight or eighty four, and whether you are working on a book or in a burger joint. How do we live and how do we die?

Resheka's writing experience, when she shared it with me later, was moving and fascinating. I wasn't sure what her output would be about, as we have discussed her book's direction many times over recent months and I assumed that it would be more work-related owing to the location of her realisations and time at the keyboard. It turns out that she wrote about facing life and death. We went for a long walk on Sunday evening and I asked her to share more from what she had said initially so that I could get a better handle on it and write it here.

She talked about a turning point she faced last year in the middle of that chemotherapy treatment. The realisation was fundamental then and still revealing itself and its power now. For the first three intravenous sessions, which were three weeks apart, she went through living hell. The pain and discord she experienced in her body seemed insufferable and inexpressible, except that she somehow endured them. Looking back at this initial stage she reports that she was still in the same resistant state that had characterised her whole life up to that point, which was the stance that was formative in the arising of the illness. Her anger at life was still in full swing. However, she was also hell-bent on needing fewer treatments than the prescribed six to eight forecast by her oncologist, which was further fuelled by her agony, but she was not out of the woods yet and had to face more suffering. Her body was responding positively, with cancer counts dropping and the growth in her hip reducing in size, but the results were neither strong enough to feel safe nor advanced enough to change the treatment. She had to continue.

She was furious, which turned into a fight with the doctor during the consultation between sessions. When she expressed her rage and he saw it, he told her that he had been waiting for her to reach that point in the therapy, and that only now was she ready to get well. Up until then, he said, she was not fighting for her life and his treatment could not be effective. With her getting over herself and finding the will to live, and being ready to work with him, he could now treat her properly. It was her responsibility to get well and his to help, which he could do once she had got her head straight. She had to let the old her die so that she could achieve this. Looking back now she explains that she had always wanted to die, throughout her life, as an escape but also a dare to existence out of resentment and spite, and the illness was simply life responding to an intention she had been putting out there for forty seven years. Faced with death for real, though, she found that she didn't want that either, and so she was stuck in an agonising quandary until something gave way, and that was her stubbornness and repressed anger. That was her false self.

She had willed her death to avoid facing life, and now that it was in front of her, she saw that she still had to face both. Death was not a way out because the only way to deal with it is to live. There is no way out but to live. As important as it was to realise that, she also processed admitting to herself that she had always been playing a manipulative game with life and that it had now called her bluff. She had always been angry and now she was faced with more than she had bargained for. To die, which was her childish scheme to get out of the commitments of living, she now had to suffer immensely, which wasn't part of the plan! For the first time, she truly knew that she did not want to die. She was prepared to face the suffering and learn from it. She wanted to live.

She was ready to stop her games and get real, and the doctor saw and validated it. This was also what I had been addressing with her all along, as part of our relationship and then as an enduring issue now amplified by the illness, which I was facing with her. She was grappling with all she had churning within her, and I was working alongside, facing my own stuff and having it highlighted and triggered by hers. I would never equate my struggle with what she went through, but it was certainly colossal in my own right and in support of her. I was going through hell too and learning on a level beyond previous bounds. I was feeling by osmosis, as I do, and handling on her behalf the emotions she had always repressed, while she steadily made sense of it all, endured the medical procedures and physical symptoms, and waded her way through frightening emotional territory. From that halfway point onwards, the treatments started working well and wearing her out less. She had found what she was looking for and begun to get well.

It took death to give her life. Now she is more vibrant and vital than ever, with her hair growing back thick and curly. I saw a photo the other day of her a few months ago when it first started growing again and I felt the contrast with her now, which made me revisit what we went through. It took such suffering to wake up and be aware. Is this not happening to humanity as a whole? Is it not a matter of life and death for the species and our planet? Are we not facing a self-induced demise that is forcing us to shift our bullshit and choose to live? Will this new life not be in a whole new level? Are we not finding how to be real, responsible and healthy? Is this not the cure for not giving a fuck? Death is the great healer.

In Simon's car the car that afternoon, while telling us about having his name on the list at the Swiss assisted-suicide facility, he said that he wouldn't put himself through chemo at this stage in his life. He didn't know anyone at his age who had lived more than six months after having it, months that were typified by great suffering. He had his pragmatic approach in place in case it was needed: say your goodbyes, and go and get the job done. What he didn't know at the time is that Resheka had been through chemo only a few months before. I looked at her lovingly in the back seat in our silent knowing while he talked on. She did speak up from her experience but Simon didn't seem to hear. Some insights are your own to have and to hold. The conversation continued down its bountiful path and then later that evening at the dinner table Sheke shared more of her experience, but Simon still didn't pick up on what she was saying and where she was coming from. I listened and observed, though. This book was brewing and so was hers. Insights were tumbling beautifully into place.

On that inspired night in the liberating city, the beauty of being, the loving cruelty of death, the agony of treatment, the strangeness of our self-destructiveness, and the bounty of our breakthroughs soaked the streets outside like rain.

Chapter 27:

Club Tropicana

I am at the burger joint. The waitress has just taken my order for a beer and backed up my interest in the food special advertised on the table display.

"This," she said passionately as she placed her hand on the promotion stand, "is amazing!"

"I got that sense from reading about it," I replied, buying some time to behold her.

"I'll bring you the menu to look at," she smiled appetisingly, "but this..."

A beer and that, I thought. Two beers.

I am feeling the lift that comes from an uplifting environment. It reminds me of Thailand. That's why we go to Thailand and why I come here on a Thursday afternoon. Gentle buoyancy. Quiet happy hour, sweet scents from hookahs, and well-chosen classic rock music. Cold beer, flashing car windows in the setting sun, raucous bikes and show-off modified cars roaring past more than occasionally. That's Bedfordview for you, where I grew up and still live. The high school is over the road where thirty one graduation classes have passed through since I did. Fuck me! Let's get back to the cheerfulness, and back to 1983, when I was into music in a big way and at the beginning of my sexual prime. Wham! released "Club Tropicana", their forth single from their first album *Fantastic*, and the video featured George and Andrew in Ibiza playing the role of air stewards who have a great time on the island despite missing a chance with two hostesses played by the backing singers Shirley and Dee. The visual and sonic imagery of that song has surely stayed with me and informed some of my passions in the ensuing thirty five years. Beach life, sunset swims, warm water, and women. Exotic pleasures appeal to me. I am happy in the sunshine. It feels free and makes me happy.

Bedfordview has most of it, with some of the finest weather in the world (this afternoon is magnificent), an abundance of excellent restaurants (I live like a king), and my history here (which is an empowering as well as a restricting thing), and so it has its prominent place in my big picture. There are other places I need to be, too, though. Wherever I am, what I love is the feeling of magic in the air. The streets of London, the avenues in Paris, the shops in Kuala Lumpur...

One afternoon towards the end of our stay, Resheka and I took a ride up the west coast of Phuket, past Surin, through Bang Tao and on to Rayan beach. It was my first time that far north on the bike, and our first time there together. An immediate photo opportunity turned into a string of sublime sunset pictures, a sleep at the table waiting for our food at an ethnic eatery, and a departure from the establishment following poor service and an hour-long wait. The people sitting next to us had eventually received their food and it was awful, and they complained with no success, and so they left and recommended to us that we try the pumping up-market place next door. We had walked through it earlier on our way in, and I'd been inspired to make a video of the pool party. And so we returned with a skip in our step and a well-formed appetite, sinking into two seats in dream-like soundings with happy people strolling around, and chilled and groovy music coming from the DJ in the middle of the water. By this stage the sunset was white gold through the hessian structures between the sun beds and the sea, and paradise was afoot, evoking a teenage fantasy by making it come true at forty nine. Wham! has always been with me for the ride. Thailand is a great place to be if you like living in music videos. For me it's work and pleasure in one.

Back in Bedfordview, two beers and a strictly non-vegan meal later, I am pleased to have put down some writing via my trusty handheld device. I've just ordered a third beer. Hey, the drinks here are free.

Chapter 28:

Cowboys and Angels

"You're pulling heaven down and anchoring it deep in this book," Amanda has just told me via text message.

"That's a beautiful sense you have there," I wrote in reply. "Wow," I reflected further, "that's exactly right, you know."

"Feels so," she confirmed.

I had been updating her on the progress. It's Monday morning and she was saying hello after the weekend, checking how I was going, and seeing if her giving me space to write was working for me. I was busy with a piece of writing already, which I then finished and added to the manuscript before giving her the latest word count. I shared some of my experiences, too, like the shift in gear from last week and the seeming shift again at the beginning of this one. That led to her insight into what I am busy with.

My sense is that she was speaking intuitively and, in that, voicing something as she felt it. She's talented that way and should be writing herself. No pressure! I'll do it for us in the meantime. Maybe she was incorporating my mention of what this book feels like for me and reflecting that back to me, hearing me. I'm not sure how she could have got her understanding that way, though, since she has seen none of the content, but it is definitely the direction and outcome of this book. Her phrasing is a poetic way of putting it, with the reference to heaven, but it articulates the essence of the feeling and message as well as the process of my writing pulling something down onto paper. It's as if I am channelling it, anchoring a higher sense of things in an art form, structuring a series of images that hang together, and speaking in a vernacular that is accessible to the current consciousness and modern palate. I am doing the shaman's job of articulating the abstract into the tactile and, thereby, taking the tactile up. This could also be called tying a taste of the horizon into the steps of the now. That is what I do with all of my work.

This experience of 'channelling' is one of plugging in to a source of energy, inspiration and insight, and then using my craft of writing to give it expression. I am happy with the word because it does describe what I feel I am doing, but I am not saying that what I do is channelling. I dispose myself to a space and I write what comes from this space. It flows and picks up on all I have gathered in my consciousness, weaving it together into a picture, and I go along for the ride, doing my best as I go. I discover as I create, which means that it is receptive and proactive, paradoxical and contradictory when you try to analyse it, like all of creation itself. It combines the feminine and the masculine, but these are just words and tools. What they point to is what counts. Use the words to cross the river and then leave them on the bank and proceed on the other side.

And so I am not saying that there is a heaven, as I am more likely to be saying that there isn't, but I am saying get past the words and, most important, find out for yourself. Don't believe, go into everything consciously, and stay present. Find heaven in the here and now and in your interiority. If I can help you be more aware, give you flashes of perspective and insight, inspire you to live more vividly and happily, encourage you find yourself, put you in touch with source energies and show you how to give them form, shift you to live the life you want and need, and help you to be sensitive and responsible as you love and die, then I have fulfilled my function. Then I have lived it as I have done it, which is my joy and my profession, my personal journey and my coming into bloom. Then I am being myself for a living, which is the message I leave with my life and my death.

It is my message in that it comes through my uniqueness with my voice, with my individuality distinctly involved and my subjectivity forming the reed in the instrument through which the universe plays its music, but this must not be confused with my ego. This work is not my endeavour or my doing because it happens when I get my ego out of the way and let the beyond have its say, with my dedicated yet playful co-operation. The beyond needs someone to speak or write for it, and I am one with the beyond, and so my surrendering to the mystery and frolicking along with it in my idiosyncratic way is the universe expressing and enjoying itself. If I get that right, this is you doing the same by reading, and then getting on with your life having been touched and even transformed by it. I can work with and enjoy my subjectivity without getting identified with it and you can do the same. It's just part of the picture and all parts feel best when they are aligned with each other and the whole cosmic orchestra.

Traditional African spirituality here in the southern region of the continent works with the notion of communing with the ancestors. These spirits, if you will, are living, but not on the same plane as people in bodies, and so people in bodies can get in touch with, communicate with and relate to them. It is the very 'not getting on with them' that brings us troubles in the physical world. This is a similar idea to having a separate self, or ego, with its own agenda outside of the natural and spiritual community. This is where we have all gone wrong, 'been banished from the Garden of Eden', or lost our way en route to reuniting with ourselves, which is what life gives us the opportunity to do and return to the 'kingdom'. And so getting lost in the separate self is part of the trip, and restoring harmony and integration are the way to be found again.

The relationship with the other and the whole of existence including the ancestors determines the relationship with the self. Southern African ethnic culture is inherently communal and has the qualities of what could be called aboriginal awareness. Similarly, the older people of Australia have an awareness of dreamtime and an entirely different relationship with the earth and natural energies to what we call the Western one. The shamanic consciousness of central and South America has similar qualities too, also relating to the earth, to energy outside of five-sensory perception, to inorganic entities, and to death. Westerners have lost touch with this knowing but it can and must be rekindled. This is the work at hand.

The ancestral realm is readily available and a guide for us on this earthly dimension, whether we are aware of it or not. The magic, healing and quantum evolution are in being aware. Dreamtime is still available to our consciousness, although we have strayed from it and suffered as a result. The vast mysteries of direct energetic experience await us just outside the conventions we cling to as our feeble attempt to make sense of the world while insisting on our separateness. If we can free up our energy from this inertia and resistance, we can experience true wonders and function on a far less dysfunctional level. The ancient Greeks speak of the gods living on one plane and the mortals on another, and describe the drama of life using the relationship between these planes. Dismiss that all as myth, you may, but myth makes the human world go round. Myth is the story that ties it all together. Myth is the language of the soul played out on the planet.

Joseph Campbell's astute and transformational work about the mythic structures in social and individual psychology cover this clearly, and Jung's penetrating efforts go a long way to opening up these realms to popular awareness. Within us is a structured narrative perception which is mirrored by life around us, giving us circumstantial encounters to face and manifesting lessons we need to learn as we live our unfolding story. We are bringing our inner our seed into material form, and constantly in a dance with the gods, who employ us to enact their inspiring gifts from their plane.

Maybe there's a muse behind this book, a sassy custodian bestowing the blessing while another meatier one does his job here on the physical plane. If so, she's young and nubile, the kind I respond to best, or an aging Greek pop star who got tired of fame, fortune and the fucking paparazzi. The point is not whether these realms and entities exist, though, but the open and flowing acceptance that they *could well* exist. Like with words, it's about what works and points us to the truth. And so it is not a debate of disputable fact but a growing of awareness and an ability to play. Awareness is utterly expansive and most mischievous. Let go into eternity and have the time of your life.

Having a sense of the gods and their ways can help you enjoy being a player in the world. It's a big theatre anyway and all of us are in costume with masks, fulfilling parts while knowing our higher selves at the same time. We are on stage performing our role convincingly by taking our character very seriously, all while being entirely different people backstage who just do this symbolic shit for a living, with families at home and whole other stories there to tell. The backstage and back-home self can be delighting in the performance while the on-stage character is weeping or getting stabbed in the back. There are various levels of awareness and engagement, and being our true selves means being transcendently aware of this while playing along in the mix of forms functioning at any moment in time.

Perhaps we are ourselves gods on one level and mortals on another, since we are all one. We are living the paradox of negotiating this unfathomable yet liveable and marvellous mystery unfolding, which it is doing for the fun of it or no reason at all, going nowhere in a constant flowering of bliss. Everything is constantly arriving, coming and culminating in this moment for the entertainment of it. It's a celebration!

Awareness opens the way. It is the way! Everything is orchestrated precisely as it's meant to be, is it not? Become aware and get back to me. Our collective unconscious is characterised by mythic structures, not so? We are born with individual sagas on a deeper level that we have to find a way to live out in the world of material form and symbolic story. We are giving expression to these inner selves out in the arena of life, where the battles, romances, glories and deaths occur, and awareness is what transcends it all and watches in detached wonder. Awareness laughs at the drama, both aloofly and compassionately, and keeps on growing indefinitely. Awareness is timeless and thoroughly in the here and now. Awareness understands death, because awareness is life. Awareness is orgasmic.

Chapter 29:

Heartbeat

Most if not all of us have a death wish. We are all committing slow suicide. In Resheka's case she was presented with that realisation in no uncertain terms and this precipitated an eventual let-go and realignment, one that continues in her ongoing spiritual, emotional and relational work. Death wakes us up and shows us how to live. Most of us couldn't be bothered, though, and are actively pursuing escape, boxed prettily, tucked into a top pocket, and spread out over forty years of poisonous puffing, or something similar. The problem comes when that escape presents us with its price, and that puts us in touch with our process, and that confronts us with our death wish. Then our will to live asserts itself, not just as a fighting spirit and willingness to learn, but, after those phases, our happiness beyond previous comprehension. This is living on a new level, perhaps living properly for the first time, and feeling calmly ecstatic. This is the way it's meant to be.

All of us have this deeper drive but it is clouded by the suicidal tendency. We are thwarted and repressed. We are wounded and in pain. Whether this self-destructive urge is built into the package deal of being alive, something conditioned into us from the outside, something perpetrated against us from behind a curtain, a fitting reaction to an unhealthy society, an indulgent characteristic of ego, or whatever, the wholesome, healthy and deeper will to live is truer and stronger. It's the real deal, closer to core. We want to live and that means embracing death, which means going through a process of encountering it deliberately or unintentionally, and waking up through the process.

Maybe life is a constant conflict between two wills, the one to live and the other to die. Perhaps both are needed to walk the knife's edge that they create. I can see that as possible on one level but it's not my overall sense. My experience is that we function on the level of duality, which is frictional by necessity, but we come from a consciousness higher than that, which, if aligned with, lets us flow through the dimension of duality with transcendent perspective and more harmonious happenings. By being more conscious we can keep going up.

And we are doing just that, under duress, because it takes pressure to push us through barriers. Dealing with death is part of that. Birth and death are the ultimate dualities and we are beyond them, and so we must encounter them. Being beyond is the real ultimate. It's not about dying at the end of a linear life but dealing with birth and death all the time, from an integrated awareness. It's like sun coming up and going down when perceived on one level, but not actually doing so, which becomes clear from a higher perspective. The sun is steady but the world turns, and similarly our awareness is timeless while life comes and goes (and comes again. That was a sexual reference). It's a state of higher consciousness that characterises healthy living, and a freedom from duality while thriving within it (with a sense of humour). This is the right way to live and die.

The shamans of antiquity, according to Carlos Castaneda and Don Juan, we able to manipulate their awareness, by leveraging it off death, to such a degree that they could catapult themselves into remote states of consciousness and distant dimensions of existence and hold off dying for grotesquely distorted periods of time. The contention is that these men and women who lived as humans ages ago are still alive today in different energetic configurations that are still linked to the human form but also unfathomably far removed from it. From the lessons learned through their lineage, it sounds to me like, for all the insight and power they gathered about the possibilities of consciousness, the main discovery was that distorting things to avoid dying is a long and winding detour to a dead end. Death is to be embraced, not use to get twisted. Awareness should be leveraged from it, but life should be loved and death not feared.

The will to live is primal but also spiritual. It has the animal quality of self-preservation but also the mystery-inspired mission of doing what it intrinsically feels it needs to do here in this lifetime. This is where biology meets mythology, or where body meets soul. When we are in the flow, aware of our oneness and acting in consciousness, we bring to bear our inner being in a co-creative ecstasy, not dissimilar to making love. This is the spiritual attained through the physical, or the real revealed through the dancing illusion. Unlike Simon's contention that sex was a waste of time, it can be used to enter higher consciousness, and it can be used to understand and prepare for death. It can bring us closer to our being. We can approach it with light reverence and deep playfulness. We can gain experience from this taste of the tactile meeting the transcendent and then approach the end in the same way. After all, that's how it began.

And so keep that heart beating as long as you can. Do not go 'gentle into the good night', as Dylan Thomas phrased it, only when it's time. It is our birth right and dignity to stand our ground and do our special dance in the face of certain death, as much as it is to embrace death trustingly. We should hold off that moment for as long as we can so that when we finally do go, it becomes our ultimate glory and parting statement to humanity.

You don't want to come too soon...

Chapter 30:

Patience

I'm back at the burger joint. There's no-one here. It's raining on a Tuesday afternoon, or more like drizzling steadily at rush hour, and I slithered through the suburb in my sleek and ebony feline machine, avoiding traffic and finding a parking spot out front. Then I found a writing spot inside with that soft precipitation sending scent through the folding doors, and speakers dropping soft rock from the ceiling. It's wonderful weather, just probably keeping people away, as such weather does. Suits me fine. The manageress, Thando, came over and joined me by invitation for a few minutes and we spoke about deep stuff until she left more energised to attend to the ringing phone. I'm half a glass of perfect Pinotage down, and feeling the music and the scene, as you can see.

Thando and I discussed meditation and meditativeness, or I told her about it and she asked and listened. It followed from the topic of Thailand, my having a five week holiday there with Resheka, and the power of living in the present. This is what we all should do, she agreed. "Meditation," I replied, "can be a tool when you first start out. At that point it's something you do, but after a while you reach a state of meditation, or meditativeness, when it becomes a quality of your consciousness that you carry wherever you go."

"Very interesting," she said entranced.

"Then you are in a state of presence, with space around you, with leaves you moved but untouched," I continued. "You are centred and calm, and alert and responsive to whatever happens, using your sensitivity and best intelligence. You are happy and feel good just by your being, and things work optimally and effortlessly because you are in the flow."

This, I explained, inspired by wine and weather, is the state of consciousness we are being forced into by circumstance, but it is also what the great teachers of all time have all been directing us towards all along. It's brand new for humanity, an awakened era in history, while always having been there for our discovery, and well explored and documented by a good few over the eons. It's reached the point now, though, where everything is happening so fast that time no longer exists and we have to take each day and each moment as it comes. We have to die psychologically to the old selves that we upheld and that are no longer serving us. It comes across like an unprecedented crisis but it is what we need and want and are grateful for once we move through the struggle and let go into wisdom. It makes sense to us when we see it while it leaves us with all the aspects of dealing with death, like grief, mourning, healing, and new life. We need to get back to being able to feel fully, because presence is feeling and if we block that we can't be alive. Feeling happens happily in a state of awareness, which is more than able to contain it effortlessly.

Speaking about this reminded me of earlier today at the kitchen counter as I stirred my post-lunch plunger coffee and observed my motions with the teaspoon. Resheka had commented the other day on the action I use, asking light-heartedly if I was aware of and deliberate about it. I said that I did it that way for maximum sugar-dissolving efficacy and karmic efficiency! I swish sideways and mix up my moves to keep that sugar guessing as it encounters affectionate friction that you just can't beat. Also, I barely touch the sides of the mug or cup, and so there will be no disturbing sounds coming from me.

Today as I observed my stirring it reminded me of how I like to make love, always mixing it up, keeping the unpredictable variety coming, surprising myself and my lover with my spontaneity, and rising with the cosmic pleasure intensity. The slight crema on the coffee surface was whirling orgasmically like a milky way in the black of space, a galactic coming in the vast emptiness of total presence. I was feeling it as I did something utterly mundane, with the touch of a dervish. This is mindfulness, meditation, ongoing lovemaking, and divine death in every moment, all for lunch. Joy.

On our second last day in Phuket, Resheka and I rode down south to Kata beach, which is two bays away from Patong. It turned out to be a clear evening as the sun set, and we went into the sea in an isolated spot mid-beach where it was just the two of us and the occasional yellow paraglider sailing past directly above us in the pastel palette of a sky. Of course we chatted, but we fell silent for stretches too, floating in the black sea on our backs with ears submerged and eyes closed. "Try this," I suggested at one point when our heads were above the water. "Look at the orange glow on the horizon but don't think about it, just see it as it is. Don't describe it to me or label it in your head. Don't drift into words. Suspend your thinking and merge with the scene with your whole being. Look with your totality and let the perceived boundaries disappear and see what happens." We both did it together and the whole universe stood still for a moment. We weren't there but eternity was.

Our minds stopped and we tasted the realm of no-mind, and so we experienced reality with no filter, distortion or reflection. Our beings were cleansed of the illusions usually screening us from the truth, and both the outer and the inner were revealed as one. You can do this with a flower or with your lover, and you can touch the eternal anytime. In the same way as an orgasm stops our identification with otherwise incessant thinking, so can such an encounter with nature and beauty.

With frequent experience and growing familiarity you can soon drop the mind at will, since you have had enough tastes of the awakened awareness to access it easily. This will transform your life and enlighten the planet. It will also prepare you to go to your death. It is a form of death, a dissolution of the self and a return to essence. When the big day comes, it won't be big at all but a natural remembrance of all you pretended to forget. In the meantime you will be much more alive.

Chapter 31:

Move On

"What do you want for your children?" I often end up asking people, especially towards the end of a first coaching session. They are usually conflicted about their dreams for themselves but have no trouble identifying and voicing them for their kids.

"I want him to be happy!" Thando said without hesitation, smiling brightly for the first time.

"Then you need to give that to yourself," I said in summary.

I had put the same point to Nokwethemba a couple of weeks before, at the same location, in fact. All of her over-calculated concerns for the future evaporated and she knew exactly what she wanted for her son and, thus, for herself. To take my point further, I suggested that she go and ask the five-year-old what he proposes she do next in her life. She did so when she got home and was shocked at his reply, which she sent to me straight away.

He said, without hesitation, "You must write about being a doctor and about being a manager," which is exactly what I had outlined for her proposed book.

"It's as if he was eavesdropping on our conversation!" she said after she told me.

"You see," I said. We know what we want and need to do, and kids are in touch with that wisdom. It's all in the ether, the ancestry, the mystery and the moment. It's all within us and you can plug in from anywhere. The problem is the muddled mind. Drop that or trick your way past it and all the strands flow together into a constant and converging climax.

Loving the other, particularly our kids, comes more easily to us than loving ourselves. For one thing, the other is an external occurrence onto which we can pour our affection. Subject verb object - I love you - makes sense to the rational mind. But how do we afford our inner being that same essential appreciation? How do we turn towards loving the subject? It's odd to get a sense of it, and to do it. Subjectivity sees through the eyes and, therefore, cannot see itself except for in the mirror, which is not itself at all. Wherever we look with our eyes, we are never there, unless we see a reflection, which is not a true depiction.

Another reason we struggle to love ourselves is because we are so taken for granted that we forget our own presence, like a fish forgets the sea. We miss the most obvious manifestation, our own. We are simply here and, we assume, always will be, while it's other people who die, not us. We haven't died so far have we? So why would we assume differently? Death is an external phenomenon. We can be forgiven for forgetting our subjectivity, over-emphasising the object, and then going in search of what can never leave us and, thus, ending up tied in existential knots, like a dog chasing its tail. The subject seeks itself as an object and spins in silly circles.

A more sinister reason why we can't love ourselves is because our entire earthly experience has discouraged it. Society condemns us at every turn, and conditions us out of our essence and into a corrupt facsimile. Healthily and happily being who we are is as taboo as sex and death. We have to wake up to this, usually the hard way, and then turn back into our nature. This is the beginning of the journey back to the truth, often agony-induced and always infinitely worthwhile.

We have to encounter who we are from within our subjectivity, not try to look at it from the outside. We need to direct our awareness inwards make the unconscious assumptions conscious en route to seeing what lies underneath. This is part of mediation. Close your lids, shut out the visual distractions, and see with your inner eye. Don't regard the apparition in the looking glass as who you are, but enter your infinitely intriguing inner sanctum and explore your being. Go into what you have always taken for granted and become aware in here. A new world will open up, a more vast and magnificent world than anything out there. The galaxy and the cosmos are pretty specs by comparison, plus they come alive in a new when you look at them from a place of know yourself.

What you behold out there is determined by how clearly you understand and occupy the observer, and so subjectivity is the first and defining journey. Who we are is the feeling inside, the surrendering and sinking into this feeling, the venturing through layers of tension into expansive spaces of insight and mystery, and the coming to the core of pure outpouring of endless love and boundless joy. This source of self is the same source as that of everything out there, and by finding our centre we find the centre of it all. By returning to myself I reunite with you. By coming home within I find my home everywhere. By living in love I am the source and recipient of it. The dog and the tail are one and at peace in paradise.

Until we experience this love from within, loving the other seems more immediate, but it cannot be whole and sincere. Once we taste the truth, though, we realise what real love is, and the love for the other takes a quantum leap. Love is not directed, but a state of being, not subject-verb-object from me to you, but subjectivity and objectivity understood and enjoyed, and marvelled at in delight. It's a rapture, baby, an explosion of ecstasy.

We cannot give this to our kids any way other than by living it ourselves. You can work fifteen hours a day as an immigrant greengrocer and put your children through private school and university, thereby giving them the economic mobility and social standing that you did not have. You cannot, however, buy them happiness or spiritual understanding. Those they can only find for themselves, although pointed to by your discovery and example. You have to live it. It's more than just example, though. We literally set our ancestors free retroactively, and our unborn children in advance, by our own freedom. We unlock the spiritual across the generations by living it now. Spirit does not subscribe to any time but the present and it is in our presence that the power lies. How we live and how we die are our ultimate deeds that ripple through space and time while transcending both. Mystical. Orgasmic.

Church, state and corporate structure have been against this for all of human history because it is the source of our individual power, and those structures have wanted that power enslaved to them. Weak people pray, vote and traipse to work every day, while empowered people need do none of those. Severed souls seek leadership, and fearful masses support religion and politics, but awakened individuals are happy being responsible for themselves. If Alexander, the great protagonist of false power, could see that you cannot control someone who does not fear death, he can point us to freeing ourselves from tyranny like his own. Don't fear death. Face, embrace and enjoy it. Lie in the sunshine and tell the so-called leaders to move aside. They may even see the error of their ways and join you. Don't look outside for answers and get hoodwinked. Be brave, grow back your roots in presence and awareness, and stand your ground. This is love in action and a global game-changer.

Like someone who has been broken and then begun from below zero to rise from an abusive relationship, we are all awakening to our true selves and coming into our authentic power. Most of what we knew will fall away. We are undergoing a rebirth. Self-discovery is the rebellion and self-love the revolution. Be yourself for a living.

Chapter 32:

Soul Free

An orgasm doesn't happen in your hole or your hard-on. It's not genital-specific, and when you get it right it's a whole-body experience, or even beyond. It should be an out-of-body experience, or is, no matter how minor. Orgasm gives access to your being beyond your physical form. It's not only sexual climax but non-sexual calmness. It's where the two meet, where the worldly and the other-worldly come together. As the peak of the physical occurrence it is also the entry point to the non-physical plane, where body and spirit merge for a moment, or remember that they are one. This is pure presence and clear consciousness. It feels good because it is a coming home to ourselves. Orgasm is death without dying.

Of course, it can just be pleasure and escape, but where are you escaping to? A moment of relief, really, like a sneeze, lost in the opposite of pain for a few seconds, which will bring a balancing effect sooner or later. Pleasure is superficial and one pole in the duality that requires the other, plus it is dependent on and, therefore, exploitative of the lover. Fuck me, baby! Pleasure is the mind's pursuit at the expense of the system's balance.

As soon as we have an experience of transcendence, say a silent sunrise or a spontaneous opening in the fabric of thinking, we pounce in it so that we can replicate it. The mind was not there for a moment but it takes over again and tries to take what was an unplanned state and turn it into a goal that it can control. The mind asks, 'How did this formidable feeling arise?' and 'How can I conjure and replicate it at will?' Of course, in this, the very nature of the transcendence is throttled out of reach by the self-agenda, and all access to the beyond is lost. We push away what we want by trying to manage it. We go back to forgetting who we are.

Thinking is not the way but the opposite of it. No-self is the way but how do you bring it about from the self? How does the ego see past its limits and manage a release from identification? It doesn't and cannot. The self that strives enforces itself, and the seeking of enlightenment is what keeps enlightenment away. This is the conundrum. How do we get past ourselves? Well, we stop trying. We drop doing and let life be as it is in the now. We accept and appreciate, and do not attempt to change. We allow it to happen and, in that, stop asserting ourselves.

Similarly, how do you fall asleep at night? You cannot create that state actively because it arises from inaction. Restful slumber comes about of its own accord when you stop making an effort and let yourself sink into it. If you pursue it you will be kept awake by your pursuit. It requires a receptive or feminine approach, not the masculine. The doing in this instance will be your undoing, whereas being allows it to happen. Finding your being is the same. Paradoxically, doing can ultimately bring you to being, because it is sometimes in making every effort first, and then finally giving up in all sincerity, that the truth makes itself known. Buddha was born a rich prince but renounced his inheritance to seek the truth, but only after he made every effort to find it did he finally see the futility of his pursuit and surrender, at which point enlightenment descended upon him. It was there all along but needed him to exhaust himself to become apparent. At that point he died and was reborn, and he threw back his head and roared with realisation and laughter. Only as a last resort do we find ourselves as whom we have always been.

Sleep comes naturally and optimally at the end of a satisfying working day. By doing to the full we find that we can finally fully be, like a fist tightly clenched can totally let go. Doing and being are in a dance. This is the seeming contradiction contained in being alive and having form. Some things, to achieve them, need us to do, and others need us not to do, with enlightenment at the zenith of this, a state of pure being. When Buddha found himself weak and defeated from years of following the misleading advice of all the so-called experts, his self suddenly subsided and true knowing took over. This state is here for us all when we are ready. We are all buddhas waiting to be born. What does it feel like when it eventually happens? Have you ever had an orgasm?

Have you ever been in deep sleep? Obviously we are unconscious when that happens but we do know the feeling. It is an entirely natural place we go to every night for essential and refreshing patches. It is an unaware state, though, a time where we sink below mind and rest from it, and reconnect with source energy without the ego. In a dream state there is still a self at work, grappling with issues it couldn't contain during the day, but in deep sleep there is no ego. Here we get properly replenished because there is nothing to uphold and, therefore, no doing. It is not just downtime for the body but for the mind and the whole strenuous sense of self, and it is a return to our true nature for that brief and redemptive time. Following that we can wake to face the day.

The problem with sleep is that, for whatever if gives us, it takes away our awareness. We need its gifts but ideally while we are fully conscious. When we emerge from slumber, or even before that in the less deep stages of sleep, the trouble starts again. Dreams, thoughts, and the notion of the 'I' arise, and by the time we are walking around in the world we are riddled with ambitions, desires, interpersonal struggles, and the need to improve the insecure self. Comparison, competition and conflict come into it because separation has been assumed and asserted again. Beneath that we are still blissful, though, like we were in the womb and at one with the universe, but above the ground we are lost in the illusion. We are identified with the mind and its partner in crime, the ego.

What we need is the connected experience of deep sleep combined with heightened awareness, not at the expense of it. We need the serenity and bliss of oneness and the ultra-lucidity of conscious presence. We need to wake up while we retain the qualities of sleep, and enjoy our transcendence while we're worldly. This existential space is what death of the illusion leaves behind, a state of meditativeness and orgasmic consciousness.

To access it, you start by sitting still with whatever turbulence is inside you without resisting it. You accept and watch, and instead of acting on any tension you feel to try to relieve or avoid it, you let it be there, feel it for what it is telling you, and then slip through the portal it opens by releasing it. You surrender through it and transform your attachment into freedom. This liberates a gush of good energy. Then you go deeper, finding the next layer of tension, feeling it, and letting go. This lets you sink further into stillness, more and more into yourself as you peel away the layers of dense energy. It is like falling into a deep sleep except that you are not only retaining awareness but enhancing it. While you are settling into centeredness you are also rising in presence, with a clear and expansive meta-perspective. Inside, you are soil and soul, and above you are the sky. It's a beautiful day.

The drug ecstasy can give a gateway experience in that it brings everything up to meet you. Instead of feeling shredded by separation, as we usually do, you feel whole. It's not some firework high like you've been shot into the stratosphere but a cool calm where all of creation harmonises lovingly with where you are. It's a

217

feeling and a knowing way beyond happiness and it's the most effortless you've ever been. This is a taste of death and a guide for finding it in the everyday. That's why it's called ecstasy.

Death is not separate from the everyday. Approximately one hundred and fifty thousand people die each day, and one day that number will include you, me and everyone we know. Every day we are all born when we wake up and die when we go to sleep, and we go through a few birth and death experiences in between. Even every breath we draw is a rebirth and every exhalation another expiry.

When you are aware, life and death are two sides of the present moment. It's all immediate. Death has no hold on you.

Chapter 33:

Chapter 33:

Nothing Looks the Same in the Light

"Hi Simon," my message to him read yesterday. "It's a month today since we saw you in Pattaya. I have written 30000 words of *Death is the Ultimate Orgasm*."

"Wow! I'm impressed," he replied shortly afterwards. "Can't wait for the finished thing."

Finished thing coming up, as swiftly as I can manage. Sharing the news and receiving his response today was a kick that brought new energy. The path ahead pulls and pulsates as my boots crunch the gravel on the road beneath them, and my lungs draw life from the clean air.

A bird was just caught in my spare bedroom. I was carrying some folded laundry down the passage when I saw the feathered fucker flapping up against the panes. That's not outside, I thought as I turned back to find it going wild to escape. I put down my pile of clothes in my master suite and returned to the guest one to open a window to let the fellow fly free. As I walked in I noticing that it had been there long enough to shit on the bed, twice.

"For fuck's sake," I grumbled, being my sweet-tempered self.

My entering the room gave the defecating guest the boost it needed to find and exit the skylight through which it must have entered. Its panic-induced stupor was probably intensified by perceived threat, to the point of clarity, and it flitted free from its self-induced incarceration while I shook my head and muttered blasphemies, as I am prone to doing at the slightest provocation. It's a British thing. "Oh, right!" I said to it sarcastically as it darted to the shrub across the lawn.

We all know how the body's chemical reaction can send us into a spin, and then a how a little life-or-death situation can put things straight again. I looked around and cussed again at the droppings on the duvet cover, and then left the room with heart aflutter and mind reflecting. That was odd. A sign, perhaps. I associate with birds, being a robin myself, and feel a certain affinity. I can talk their language. That one might have had a message for me.

Can messages be made obvious to us from nearby realms to draw our attention to things we may be missing? An awareness of the intricate orchestration in everything brings with it a trust and a knowing, and a sense of singing symbolism. Flashes in the matrix might make us more mindful. The gods could be holding everything by the marionette strings and the angels may well be guarding us. An odd occurrence might be most ordinary in the mythical world.

What vernacular works for you? What speaks for your being? What reaches out of the dream and wakes you up a bit? It's pretty personal. When you learn to see, it is not the objects out there that change but the seer in here. The transformation is in us through awakening of perception, and the world transforms around us. Death is a transformation of awareness, and awareness is an open window and a way out that you forgot was the way in. Brush the sheets, wipe your eyes, thank the gods and fly free, my friend.

"The job of a waitress is to give the customer permission to do what they know they want to but feel guilty about," I said. "That's what they come here for and nine times out of ten they say yes."
She laughed in guilty agreement.
"People like to be talked into what they desire," I added, "and your job is to give them permission and encouragement at the right time. It's sneaky!"
We were negotiating her opportune suggestion that I have a third beer, backed by her sound argument that it was happy hour, and intensified by her bending of logic to suggest that I had effectively had only one because of the half-price special. I gave her credit for her ingenuity but clarified that I had come here for one beer and was already finishing a second, all things considered. "Cost is not the deciding factor," I teased in return, still hoping that she'd talk me into making it three for the price of one and a half.

"So you're having a third..." she's just said more than asked a few shrewd minutes later. Another waitress was here in the meantime and patronised my description of my decision-making process as I underwent it. In summary, she said, "So, another one, then?"

"Yes," I'd conceded, which is when the first waitress passed by again and knowingly confirmed the order that she had been facilitating a few minutes before. Teamwork, I tell you.

"The only thing better than a woman making decisions for you," I told her, "is two women doing it."

"How's that third beer?" she's just joked a few gulps in.

"Very sneaky, Nicole," I retaliated feebly as she laughed.

"Books are a uniquely portable magic." Stephen King

Amanda sent me that quote earlier and I have just written back saying thank you and adding, "Writing with beer and waitresses."

"Good stuff," she replied.

"I reckon so too," I agreed.

"Let the writing flow," she finished after a pause. Good guidance, I thought as I loosened up.

Leandra, the long-maned beauty who had met me at the door, led me youthfully to my table, taken my first order, and chatted about being included in my writing, came outside to say goodbye. A new waitress had taken over her tables, explaining that she had finished her shift, and I had pondered why she had left without saying goodbye. Then I looked up from my phone and she was standing there, out of uniform with sparkling eyes and brush of fresh make-up. She had come to say goodbye after all.

"I'll see you," she said as she dashed off.

"Look forward to that," I replied with feigned maturity.

The gods are good. Let me loosen up a little more.

Chapter 34:

Happy

"One thing I can tell you for certain is that I am not gay," I said to Resheka, spinning around in the street in late-night Patong. "Not gay and not bisexual." We had a good laugh as we entered Bangla Road from Sea Dragon Soi where I had just seen one of the multitudes of dressed-up people trying to entice you into the clubs along the way, a woman with her breasts positioned perfectly for visual perception. They may not have been great in natural shape, I know, but propped into an optimizing bra, and creviced by that opening in her white top, they looked peachy. My instincts were spoken to sharply, and I felt my hormones rush in reply in the split second that their cleavage flashed before me.

Effective marketing indeed, and cause for my spontaneous statement, which was in delayed response to something Simon had said a few days before. "All artists and creative people are bisexual," he'd opined, speaking for himself as a prime example but making a considered point. Later that day with him, as we arrived for lunch, I had joked back about it saying that one thing we'd realised so far was that I was bisexual too, but meaning the opposite. A few days later now and back in Patong I made my statement more directly. Those Thai tits made it as clear as ever and Resheka enjoyed it.

As much as I was voicing an impulsive confirmation, I was being funny and cheeky and having a dig at Simon's certainty on the subject. Everything I say is funny, even if that's not obvious at first. Just look more deeply into it. Drink half a bottle of wine bookended by two joints, read it again, and call me in the morning. Text me, rather, I don't take calls. Or speak to my manager, since I'm focusing on my writing at the moment. Everything I say is serious, too. Have a laugh and know that I mean it.

Gender identity and sexual orientation have been so up in the air in recent times. It's good to question the status quo, to overturn entrenched assumptions, to experiment and explore yourself, and to find freedom, but it's also really good just to know and be who you are. Women are redefining themselves, the LGBTQ concept is gaining letters, and sexuality is still discovering its liberty, and a trip to Thailand is all you need to show you the extent of that, plus liberate your leanings and, more important, restore your settings. What we need in all of this too, though, is for men to be men and women to be women. A new and healthy community will arise around steady certainty. I'll write a book sometime soon about being real and handling relationships, probably my next one. It has been brewing for some time and just needs to drop from the ether like this one did.

In the meantime, gentle rain is tapping on the terrain outside and sprinkling sounds through the open summer doors, and George Michael is playing smoothly on the high-end home stereo. I've been thinking about him and noticing his explicit absence in the recent writing. He's here, I assure you, doing double claps every four bars and layering subtle touches into the deceptively simple mix. A drummer would appreciate the instinctive accentuation, clever repetition and musical precision. His song "Move On" from *Older* is on a compilation I made last November, and the pure class of it alone makes me happy. It's good to work with the spirit of a long-time hero and now creative cohort, with his business manager from when I was a teenager, with my beautiful companion, with special friends, with spicy acquaintances and seductive waitresses, with surprise path-crossers in the ascending story, and with you reading this now. We are all in it together, making our way. How can we continue to pretend to be separate? The illusions are shimmering as they fall away.

In the mix too is a collection of potted trees I've owned and gathered since the late eighties when I was given one for my twenty first birthday by my girlfriend back then. Plenty have died over the years but there are fifteen or so stalwarts still standing regally around my garden. These are companions between thirty and fifty years old, some of which were gifts, some bought, and some uprooted as sprouting seeds from the shade beneath their parents in Bedfordview and Irene. Once you begin a relationship with a Bonsai, you are in it for life. They depend on you, reflect you, grow with you, and live and die with you. Their roots are contained, which makes them needy, somewhat unnatural, and your enduring responsibility. You cannot get out of this bond. What would you do, sell them or give them away? To whom? That would effectively be killing them. You might find a custodian but it's unlikely. You could perhaps plant them in the earth somewhere and set them free, but where? All you can really do is love and enjoy them.

Cutting them back can feel brutal but you have to do it sometime. If you give them too much space to grow they become unhappy and you become unsettled inside owing to their unruliness until a day comes when you do the job. This is a symbolic process that cleans out much of the dead wood in your inner space and sets you up for a bout of fresh growth. The trees appreciate it with a showing of just that, which gives the garden a new lease of life. You feel good and the shifts ensue until it is time to do it again.

Bonsai are not plants, they are trees. You have to water them almost daily, feed them weekly (in spring and summer), keep them free of pests, and groom them almost continuously. You have to find the time to do all this, because they matter, and use this time to face yourself, because you matter. You have to get into the mood and move with it. It's an intimate and instinctive relationship, like with people and animals. We are all living beings.

One of the oaks died recently, not long after I returned from Thailand and was writing about death. It wasn't neglect while I was away, because I had someone watering them for me and the tree was alive on my return. But it hadn't been strong for a while before that and must have died from steady decline, combined perhaps with simple readiness or sustained unhappiness where it was standing. I was told once by an expert in my early days of learning that, "Bonsai don't just die, we kill them. Ninety percent of the time it's lack of water." This one seemed to go for other reasons, though, perhaps from over-pruning on my part and an attack of parasites that it was unable to withstand in its frailer state. With being away and otherwise engaged, I hadn't given them the love they need, and so this death may have been a sacrifice that came with my writing and a pointer to this topic. Maybe it just had a message for us all. Trees teach us and trees die.

And trees are born. Last year Resheka was given a bag of lemons by her aunt who has a tree in her garden that originates from one in Durban planted by Resheka's father. We experimented with making a batch of limoncello and I planted eight of the remaining seeds in some pots at the back of my house. Seven of the eight sprouted and have become sizable shoots, which were ready this week for transplanting. One evening after working with my gardener in the day, I separated them out into new homes, putting one in the ground in a gap in the front garden, three into vacant bonsai pots around the property, and three into plastic containers I'd bought for Sheke. With that the death of one old tree turned into seven new lives. With the growing green, I felt the beckoning of the Irene house and the regeneration of its English garden.

Chapter 35:

You Have Been Loved

It's ten years ago today that Frank died. He was sixty eight and I was thirty nine. Dying in your son's presence is a most intimate thing to do, especially for an accountant, but he did it. After all those years of calculations he had the spirit in him to be raw and vulnerable. I had been thinking ahead to this anniversary, Resheka reminded me of it yesterday, and then Heather sent a message this morning: "Thinking of our dad today and how hard it was for us to lose him, how much our lives were changed by his death and how much we love and miss him." Ten years. Time to feel. Time to reflect. Time to write.

I spent much of last year terrified that Resheka would die. The prospect tore me to shreds and still stalks me sometimes. Part of that was dealing with the real possibility presented by the illness she had, part was the parcel her presence presented in which it was her dynamic, and part was remembering how my dad had slipped away through my fingers. I was mourning that still, I saw, not because I hadn't at the time and since then but because it takes a long time, perhaps a lifetime, to fully process these things.

Loss is a core theme in growing up and growing older. Wisdom knows about letting go. There are always plenty of feelings to process as you age. It's part of the process in the emotional digestive system. Just like the physical body does, so the energy body breaks down, integrates and discards, keeping us healthy and humming. Emotional blocks are as troubling as physical ones, if not more. It is our job to feel. Feeling is being alive.

Keeping a stiff upper lip is the method Simon spoke of as his way, based on his British upbringing, and I can relate to that, but being able to feel is fundamental and so I have taught myself to inhabit and enjoy it. If you dull the pain, you kill the joy, which is not well. Maybe that was behind Frank's terminal disease. Holistic healing suggests that repression results in a cumulative backlash from the body, and, illness aside, to be ecstatic you need to experience all extremes of the spectrum... sorrow, rage, despair and terror. Feeling is existential, and that's perhaps one reason that Simon finds the word meaningless or offensive. We were able to laugh at it in Pattaya, which shows acceptance and understanding, but 'existential' is very much the word. If you think about something, it is conceptual, but when you experience it with your whole being in the present moment, it takes on genuine meaning. It becomes real and you remain free.

That other word that Simon said he can't stand is 'spiritual'. Spirituality, too, is empty until you live it, at which point you will not even need a word, as it will permeate your being and speak for itself. Words are only tools to describe experiences and point to those existential realities. In a sense, the truth becomes untrue when you state it, because it gets lost in translation and we get distracted into the thought instead staying in reality. The truth is best experienced and shared in silence. Poets reach out and come close with their words, drummers speak distinctly with sticks, and mystics say nothing. All of them feel.

Feel! Frank couldn't do it, as he was also from the stiff-upper-lip generation and English culture, and his body turned against him in the end. Was it years of violence to the self that resulted in that reaction? Resheka and I worked on that level throughout her chemo treatments and she credits what we did with her healing as much as the medicine. She became aware along the way of her process and how she had, on one level, brought on the situation she faced. Then she had to feel her compounded feelings acutely and free herself from them to be healthy again. The intense suffering amounted to that, which she continues to work on. This is the price of freedom in a world gone wrong. We are making our way back to getting it right.

I feel intensely in my own capacity and I feel as much on behalf of others. It makes me too empathic, but that's my plight. I am always learning how to manage it better. Feeling Resheka's pain and grief meant that I could show her how to do so, too, which taught me a great deal but was perhaps outside the bounds of my business. I was forced into fierce healing, helped along by my own abdominal surgery during that time. Before that intrusion, my body was carrying a build-up of emotion, especially in the belly, where we hold so much of the sensitive stuff, and having that soft space stirred up and symbolically shifted was what I needed to happen.

The body shows us what it wants us to hear and we need to listen to it, otherwise it is forced to make the messages louder. We need to be aware, in tune and good with emotion so that we can grow, hear and process energy, deal with loss, live in joy and embrace death. Being a healer is particularly intense and means feeling for yourself as well as helping others with their healing. The ability to inhabit your physical and energetic levels of existence, sit with intense experience and hold space for it in yourself and others, and stay vividly present, is part of the language of a new humanity. This is wisdom and wellness for a fresh generation of our species. Repression and taboo are history. Sex and death are part of the weather. It's a glorious morning.

Feel...

The transcendence of death as I experienced it with Frank that Friday afternoon ten years ago today was a function of feeling. Because we had done the work, we could go through the gate unhindered. From that enlightening access to essence, I have been able to advise people since. A few years back an old school friend, Roger, announced on social media that his wife, childhood sweetheart and soul mate, René, was undergoing treatment for a few forms of cancer found throughout her body. It didn't look good from what he described but everyone always fights first for any chance to preserve life, and we all backed her and him in that. I knew, though, that it might be about something else, and I watched and waited as they faced their challenges, sending Roger supportive messages saying that I was here to talk whenever he needed to. I remembered what I had gone through with Frank and imagined how hectic it must have been for my old friend for whom it was his beloved, and with whom he had two young sons and the pressure to hold a family together.

I sent them love and held out a sturdy hand in the ether, as I do for people, and I kept in tune with what was happening. Then I bumped into him in the supermarket and we had a heart-to-heart talk amidst customers, vegetables and fridges, with his boys sitting in the trolley. He thanked me profusely for my support over that time and we proceeded into our lives feeling connected. At this stage the agenda was still to do everything to save René's life, but I was ready for when that might switch to dealing with her death. That day came, and Roger summed it up in a sobering post that followed a string of heart-wrenching updates of their suffering and struggle, with distressing photos of her disappearing body. At that point she had only weeks or possibly days left and there was nothing more they could do. It was time.

And so I wrote to him and shared from my experience what I felt he should do. "It sounds like you have shifted from fighting to accepting," I said, "and now you can help her die in the right way." He responded and was with me and ready. I recommended facing and feeling everything and avoiding nothing. I encouraged having the conversations that needed to be had, and letting love lead the way. That's what the two of them did and a few days later he announced online that she had died, posting a beautiful description full of light about how perfectly it had happened. At the funeral he thanked me in front of friends for how I had helped, and I filled even more with the love and the bitter-sweet joy that comes with facing the realness of life. It's difficult, but more than worth it. There are many rich experiences, and death should be one of the most beautiful.

Roger has since met and merged with a new love in his life, Alison. Amazingly, she lost her husband in a similar way around the same time, and has two kids, too, and so now they are a happy family of six! The two parents can understand each other's heartbreak, needs and challenges, and care for each other while the offspring have double the vibrancy they may have initially lost. Roger still posts occasionally about René, sharing pangs of recollection when the memories come flooding back. He can have two loves in his life because they both understand. Death brings us all together.

It's been ten years without the physical Frank, ten years since that transformative day, and ten years with Frank closer than ever. I am not explaining, but I am feeling, and I feel him here. I am sure that René is with Roger and her growing boys. Our being knows and we have to trust it. Frank is in the silence of the afternoon in this house that he left behind, and in the blooming garden, most of which he planted and I have nurtured since. He is in my heart and mind, in this book, and in my words. Presence is rich with layers of life.

Back then Heather, Jason and their three young children flew out from London and we held Frank's memorial service at the Johannesburg Country Club where he used to love to go for lunch. Belonging was important to him and the venue was an ideal representation of his values and roots. It had no religious element, as he had long since let go of his Anglican affiliations, and I conducted the gathering, speaking as facilitator and firstborn child and son. It was daunting, but it was my forte and an opportunity to continue making the most of the once-in-a-lifetime experience. My speech came together on the morning and the rose garden was resplendent when we arrived to honour the good man. The two Wheeler brothers, my uncles Peter and Denis, had driven out from Pretoria and brought their parents along in spirit. My mom and many old family friends were there, and peers from my past had come to pay their respects too. It was powerfully perfect.

The club's event organiser had advised me to expect an attrition of ten to twenty percent of those who had confirmed that they would be there, but the senior partner at KPMG had sent out a circular and a stream of accountants in blue suits poured in until double the number of expected people covered the lawn around the packed rows of seats. It looked like a board meeting in heaven and there weren't enough tea cups to cater for them all. I had auditors come up to me in tears and tell me that Frank was the last of his breed, a true gentleman and a proud father of his two children. After his lifetime of numbers and balance sheets, his special day was full of feeling.

Chapter 36

Do You Really Want To Know

My mom called me one afternoon in November 2007 to say that she had spoken to my dad and that he didn't sound well. She thought I should perhaps go past his house check on him. A few weeks before that, at the launch of my book INSIGHTS, where I did a talk and then played a short show with the band I was in, Frank didn't look well or seem himself. He had lost weight suddenly and seemed to have aged ten years in a couple of months. When I arrived at his house, he was so weak that he could hardly walk around, and hadn't eaten properly for days. We spoke in the lounge for a while and decided to go and have him checked out. I can see now, looking back, that he was in the early stages of facing his death. I drove him to the hospital and they admitted him for a set of tests. By that night we knew what was wrong and that he was "very ill," as the oncologist put it. He stayed in the hospital for a while as the doctor began treatment, and we processed the situation and where it left us. Heather flew out for a fortifying visit, Frank responded well to medication and, as he felt that he was on the mend, he insisted that I go on the scheduled summer tour around the South African coast with the band. And so I did.

While I was on the road, eight dates into the mounting mayhem, he was discharged to go home, and something about that brought out all of my contained emotions, way out there in the wilderness with the wrong company, partying people who didn't care. I was flooded with release but surrounded by the loneliness that only a callous crowd can provide. Twenty five drinking and marauding musicians and road crew in moron-mode, and three trusted cohorts about to betray me, were the opposite of what I needed, but exactly what I had to contend with when I needed to talk to someone, feel connected and heard, and to process what was happening back home and inside me. Plus I had to play in a different town every night and sit in the bandwagon all day listening to endless, careless, hung-over bullshit. You'd have thought that there'd have been one human being in the touring party but mobs are never intelligent or nice.

I called Heather from Mossel Bay and managed to vent as I paced up and down the small shopping mall near the venue for the four-band show later that night, which helped. Then I hired my own car so that I had space to myself to deal with what I needed to and listen to music I liked. Still, I shouldn't have been there in the first place. The bond with the rest of the band had broken a while before and I had pushed on instead of reading the writing on the wall. I'm like that, at my expense, in all intimate relationships, plus I loved the music so. I didn't want to let go. Death doesn't come easily when you are hanging on and in denial. The nights, towns and shows blurred by and, while the touring party stayed in Cape Town for two days off over Christmas, I flew back to Johannesburg riddled with chest and throat infections to get some medication, sanity and sleep. I couldn't get near my dad with his compromised immune system, and so when I went to see him we had to sit across the room from each other. The rest of the time I stayed in bed, and then hauled myself back to Cape Town to honour my commitment to lunacy.

By the time I got back to Bedfordview at the end of the tour, which was early in New Year, I was under fresh pressure, first to recover and then, as soon as possible, to get back to bringing in money, which had taken a back seat for some time with the all-consuming nature of making, recording and playing live music. But as fate would have it, in my dark hour, my dad called having taken a turn for the worse. I dashed to fetch him and found that he really was bad. At the hospital he insisted on walking in from the car by himself, but he collapsed onto the seating outside the entrance, head slumped forward, and I ran inside to get him a wheelchair. The diagnosis was that a different strain of leukaemia had arisen and that he needed intravenous chemo, which he chose to go ahead with. Day by day I watched it systematically strip him away, dragging me through extreme ups-and-downs with him.

He'd suddenly make progress, be sitting up strongly when I arrived there in the morning, and then, just as unexpectedly, take another severe downturn, all within a single day. I'd visit him three or four times between running our two lives, and eventually get home at eleven at night, where it would take me two hours in solitude to process everything that had happened. I'd eventually fall asleep in the early hours, leave my phone on in case the ward needed to get hold of me, and then be woken at 6.30am by an old and out-of-touch friend of his calling for an update.

"Robin, Dave here! How's Frank?"

'How am I, you fucking arsehole?' I felt like saying to him and perhaps should have. 'How about considering what I am handling and that I am likely to be asleep at this hour, you stupid prick,' I might have added, had I not been too ravaged to fight. 'If you want to know how Frank is, go to the hospital during visiting hours so that he can tell you to fuck off!'

When he died in early February, his home was exactly as he had left it that afternoon when I fetched him a month before. I had been in and out to look after it since, but now the job was entirely different. I had to head into his heritage head first, see what I could make if it, and start to clear most of it out. Steadily I assessed shelves of files, processed years of paperwork, and worked through his personal possessions, all of which put me through all sorts of intellectual challenges and emotional upheaval. My life was still on hold because I could not get to any of it until I had made space by sorting through his, and there was simply no way to hurry up handling the heavy load. I wasn't paying the price for my father's sins, but I was inheriting the flames, as Springsteen described it in the song "Adam Raised a Cain" on his album *Darkness on the Edge of Town* in 1978. I picked up where he left off and did the work he couldn't do. Like Bruce, I was trying to shatter the shackles of ancestral history to take the myth forward, but first I was being baptised in the unforgiving fire of the family furnace.

What I learned from this tremendously taxing time is that I could handle anything. It made me truly come of age. I could rise out of any-sized pile of ashes, no matter how steep, soft or sinking. I could overcome, if only by a dusty breath, and I could live to rewrite the book. And then I could keep writing. I learned that one human can sort out some of another human's shit, and that such an act of love and intimacy brings two souls together forever. That's what family is for, after all. I learned that it's still better to sort out your own shit, if you can, while you're on earth.

When I distilled what was left of the man's physical life, there wasn't much to it. It is in spirit that our legacies remain. The rest rusts away pretty quickly. If someone bequeaths you something in the material world, what better way to value it than to invest it in the realisation of your ultimate dream for life and vision for the world? This way you can keep it alive, carry it forward, and fortify it in the ether for when you slip away yourself. If a string of forefathers leaves you standing on the shoulders of giants, is it not fitting to honour and further their work to the best of your ability?

Frank used to tell me as a child not to criticise something unless I had a better solution. And so I have systematically presented my solution, in my lifestyle, a universal brand, and a series of books, and I have been loyal to it all through thick and thin. I have captioned it succinctly, personified and presented it poetically, proved it relentlessly, and grown it globally from the same soil he was seeded in. After a lifetime of figures, his assets were all heart, and my inheritance is beating in my chest.

We cannot preserve possessions even when we're alive, but we can burn bright with the light of our personal and familial soul, and live with self- and ancestral-respect. We can stand for something that stands forever, and make it more powerful and beautiful. We can grow grand new trees in the old soil and make music from the studio in the back garden. We can integrate our heritage and our individual expression and give the whole world something truly special. We can come together in oneness and live in liquid love. This I know. It's been inside me since I was born and it was taught to me by death.

Chapter 37:

If You Were There

I find that when I am being creative I have less inclination towards sex. Partly it's the inward direction of attention, the intent listening to the inspiration coming through, and the focusing of effort and ability on the vast task at hand of turning the ethereal into the convincingly real. It takes devotion and all of one's energies, and I can't afford to be distracted or have my efforts dissipated. It takes time to get to the depths of awareness needed to work on the emerging manifestation, and surface-level stuff has to be put aside, as obsessive-compulsive as I can be about it usually. Sexual energy and creativity are the same essential power, and they all go into the artistic work.

I've heard that Einstein's wife was under strict instructions not to speak to him unless he initiated conversation, which makes sense. You can't reach new heights when you are kept on the same stratum by conventional consciousness. It sounds like he was far from the best husband to both of his spouses, though, and so his genius in one field came at a cost to another. Balance isn't easy.

Sex is creativity in raw form, and another pure form of it is consciousness, which is at a higher vibrational level. And so the exact energy that can end up finding expression in a naked romp can be applied to other inventive endeavours and to the awakening of individual and collective awareness. Your inner thrust can be a way to distract yourself with (possibly pointless) pleasure or one to take you (and all of us) into nirvana. In that, being creative is inseparable from having sex, and they both have their respective places in the spectrum of positive pursuits. Both are invigorating, exhausting, intimate and orgasmic.

Importantly, the way to the higher is through the lower, not in denial of or at the expense of it. And so, embrace sexuality and live it fully but do not stop there. Integrate it with your spiritual awakening so that it can take you up. The lower may fall away as the higher prevails, but you needn't repress it or make any sacrifices. Celibacy results naturally from profound creativity and awakened consciousness and needn't be conjured or forced in any way. If it arises from getting older in body, then it is a symptom of having ripened to a spiritual age. Instead of being tied to your physical form, you are able to stay resident in your higher self and let your light shine through into the world. This is the quality of wisdom and grace. Don't fight it but embody it.

Creativity and sex are both spaces when time stands still. It flies by without you noticing because you are so in the moment and fully engaged in what you are doing that the illusion of linearity evaporates. The present opens up and goes on forever, and mind is not dominant. Thinking becomes a servant to higher consciousness, thereby taking its rightful place in the hierarchy of layers of awareness. Mind and time go together, the latter being a construct of the former, while presence frees us from both. As a crude example, I pressed play on the stereo here, sat down to work on my writing, and then noticed that track four was playing, which implied that tracks one to three had somehow transpired. In the same way, time flies when you're having sex. Both of these existential places are a taste of the transcendent where life is not linear but quantum, not time-bound but eternal, and not horizontal but vertical. Instead of being a sequence with a beginning and end, it's an infinite up and down. We are in a mystical and spirited state, the present, the here-now, the moment, where we can keep going deeper and higher. It is the only reality there really is. Here we are being ourselves and, paradoxically, there is no self there, only presence. We have transcended the self and transcended time. How happy are we?

It's the same thing, or no-thing, as being on stage. Bruce Springsteen is the best example of this that I have seen. He totally inhabits the moment. While he is up there, nothing else exists, let alone matters, yet, in that, he is one with everything and, importantly, bringing this access to the audience. His job is to open the present and be a portal for it into the lives of those who love him and his work. This is, in fact, what he sells, although it is priceless and immune to financial quantification. It is so precious that people will fly across the world to witness it, or follow the band around the continent to witness every show. It is literally salvation through rock 'n roll because it puts us in touch with ourselves. Also, the music makes us feel. In a state of presence, awareness and emotional resonance, we are fully alive, and being fully alive is all we truly want and need.

Every hankering in us is a twisted search for just this one experience of total aliveness. Monetary wealth is an empty substitute, fame is a dangerous surrogate, and romance is a dreamy replacement stalked by a potential nightmare. Aliveness is all, and it has no downside. Until we have it, we will resist dying, and when we have it, we will have no trouble with death. The two come and go together. Peddle drugs and you can make money, and sell substitutes and you can amass assets, but give presence and vitality and you will be truly rich. I call it being yourself for a living. It's the new world for a wholesome humanity.

Time out of time is the best time because it is actually the only one. Time itself is a type of torture and presence is paradise. Now is forever. Sometimes the music disappearing is a symptom of merging with the moment, and other times you can use the music to find the moment. Use whatever is happening because the now is always here for you to rediscover and, in so doing, return to yourself.

Start with your breathing. That is with you all the time, immediate and taken for granted. Become aware of it. The physical and formless realms intersect with the breath. Return to it repeatedly and you will reside there increasingly. Natural, vital and mindful inhalations and exhalations, and engaging the world from there. Be attentive the body too, and inhabit it fully. Fill and feel your feet, and wiggle your toes to bring your awareness out of your head and down into your other extremities. Then be conscious of your emotions and their energetic and transient nature. Let them be there and look into them as they move and morph. And watch your thoughts come and go, too. Be the watcher.

I use day-to-day household maintenance tasks as meditations. It's one Zen way of living that I love. I do my own laundry and hang it like I am sculpting art. The towels drape symmetrically, ready to come off the clothes horse crisp and prepared for folding. The kitchen tea cloths, when it's their turn, get my loving treatment too. I shape each one into a neat parallelogram that I pivot over its middle on the rail so that when they are dry I can take them off efficiently and pile them prettily. This makes me happy. The stack then goes into the allocated corner of the convenient cupboard for ease of access, and fits into the art of being in my kitchen. Even mundane chores by the mind's assessment are the creative spirit's playground. With the music so intensely present throughout the living and working area, I am in the contented and inspired flow while I am living the life. Mixed into that are all my other creative endeavours, like typing out one-liners, compiling picture quotes, managing social media profiles and connections, corresponding with clients, and reading and writing books. Everything else needs to find its place in this for it to have a home in my life. When it does, it is as rich and as thrilled as I am.

Creativity is sex, just slightly differently applied. Some men spawn children, fulfil the fatherly function and do their creating that way. I fashion stuff like this. It's less messy! I explore consciousness and enjoy freedom, live as an artist, voice a mystic's life, and encounter the void without external structure or company pension. I build my own entrepreneurial foundation. I've stuck at it for twenty two years when others have left the room clutching their hair in their hands just at the mention of it. Then I kick in at fifty, more creative than ever and just warming up. Just wait until I die...

Creativity is death. You throw yourself at that canvas, crucifying yourself in an orgasm of colour on a cross of virgin white. Creativity is surrender, nails in artistic arms and feet, with blood dripping from the brow onto the page. Creativity is forgiving the masses for not knowing what they do while you do it all up there alone, all for them and for its intrinsic value until one day it might pay. Creativity is giving it all up and letting it all go to be true. It is death and resurrection in one, the truth coming full circle, the big payday every day, and living forever in a global shift. Creativity is worth it.

Chapter 38:

Precious Box

Why is Simon working on seven movies at seventy eight, Quincy busier than ever at eighty four, and Frank ten years gone already? Why was the conformist dead just a handful of years after he retired early when the rebels haven't retired and don't plan to? Does having an inspired reason to live have anything to do with it? Why is Resheka still here, healthier than ever, after a close call? A reason to live has a lot to do with it. That's what the doc was looking out for in her and he validated it when he saw it. She then grabbed onto it. After all, she did not want to die. Her old ways were just a manipulative game and she was ready to wake up from that nonsense.

Frank had taken a handful of big blows in the decade before he died and he didn't deal with them openly or wisely. It seemed to me that he took them silently on the chin, on his own, and then carried them in his blood and his bones. His career was over before its time and he had no drive to do anything else after the series of hard knocks, plus he didn't process his experiences and take his opportunities. There's an entirely different energy behind feeling defeated and directionless to having huge work still to do and an excitement about how it all can and will happen. There is a basic difference in life when you are engaged and happy, and trusting of change. The hard knocks are blessings in disguise pointing you to the new way.

Life's purpose and your happiness aren't the biggest predictors of longevity, from what I can gather having scanned a little research, so I am not making that kind of direct correlation, but George went when he ran out of reasons to live. Frank's work was done and seemingly he had better things to attend to elsewhere, plus he could collaborate more effectively here when not encumbered by physical form. It's not necessarily about longevity either. Some of the very best of us have burned brightest for only a short time. The bottom line, though, is that you are better off with a vein of spiritual gold running through your life. If I make eighty four, I might be doing my best work then. That happens when you follow your passion and keep growing and giving. Richness keeps unravelling and doesn't depend on your hormones or structured employment. Quite the opposite, in fact.

Last year and for the few running up to it, when I was feeling so terribly stuck, I was working in a most insular way, which was fitting for a seven year stretch characterised by writing and inner growth, but it had gone too far. It wasn't bringing me what I needed anymore, and was keeping me in too much pain. I was struggling to deal with and then recover from a relationship, couldn't seem to attract enough external traction in business, and was feeling so down that it could have been called depressed. Then energies shifted but needed something as strong as abdominal surgery to stir up such enduring intensity and help me surface from that insular era. Later in the year it culminated with five weeks in Thailand, which brought everything together in accomplishment, release, reflection and celebration. It was only then that I could claim to truly know that it was all meant to be the way it had been.

In the years since Frank died I'd written nineteen more INSIGHTS books, plus my autobiography, which are good numbers for a writer and an accountant's son. The stuck feeling was part of the creative tension much of the time, part of the friction that kept me firing on all cylinders in my introverted way. As tortured as I felt at times, I was indisputably productive from an outward perspective, which was a comfort, but even more so inwardly. I was growing vigorously and gearing up for the next age of creative life. A soulful spin in Southeast Asia catapulted me into that, and the precipitation of this book gave the accumulation a channel to take form as well as open the way into the new era. It may take seemingly forever, but spiritual growth knows the way and has impeccable timing.

Thailand was a flower bursting into bloom in bright sunlight after a growth cycle underground. Travelling up to see Simon in the last week was a powerful climax that gave me something to come back with, the very thing I was looking for. What I sought was within me but the voyage and connection outwardly were needed to mirror and trigger it. It transformed my readiness into an inspired thrust, a taste of the treasures of trust, a drop of pure inspirational gold, a burst of rejuvenation, and a most compelling reason to live. It was a new voice, a worthy challenge, a tantalizing tome ready to be written and born, and the wave of energy that it came on. I began without delay and haven't stopped riding this chariot of fire since. This is what we all want to take us and far and as wide as we can go. We want to live. Death is not the problem. Not living is the problem. Live and there will be no problem. Live like the music and the rain. Live like your life is the love the whole universe is looking for.

But before we went to Thailand, I had to go through feeling tied down so that I could get here. It was the big lead-up, we can say now, looking back. I felt like a failure when the opposite was the case and requiring my realignment with it. I felt out of synch and in need of a shift, but it was a necessary discord. In my hell of troubling thoughts, I was able, with Resheka and Amanda's help, to reframe my situation to my advantage and keep going. And then we met Simon, this book began, and I had a clear path ahead of me to all my dreams coming true with the fruits of my labour to enjoy.

My Thai massage therapist in Johannesburg had advised me a few months before that I needed to be happy to avert illness and I had kept working my way into joyfulness and switched back into trusting and finding the flow. I knew exactly where she was nudging me to go because she did so at the right time. The build-up to the Thailand trip pulled me forward and the trip itself shifted the impending birth into the existential realm.

Your life's purpose is important. You need to find it or be finding it or living it, which are all the same thing really. You need to know and trust that it is there because, well, you already know that it is. The bullshit is a game, but you know that too. Getting lost is part of the picture. You need to go with that knowing and keep going, growing into it all the time, even when it hurts. Your life's purpose kick-starts you on your spiritual quest, shows you the way all the way, keeps you together through tough times, and awaits your breakthroughs, beaming as you burst gloriously from the clouds into the next dawn of your realisation. If you are struggling, hang in there while death and rebirth do their timely thing. The grappling is all part of the impending glory.

Your life's purpose is not a purpose per se, as there is no purpose to anything but continuous celebration. We impose meaning and interpretation onto an unfathomable existence that keeps culminating every moment for the sheer delight of it. Every moment is purpose itself attained, and we are the attaining. But for the sake of description, let's say that your purpose is total alignment with that, being yourself, doing what you love, being creative, being a rebel entrepreneur, living fully in the moment, navigating the hardships, bringing your brilliance to bear for the benefit of the transforming world, and all the rest that you already know. The trick is to feel it and let go into it. Risk it and be it. Leap in and write it.

Bust open the precious box you carry within and send those jewels sparkling into the air. Bring the actualisation of your burning potential into form and make the planet more beautiful with your joy. Transmute your pain into triumph, live out your inner myth and temper it with the teachings of death. Give a fuck and give it with all you've got, making shameless fuck-faces whenever necessary. Keep a stiff upper lip, too, if it works for you. We all have our uniqueness to bring, and we all have our role to play. Yours is the royal way.

This mystical trip sometimes means feeling like you're fucking up. How much do you think a star like George suffered behind the scenes? Eventually he was suffering in full view, and he went down suffering. It's not so much sad as it's real! Face it in every genius who has enriched your life, and face it in yourself, you genius. His story is ours and mine is yours. Hiding behind sunglasses isn't much help, whoever you are. Do you think Simon hasn't been through the throes of depression while admiring fans lapped up his tales of the high life? He told me about some of them. You can't be on a high all the time. The crests have the troughs to thank for their frothy ride. Do you think that being myself for a living for twenty two years has been easy? Do me a favour.

Quit your day job, stick to it when there's no money, and get back to me. Do something true and visionary, and keep going when the business world shows steady indifference. Dig deeper as the desperation mounts and keep coming up with the same answer: keep being true! Evolve your offering, overcome yourself over and over, learn to value yourself and charge your worth, find the joy again that you set out with, and you'll find the your sweet spot.

I have to be paid fittingly for what I do, and clients must have something as compelling to offer as what I am already engrossed in and enthralled by, otherwise I need to walk away. No more dysfunctional dynamics, please. As a result, I have a hard-won set of criteria for corporations, the three 'R's, distilled from two decades of doing it: realness, readiness and remuneration. You have to be real, you have to be ready, and you have to pay commensurately and handsomely. BEntrepreneurING is the only brand in the world that can do what we do for you.

Can you afford it? Can you afford not to have it? We are not in the business of fitting in with your agenda, do not submit proposals or attend pre-sales meetings, and charge to consider your proposal. We accept non-refundable payment in advance before any discussions to establish whether you are real and ready, and if you are you will understand and accept our terms. If you have issues, go and get real and ready. Like your company, we have selection criteria. We're niche, bespoke and boutique.

Two factors temper you into realness. Either sincerity and insight into the truth and direction for your brand and organisation, or desperation. In other words, either inspiration, or the chilling sense of imminent death of business as you have known it. Only then do you get real. Often it's both factors at the same time, a combination brimming with potential. If the old ways seem still to be working for you, though, you might have to continue in your contrived way until transformation is the only option. I prefer not to deal with organisations like that, owing to the unpleasant nature of it and the abundance of better things to do. If you find the present and can see the future, though, you will want to work with me, and if the past has betrayed you, you will need to work with me. And so, get real, and put your money where your mouth is.

One factor determines readiness and that is readiness itself. It is a function of the whole, and it cannot be rushed, accelerated, driven, purchased or bribed. Equally, it cannot be slowed down, prevented, stopped, delayed or corrupted. Before it is there, there is nothing you can do but the work of trusting and opening to it, and when it arrives, you can do nothing but go with it. And it is coming for everybody...

Getting real and getting ready also means understanding my business, my life's work and purpose, my vision and direction, and my working style. How else would you know you need it if you haven't become fully au fait with it? I learn about you after payment. If I were to try to sell my stuff to you, I would be reinforcing the fake structure that doesn't work, trying to convey what I do on your terms, and giving away what I do for free. When, then, would you begin to value it and pay? Never, of course. You would stay where you are, take what I do for granted, and treat it with disdain. I know this from experience. Plus, you corporate chaps tend to be quite mercenary, and understand well the language of putting money first, so I am doing so too. If you don't understand what I am on about, you will begin to get me very clearly when you are financing your access.

If the Financial Director is foolish enough to get touchy about return on investment, which so many of them still are, I will meet and raise their bets, saying something like, "You're the numbers person, so you work it out. Translate the value am I about to add into a projection expressed numerically and then pay a percentage. I am sure that you will regret not just taking the initial figure upfront. Your limited thinking and your attitude will cost you, and it's too late to turn back now. Let me know when you have the figures and you can transfer the first instalment."

This remuneration matters mostly for you and your process. How much is transformation worth? If you can patronise it, you are attempting to keep it is beneath you, which means that you are still faking control and not ready yet. But when you are sincere and positioned to pay, like when it is a life or death scenario, you will make the right financial investment and gain optimally from it. Then and only then can you transform.

It is a total occurrence, not some strategic initiative. The paradigm is qualitatively different to your past, and this is my turf. To help you, I must keep my footing, stand my ground, and represent 'being yourself for a living' respectfully and rigorously. There can be no compromise and you will thank me profusely. There will be invigorating growth, fun and fulfilment beyond your imaginings, quantum leaps and shifts, and success on a whole new level. Payment is for your benefit and at the heart of a successful project. In advance. Thank you.

Chapter 39:

Cars and Trains

Wine. Water. Wellness. Woman at the next table. Beautiful vision. Someone's wife! Inspiration, perhaps a little too much. Her husband and kids are back. Simon's book *Black Vinyl White Powder* is on the table in front of me. Enjoying that. Saturday lunch. Creative tension. Sexy energy.

Rain arriving. Staff mayhem. Angry owner. Greek drama. Good fun. Writer's moment. Hail warning. No problem. Closed doors. Different feeling. Food coming. Present moment. Turquoise bottle. Tall glass. Empty carafe. Nourishing meal. Writer's life. Americano and ouzo.

You can write anything you like and you will be writing about death. I am stirring my current coffee the way Resheka pointed out. The Milky Way on this one is thick and stormy. Stirring is death, death is art, true art always points to the eternal, and the eternal is the present moment. I am going to swallow half of that pungent aquatic tot and back it with a black hit of the hot galaxy in my white cup. The other half of the aniseed firewater and then more bitter-sweet sips from this precipice of porcelain. Worth sharing.

The family of four with the riveting wife left a while ago and was replaced by three people who have just prayed before they began to eat. Their food arrived and, with it in front of them, they held hands and closed their eyes, which made me look away, in uneasy reverence. Private moment. Strange stuff. It's good to be grateful and mindful, but my goodness. Anyway, I'm praying too as I drink and write this. Thank you, thank you. My life is grateful worship, packed with grumpiness, a continuous prayer of undirected love and more than occasional moodiness, my own brand of growing goodness integrated with creative edginess. Where on earth could I send all of this? Everywhere. Thank you, thank you, for everything everywhere, here now and always.

Sounds exactly right. So death comes in that same way and you enjoy it. You relax, trust and let it come, like the best blowjob in human history. Unbridled, unbounded and biblical. You stay loose and natural, and an orgasmic oneness arises in its own time, the right time, when you and the cosmos are ready.

Cars and trains on a Saturday afternoon. No rain as yet and none likely. Clear skies. Perfect afternoon. Reader's moment.

While we were in Thailand, Resheka mentioned out of the blue that she wanted to buy a watch. She had been considering it quietly for a while, as a gift to herself to mark the healthy and wealthy ending to a trying year, as a celebration of achievement, and as a symbol of a new self. When I heard what she was considering I offered to make some suggestions, which she welcomed. I'm no expert but I have a sense of things. We were swimming in the sea when we spoke and my watch was on my right wrist.

It was carefully chosen and I relish living with it. First, it is the same brand as a pair that Frank and Beth bought each other when they got married. I remember these matching timepieces when I was young and wore Frank's for a while after he died. It had been his daily adornment for many years but then he put it away for some reason and started wearing Chinese cheapos so humble that they were less expensive to buy than their replacement batteries. Truly disposable and thoroughly non-vulnerable. Finding his old dress and work watch from the late sixties brought back the seventies and the eighties when he wore it and I was young. Having it on my arm allowed me to keep my father with me in the present. And then, a few years later, I felt ready to buy myself my own version. I had already decided which one it would be. Not particularly expensive but perfect, and particularly perfect for me.

On the day I turned forty three I walked out of the store where I had bought wedding rings, and other key purchases over the years, with a luxury bag, a charmed box inside it, and the feeling of a meaningful gesture well conducted. The esteemed procurement was the current version of Frank's, a dressy diver's watch, both sleek and sporty, and at once classic and current. It's the one I still have on six years later and the only piece of jewellery I wear. I have it on most of the time and it reminds me of the good things in life, to be present, of my father and of the fleeting nature of things. If it feels heavy on my arm, I take it off, otherwise I am one with it. Of course, it makes a statement to others too, if they have eyes to see. Even at a glance it looks gripping but a discerning person will be able to read more into it, which is what I wanted to convey to Sheke as we floated in the warm ocean water.

I suggested that she get a real watch, by a fine watchmaker, not a fashion item with the same branding as handbags and sunglasses. I'd nearly made that mistake before consulting with my erudite old friend, Adrian, who has an aptitude for such things. After that I stepped back and began again, and took a few years to reach my decision. From my experience then and since, I sketched the strata of manufacturers to Sheke, based on a pyramid I'd seen online once and saved on my phone, which I later sent to and talked through with her. I guessed the approximate associated prices, and gave my take on where she would possibly pitch herself based on knowing her and what she wants to achieve with the investment. My taste came into it unashamedly but I prepared her to investigate the range of brands and models available and make a discerning decision. We undertook to look into it as we went along.

A few days later we found ourselves at Phuket International Airport on the way to Kuala Lumpur with a delayed flight and time to see what the duty free shops had in the way of hands-on research. A sign directed us upstairs to where we found the retailer specialising in the brand on my arm, among others at that level. A browse around eliminated all but the recommended range and Sheke found two designs she liked a lot. She tried on colour variations and I photographed them on her tanned skin for us to look at again later. With careful consideration we settled on the one. It was early days in our explorations but I had the sense that this would be it.

In Kuala Lumpur we stayed in a hotel right next to the Pavilion shopping mall, which gave us an opportunity to look at other brands that held possible appeal in aesthetics and association. This was a worthwhile and educational exercise, but it really just served to confirm the original finding at the airport. That one watch in particular... We'll see. I have spoken to the owner of the jewellers back here in Bedfordview, ahead of seeing him again when Resheka's ready to buy. Last week she stopped me at the window of a neighbouring store and looked at a single-stone diamond necklace and matching earrings. Those and the watch, and only those, are what she wants to own and wear, she said. I see a picture coming together, strung stylishly by a sophisticated and soulful story.

I told her tonight about writing this watch story into my book, and asked her again to explain what the impending purchase means to her. She had no hesitation in voicing her realisations, as they were still front of mind. The watch and the simple and elegant diamonds represent the transformation she underwent through the illness and treatment last year, and the rebirth she continues to experience now. They symbolise the awakening to her truer self and the celebration of life on a new level. And, most important, she said, they depict her liberation from fear and her emergence into worthiness.

Before her trials and tribulations, and between then and her celebratory trip to Thailand, she could afford the jewellery, she said, but she felt it more pressing to cling to the money in case anything negative were to happen. Her gearing was to live in fear of some possible occurrence of a negative nature, plus she didn't feel aligned with the person who could own and wear such items in congruence and comfort. Also, at the time, she didn't realise any of this either. The encounter with death and her resulting transformation of awareness stripped away all she had clung to in falseness. It brought her into the present, made it clear that her fears were foolish and unfounded, showed her who she really is, and taught her how to live.

"A good life deserves a good death," she said tonight. "Give yourself permission to live how you want to live, and die how you choose to die."

Looking down at my clothes, which years ago I would have aspired to and I now wear with casual acceptance, and looking at my watch that symbolises so much, I see that I am magnificently rich. Of course, my wealth is without any possessions and without time, and there is no watch required, but it's good to integrate one so beautiful into my life, and to do it so discerningly and creatively with the other joys of living. We can experience the best of everything in the permanent present.

At the time of the second edit of this book, Sheke bought me some orange roses, which stood before me on my desk in a tall vase for almost two weeks, with the garden outside through the slatted window behind them. As an expression of her affection for me and support for this work, their presence and beauty oversaw and inspired my loving labour. I watched them stand stiffly at first, open the next day, throw themselves into full bloom the day after that, slowly soften and fade over time, and still look magnificent as they perished. I watched the spectrum of life.

Chapter 40:

Battlestations

Isn't fucking a kind of death? You give up your dignity and human poise and behave like an animal. You need to be drunk on pheromones and hormones to enter into such behaviour. You disgrace your carefully constructed ego by tying it up in the corner, whipping it a bit, and then making it watch you have sex with someone you put first for a while. Sadomasochism at its most smouldering. You have to die inside every time you do that. Intensifies the thrill.

No wonder we keep sex from the kids. We're fucking embarrassed. We can't show such innocent souls our secret selves. We cringe when the dogs do it, so we go behind closed doors when we obey the same reptilian instincts. Love you too, baby.

Is it not love being made? If it is then shouldn't it be happy and health? There's no humiliation in sharing love. And isn't it also biology? There's no shame in biology. There's no disgrace in dying. We come and we go. No taboos required.

Isn't fucking a death of innocence? Isn't that also why we try to protect young people from it? Before sex we are so pure, then something horrendous happens and we are sinners forever. What a price to pay for a roll in the hay. We are all going to hell for tasting natural heaven. Forgive us, Father, we have been ourselves! Christ, that's insane. Let's be real and wholesome, shall we, for God's sake? Death is real and wholesome and we need to live accordingly. No God required and, most important, no corrupting church.

Here and now I am, relaxed from a life well-lived. I have that satisfaction in me, with hi-fidelity music all around and a Highveld thunderstorm in the distance, which is sending lightning through my evening window. This song's "Tunnel of Love", from the double live album *Alchemy*, recorded at the Hammersmith Odeon (now Apollo) in 1983. Dire Straits never felt better. I'm hovering here timelessly when I'm forty nine, like I did when I listened to the same stuff with roaring adolescent love thirty five years ago. As a kid ten years before that, and before this fine band started out, I listened to my mother's small collection on my portable record player. First I'd unclip the speaker side of the case, then I'd slip the black disc from the paper sleeve and place it over the silver pin in the middle of the rubber plate. I'd pull back the arm to activate the motor, carefully place the needle in the groove, hear that magical crackle, put my ear to the speaker, and disappear into the land of sound, a mystical place so close to the one I carried inside...

Isn't music a kind of death? An expressing, capturing, replaying, and reliving of monumental moments? Isn't it being lost in the moment, life flashing before your eyes, an overflowing heart, a tear twinkling, and a traveller transfixed? Isn't death just like a Saturday evening listening to old songs with rain across town and wine in the home, all hazy on the polish-scented, cherry-wood coffee table dimly-lit by the orange glow from two corners of the symmetrical room? "Telegraph Road" reminding me of the *Love Over Gold* album on cassette back in 1982, which was one of my very early personal purchases for myself and, thus, epic investments at the time, played on my first music centre that I saved up for. A teenager transformed and now a more-than-adult looking back.

What is life? What is time? What is music? What is death? What is writing? What is the ultimate? What is good? What is real? What connects the me then with the me now? What made my hands go from four to fourteen and then to forty nine while I looked on from somewhere transcendent? What connects me here with you there, and who are we? I feel that we are approaching an answer. I know that you feel it too. You know exactly what I am talking about but you don't know quite how to word it. Don't worry, leave that to me. I have the evening free.

Dire Straits' song "Tunnel of Love", originally from the album *Making Movies* in 1980, is distinctly Springsteen-esque. Bruce's 1975 epic *Born to Run*'s influence is all over it, as is the carnival life from his first two Jersey-shoreline inspired albums. The East Coast boardwalk is mirrored by the Spanish City in Newcastle, England, where Mark Knopfler spent his early adulthood, and keyboardist

Roy Bittan from The E Street Band even played on *Making Movies*. There are youthful dreams all over the world and fairy-tale scenes to reflect them. If you can live it and feel it and get it down on record, you can live forever, or at least for a few minutes on stage each night and in the darkness of a million dreamers' bedrooms in locations you would never go otherwise. Without meeting someone you can reach into their soul and enrich their life, steering it towards the truth and helping them on their journey home. It's not just sound travelling far and wide, it's spirit transcending space and time.

Springsteen changed the global music scene with his opening trilogy of records, putting us in touch with the fantasy side of making memories and inspiring many musicians to make rock 'n' roll even more mythical. Bob Seger's grand song "Night Moves" is seamed straight from the same spiritual cloth, by Bob's own bold admission. Bruce was the seed, but he too was spawned by other influencers. Interestingly, a few years after that, his 1987 album was called *Tunnel of Love*, taking the fairground theme further, with an unexpected career-turn into songs and sounds about relationships and steeped in dark introspection. Taking a title used by a band he influenced, Bruce steered the rollercoaster out of the youthful lights of fantasy-come-true to dreams-turned-shadowy down the twists and turns of love and sexual intimacy. Bruce is the best. Isn't being the best a kind of death?

I used to listen to his *Tunnel of* Love album, the follow-up to the mammoth *Born in the USA*, in my first car driving back from Irene on Sunday nights having been out there to work on my humble machine under the mentorship of Uncle Peter. Growing up I had first heard Bruce in around 1980 when the singles from *The River* album were hits on the radio. "Hungry Heart" and "Sherry Darling". The noir and hitless record *Nebraska* followed that and passed me by for the moment, and then the world and the rock star were ready for a string of his biggest hits and an ass-in-jeans cover that would define mid-eighties culture. He toured that record and rode that wave as far as they could go, and then returned home to the East Coast to face the comedown from stratospheric success. It hit him hard, as it would, but we only got to read about it in his 2016 memoir *Born to Run*, in which he described his first full encounter with depression.

The pain of youth mixed with his creative thrust and the determination to avert his father's working-class fate had driven him to become a musician, produce great work in the studio and on stage for more than a decade, and live his dreams beyond most people's wildest imaginings. After eighteen months on the road, critical acclaim, adulation everywhere, and all the money he could ever need, he had nowhere left to go in the world. He had to turn inwards and face himself. I am sure that had he not done so, he would be dead now.

Instead, though, true to his heroic spirit, he stopped running and did perhaps the biggest work of his career up to that point. On the advice of his manager and confidante, Jon Landau, Bruce went to see a therapist, and upon arrival in the man's office burst into tears that just would not stop. This set in motion a relationship and inner journey that continues more than thirty years down the road. His towering achievements are characterised by lifelong torment and rooted in his ability to translate that into redemption for himself and his audience. He has managed to stay just one step ahead of disaster, though, by being himself for a living, which is his glory and great gift to us all.

By 1987 I was a huge fan, having loved *Born in the USA*, discovered his back catalogue and immersed myself in that retroactive world too. When news broke of the follow-up, I wondered what it would sound like and where it would go, knowing that it would not disappoint but not expecting the road it took. Recorded largely alone with a sprinkling of help from his soon-to-be-jettisoned E Street band mates, *Tunnel of Love* soon became my favourite Springsteen album and remains so to this day. It brought all his work to that point together and somehow spoke to me more deeply than the rest of it through its brooding melancholy, which is much like my own. Although I was only nineteen at the time, that music spoke to my old soul.

I found and bought my first car a few months after I began university. More than providing me with much-needed transport, though, the purchase symbolised freedom, adulthood and the materialisation of visions I had nurtured since lying in the backseat of Frank's cars as a child. I wanted to be in command of that dreaminess, to turn on the heater when it was cold, and to play music as a soundtrack to the hypnotic movement. That day dawned with the arrival of a white 1976 model Ford Escort, very similar to my mother's car at the time. It needed some work done on it and to my delight, my uncle offered to help. He had been in the motor trade his whole career and was a wizard with anything mechanical. "Bring it over on the weekend," he chuckled over the phone, "and we'll see what we can do."

With the spare parts and replacement oil he listed freshly purchased and packed neatly in the boot, I drove out of Bedfordview onto the motorway that Frank had made familiar for me, and took the turnoff I knew well just before Pretoria. Irene was to the left, where it had always been, and I was there with my own set of wheels. I arrived at the big old house and was immediately put to work out back like a fresh apprentice. "Pour some engine cleaner into an old tin," Peter told me, "and use this paintbrush to wash down the engine. Plug the carburettor inlet with a rag to make sure that you don't get water in there, and reach in to all the hidden places until the grease and dirt are loose. Then rinse the whole motor down with the hose pipe."

I did as instructed while he went about his chores, and an hour later called him over to show him the results of my work. "Hmmm," he said, peering over the much cleaner interior. "Looks good. Now do it again. See all these spots you missed? We need to work in there and we can't do that until all the gunk is off." A little put out but not discouraged, I redid the job, with more rigour this time, learning as I went and enjoying the even cleaner motor when I was done. Just one more inspection and repeat, and we were ready to move on to doing the service.

Peter had always held a mystical charm for me, as one's uncle does, but remained inaccessible through my youth. He would occasionally arrive unannounced to see my grandparents while we were there for lunch or dinner, and then leave freely with none of the family ties I saw in my dad. He never married, drove an Alpha Romeo Junior sports car, and maintained a free-spiritedness that I looked up to. He had moved back to Irene after my grandfather, to look after my gran, and would eventually take over the house. My new connection with him around my car brought us closer and I really got to know and love him as a supplementary father figure, older brother, fellow Wheeler and fiery character.

Whereas Frank had frowned upon swearing in my presence, Peter cussed like a mechanic. When I got stuck on a stubborn nut in the jacked-up car, and had tried everything to loosen it, he would lie back on the trolley and disappear under the vehicle. There'd be some silence at first and perhaps a grunt or two, and then he would send out a stream of blasphemous expletives that would launch his teenage nephew into fits of laughter. Liberated and educated, I was soon emulating his behaviour, which has symbolised my paternal tradition and typified my character since.

Not unlike Frank, Peter showed me how to maintain my material world impeccably. "If you're going to do something, you may as well do it properly," he once said. And so I have done that since. I would remove the washed engine parts, assess their condition, read the running of the motor based on their state, clean and dry the ports where they fitted, take the shiny replacements out of the boxes in my boot, smear anti-corrosive lubricants carefully onto the threads, and screw them lovingly into place to just the right tension. I'd set the firing gap in the spark plugs, put the new points and condenser into the distributor, adjust the timing gap, slot in the fuel and air filters and, when the satisfying job was eventually done and the sun was going down, put the jack back under the front chassis, take the stands out from under the car, and lower my beloved machine onto the ancestral earth.

Peter and I would chat in the cool of the Irene evening that I remembered from my childhood, with Richard's spirit hovering and grumbling around the old workshop and sometimes with Frank also in attendance having driven over to join us and attend to some family paperwork. The soul of Springsteen was there too, in my hard-working hands, the smell of sump oil, our masculine metaphors and blue-collar salvation, and soaked into the soil that fed our collective struggles and joys. With black grease still under my nails and in the cracks in my skin despite a few rigorous rounds of hand cleaning, I would say goodbye to my uncle, start my happy engine, reverse out of the stately gates and drive away gently as he closed them behind me.

My tape of Bruce's *Tunnel of Love* had been ready in the cassette deck all day and now begun playing. The journey of songs would weave through the familial and personal themes so strongly in my heart, and the forty five minutes of music mapped perfectly onto the trip back to Bedfordview. I would pull into my hometown and turn into our driveway as the last track was chiming to a close, and for a moment everything in life would make total sense.

There is no feeling in this world like driving a car that you have worked on yourself with loving rigour and deep resonance, especially with a timeless soundtrack playing. That hum around and within you is the harmony of oneness. I have carried the feeling forward into everything I do. I am sure you can sense it as I start to steer this book home.

Chapter 41:

Star People

Another interview with Quincy Jones was published last week, this one by David Marchese on Vulture.com and simply called "In Conversation". Again the man was frank, as if he is working on some sort of sincerity movement, which, between these two recent pieces, sent ripples of realness through the world. That alone is priceless, and then there was the content. One of the questions David asked was if Quincy is afraid of the end, to which the answer was simply no, and another was what he thinks happens when you die, to which his answer was that you're just gone. At that is all the attention the topic of death received from both interviewer and subject.

For all the brilliance of the life well lived and the insights given with genuine gangster style, those two answers were remiss for a man of his age with his public profile. Maybe it was just a sign of ignorance. All considerations were, once again, all on *this* side of the big day, but neglectful of anything beyond. Two questions, two blunt answers, and let's move on. Well, let's not. Don't be fooled by the big man's abruptness. The article was not lacking in art, wisdom, music, shrewdness, education, perspective and inspiration, but the mysticism you might want or expect from someone of eighty four was distinctly absent.

In the GQ piece a few weeks back he spoke about sex and twenty two women worldwide, which, as an octogenarian, may be great (and may not), but this attitude is out of keeping with his stage in life and proximity to death. It's immature. Look, part of me would probably love to be fucking forty-and-under women when I'm eighty, if Resheka doesn't mind, but it would likely have to be with the help of piles of pills at least, if not nanotechnology. That's going on my expectations, Simon's testimony and other friends' experiences. And there may be better things on my mind by then, too, or, more precisely, better things happening in my being. I might have outgrown aspects of my biology and the troubling tethers that come with them, including thinking about sex all the damned time. The mind is what keeps us stuck and, in my view, a great grandfather like Quincy with an adolescent mentality is not balanced and exemplary.

The proverbial dirty old man is someone who is still twenty one in his head and out of touch with the rest of his existence, whereas a whole and healthy man, who has loved well and fucked to his heart's content during the appropriate years might, have become disinclined to rolling around naked like a 'beast with two backs', as Shakespeare described it euphemistically. A woman of that vintage may also find the idea of getting funky somewhat unsavoury, unless she, too, is lost in thought and unfulfilled fantasy. Maturity means harmony with your stage of physical, emotional and spiritual development.

Quincy seems to have given no due consideration to his impending departure, apart from to delaying it as long as possible. In his mind, the end is two or three dozen years away and terminal, which, to my mind, is a naïve and avoidant approach. Keeping more pussy in every port than most men have in a lifetime doesn't make him the big papa. We need a more mystical example. Youthfulness is overvalued in a consumer society and someone demonstrating it at advanced age is admired more than it should be, while the quietly enlightened may go largely unnoticed. We need to turn the world the right way up, in this area and many others, by being the right way up ourselves.

What happens instead if you enter the mysteries of life and feel an increasing pull as you age towards embracing these in preparation for the dwell point ahead? What happens if the presence of death awakens an awareness in you that was there in the shadows but dormant to your primary awareness? Do you seek out Quincy Jones for his wisdom? He may be on the job somewhere, so maybe you'd leave him alone and hope to catch him for consultation on more musical matters when he catches his breath. Checking in with ethnobotanist and psychonaut Terrence McKenna might have been much more meaningful and helpful, had he not died in 2000. He is becoming more well-known now, moving from fringe to mainstream awareness, with the proliferation of knowledge from those less socially encouraged reaches of human consciousness, plus the movie about him called *True Hallucinations*, with Jim Carrey is out today as I write, 4 March 2018. Carrey himself is these days walking the contrary-mystic's talk in the public eye and causing a stimulating stir.

Wikipedia says that "Psychonautics (from the Ancient Greek *psychē* ["soul", "spirit" or "mind"] and *naútēs* ["sailor" or "navigator"] – "a sailor of the soul") refers both to a methodology for describing and explaining the subjective effects of altered states of consciousness, especially an important subgroup called holotropic states, including those induced by meditation or mind-altering substances, and to a research paradigm in which the researcher voluntarily immerses himself or herself into an altered mental state in order to explore the accompanying experiences. The term has been applied diversely, to cover all activities by which altered states are induced and utilized for spiritual purposes or the exploration of the human condition. A person who uses altered states for such exploration is known as a psychonaut."

The Urban Dictionary has this as their top definition: "An explorer of one's own mind. A psychonaut often embarks on inner voyages with the aid of psychoactive substances, meditation, sensory deprivation, binaural beats, and other means. Most commonly, one who experiments with psychedelic substances, such as psilocybin (magic mushrooms), LSD (acid), MDMA (ecstasy), peyote, or mescaline (shamanic tools). The goal of the psychonaut is to learn about self and reality by transcending normal consciousness. Psychonauts are distinguished from purely recreational users of psychoactive substances in their desire to learn and grow from these experiences." (Brackets are inserted by me.) My resulting definition is, "A psychonaut is someone you should speak to about death instead of Quincy Jones."

Terence McKenna championed expanded awareness in popular culture via his books and lectures towards the end of the twentieth century, having explored terrain way beyond the reaches of even the more adventurous plant-imbibers and intra-psychic wanderers. Psilocybin and DMT (the key ingredient in ayahuasca) were his speciality, and dissolving boundaries was his predilection. Let's put it this way. If geographical distance were used as an analogy for psychedelic space, your trip to the kitchen to check on supper is like his stepping outside the milky way of the inner cosmos. This man ventured way out there and came back to tell the tales, which he did with remarkable eloquence. He was an exemplary teacher whose insights begin beyond where Quincy's end. Perhaps he knew the psyche like the producer knows music and would have known about death before he died, which would have prepared him. Conversations with him would have helped you get it too, and be more ready to encounter the vastness when the time came. His work remains to offer you that, and even one quote of his on an internet meme gives you a glimpse.

Taking psychedelics in a shamanic spirit and even a recreational one dissolves the perceptual and actual boundaries that keep our sense of the world held together, and makes us available to experiences largely indescribable using the language and communication structure of our mainstream culture, although Terence found the words. We realise answers to questions we didn't know we had, and stumble upon a place where there are no questions and no answers. Plants are most intelligent. They help us see and understand the world and the mystery, and are perhaps the teachers we need most at this time. Even chemicals can put us in touch with a gestalt that becomes a reference point for spiritual growth. I am not an advocate of them but I have benefited.

My first trip on LSD, which I took while walking around Wimbledon Common in the late nineties, would teach anyone more about death and dying than the Catholic Church ever could. Expanded awareness will actually prepare you, and it will open your eyes to what existence is about and what your consciousness is capable of. It will show you how nature is alive, how you are usually asleep, how everything is speaking to you all the time, how you are blotting out most of it and containing your perception to cope, and much more of the like. Psilocybin on a sunny afternoon in Hyde Park, like I enjoyed with Paul once, might do something unnervingly and ecstatically similar, which I can hereby convey to you. Acid and mushrooms could teach you how to really laugh with every fibre of your form, and die to sheer terror as you keep living at an unmanageable degree of intensity, or completely disappear into music on an old friend's couch. This is closer to the nature of death, I'd suggest, than what Quincy sees. We should consider all options and be aware, prepared and open. Make the most of your older years and keep growing up appropriately.

Have you ever considered that the world is dying, that death is built into not just our bodies and all living things on earth but into the existence of the planet itself, and the galaxy we're in? Science will tell you that conceptually, as unfathomable as the numbers are to the mind, but what about the whole reality that constitutes all of this? If something is born, that means it is going to die, no matter its relative size and lifespan. We are just a shooting star, and the entire cosmos is a squirt across a bigger backdrop. All of it must end and go back to where it came from.

We could even understand everything the other way round, so that instead of assuming a process of creation, propulsion and evolution towards inevitable termination, we could see that something is pulling us forward, like a vacuum or a point of transcendence in the future. It could be the case that closure is what we are compelled by, and that death is drawing us towards it like an implosion. It is not the feared end for each of us individually, or for the earth, the galaxy, the universe or all of reality, but the big breakthrough we are all here and heading for.

At the time of writing, well-known theoretical physicist and cosmologist Stephen Hawking died, and clusters of his famous quotes made their way around the press and social media. One of his propositions was that we are advanced apes, and another was that we are bio-computers that simply switch off when the power is cut. And so his idea of death was similar to that of Quincy's, except that the same man spoke of understanding God's thoughts, and of God throwing the dice in unknown places. Which God is that exactly? Was Stephen speaking metaphorically, using words to articulate the otherwise inexpressible, or was he contradicting himself? Was his science unsound or was he giving himself away? One thing for certain is that he knows now what death is.

My suggestion is that if he were as much an explorer of his inner cosmology as he was a student of the outer, he would have understood the other half of the picture, which is arguably the more important half. He would know his own subjectivity and consciousness. Also, if he worked with his other faculties as much as he did his mind, and kept his thinking in its rightful place in the layers of human awareness, he would have been a wiser man, perhaps even a mystic. His statement that science is about romance and poetry would have reached its potential rather than stayed a seed, and his search for knowledge would have expanded into the realms of knowing, with the former being a function of the mind and the latter of the whole being. Science applied to both inner and outer brings about total understanding. We cannot know more about the world than we do about ourselves. When we awaken to who we are, we get the big picture.

Death is inseparable from life and it tempers everything in it. Death is the dissolving of the boundaries between dimensions, and it works as an element of ongoing growth. Death is the difference between the old and the new you. It is the big awakening, the softening of the box keeping us blind. Death is a letting go into the natural rising. Death is everything that is not false. Can anything be more real?

Chapter 42:

Everything She Wants

Yesterday I was writing over lunch at the Portuguese place on the industrial outskirts of Bedfordview when I looked up and saw Basil and Paddy, also regulars at the restaurant, and elders in the area. I was at primary school with their youngest son, Gary, and so I've known the family since 1980, a prominent and popular name in the suburb and surrounds. The business Basil began in 1967 is still a household name, and he made a lot of money over the years, eventually retiring fully in his late 70s and handing over the managing of matters to Gary. He and Paddy live a quiet life, still in their family home after forty eight years but about to sell it and move to Cape Town. They're to be seen around town at regular spots, going everywhere happily together, and gracefully fulfilling the role of living legends for many lifelong dwellers in the village-like community.

When I'd ended my meal, I went to wash my hands, said hello on the way past as they finished eating, and then came back and had a chat with them, as I usually do. The idea had come to me to get their take on death for this book, and when the catch-up at their table showed the way, I asked if I could talk to them about something specific. They invited me to sit down, and so I went to my table for a minute to enjoy the espresso and grappa waiting for me there, then returned and pulled up a chair.

I gave them a run-up to my question by sharing the Thailand trip, which was an expansion on what I'd already told them having seen them out at dinner on the night Resheka and I landed back in South Africa a few weeks ago. I led up to the day we spent with Simon, told them a bit about him, and then introduced the writing I am doing. I explained how the book is about death and I wanted to ask them about that, something, I said, they must have had an evolving approach to as time passes. Basil is eighty one and Paddy is seventy three. Gracefully I got us going on much of the stuff of this book, by listening to each of them and reflecting back what we discussed, with new questions and a growing sense of structure. A wealth of insight and affirmation came up between us and I could see it slotting into the story here and bringing everything together.

The conversation was a piece of perfection, one I could have recorded and transcribed, or filmed for television, in the same way as we could have done with the longer one with Simon. After that day in Pattaya, Resheka said that she had a few times wanted to record it all and share it with the world, for the powerful content that came up but for the magic too. At that one point at dinner she'd jumped up and taken photographs to catch the chemistry and flowering friendship between two men so similar in many ways. It was that similarity that Amanda had seen when she read

I'm Coming to Take You to Lunch a year before. The meeting was the materialisation of the intuitive that had been the seed of it all.

The idea of a series of television conversations is a brilliant one that Resheka and I conceptualised back in Patong, and that kept coming to me with increasing intensity and insight. This one with Paddy and Basil was affirmation and advancement of the concept and the time with Simon and I glowed inside as I watched it all unfold effortlessly while I enjoyed being part of it and in the flow. And that flow is going to keep growing. That's how easy and brilliant it is, being myself for a living.

A series of conversations with me, on topical subjects like death, relationships, self-actualising, sex, electric cars, colonising Mars, and other things 'being yourself for a living', perhaps called Wheeler-Dealings, filmed on exotic location. I'll have gracefully epic meetings with living legends and everyone around the world will share in the rich rush of life lessons. More life-and-death-related realisations have been coming to me since I saw the two Bedfordview elders, and I have had to trust the writing to take care of expressing everything in the right way at the right time. It's a huge handful to hold in your head, but I have been keeping calm and patiently making my way back to the keyboard, and here I am.

Paddy and Basil have their worldly affairs in order, which is part of being prepared for death. They have taken their time with letting go of the family home to join two of their kids, who they often visit in

Cape Town, but they are ready now to process the change emotionally, which is as important as doing it physically. The death of that era in life brings the birth of the new one, and you have to go through all of it to live rightly. Basil said that he's been close to his brother and a few friends over the years, around their deaths, and so he knows what it's about from experience. Paddy doesn't think about it much, appreciates that she is onto borrowed time in her life, and says that she is here by grace alone. She isn't afraid of dying, she said, but admitted that she is a little afraid nonetheless. "We don't know," she stated correctly.

Basil said twice that he takes it one day at a time, which reminded me of the old Greek man at the mall, John, who is ten years younger, comes from a background of having lost his family fortune, has the tortured gestalt of an overthinking philosopher, and says exactly the same thing. "One day at a time." It's a healthy bottom line for everybody.

Paddy and I joked that as much as you prepare and anticipate, there's no way of knowing what will happen. Basil's assumption is that he will go first based on him being eight years older and her family history of women reaching one hundred, but his premise could well be upturned. I suggested that, and Paddy laughed saying that their daughter, Sandy, has often teased about organising lots of young women for the old man if that happens. I know just the place, I thought, never more than a blink away from beloved Thailand. Good to laugh and be realistically upbeat about it all.

Good to talk about it all and make it part of social connection. I prefer it to football and finance myself, every time. Conversation like that carries us a long way, and it is beneficial for everyone. I'm sure our broadcast-quality chat stirred up insights and feelings for the two of them, and had a sense of goodness and readiness about it. Perhaps it will be there when their day comes as part of their preparation, as this book may be for you when your time comes. That goes without saying for me, since I am writing it.

"You're happy in yourself," Paddy said to me, "I can see it."

"Yeah," I smiled back. "I live the way I choose and do the work."

We finished up as if the scene was sculpted for global syndication, and as we left she said over her shoulder, "I want to read that book when it comes out."

"I'll keep you posted," I said with calm ecstasy.

You're going to let it all go when you die, so why not let it all go when you're alive, and live in freedom and joy?

My friend Arthur, who's seventy seven now, introduced me to Thailand in 2010 and was considering moving there at the time but ended up not making the leap, saying now that he left it a bit late. It's more a case of not really wanting to go, I'd say, the other side of which was his attachments here in South Africa. Before my first trip I finished finalising one INSIGHTS book for publication and finished writing a later one in the series on the same day and needed a proper holiday to break the tension, celebrate the achievement, and give me the resources to return and get DEEPER INSIGHTS onto the shelves. I opened myself to direction, as I had no idea of where to go other than somewhere new, sunny and beach-based, and that day two sets of friends said to me, "You should go to Thailand!" That was a sign if ever I needed one, and so I had tea with one set, Arthur and Colleen, and they shared their love of Phuket and some travel tips with me. A week later I was there for ten days, and four months after that, having fallen in love with the place, the lifestyle, and the me that could be so free and happy there, I was back for six weeks with the view to stay longer.

Two weeks into that trip, Arthur arrived for a month, without Colleen, and the two of us had fun together like boys getting to know each other and enjoying the fun of deep conversation and sunset swims between days of independent adventure. He wanted to talk about his assets at the age of sixty nine, and his possible relocation plans, which were both educational but limited, and I needed to go deeply into the turning point I was grappling with at forty one. My dad had died nearly two years before, I had finished renovating my home and put out a trilogy of books at the end of a decade, and a relationship had shown itself as over, too, and so I was burned out and at a loss for convincing direction. I needed to rest, re-evaluate and, importantly, reconnect with who I was and what I wanted. The questions I was asking were the very stuff that Arthur was avoiding.

Not at Basil's net worth but more than taken care of, he could have done whatever he wanted, but had numerous ties to Johannesburg that kept him occupied and, more significantly, with a sense of identity. I told him at the time that although I was young enough to be his son and unable to speak for him, I could still say that my view was not to buy in Thailand but stay flexible and mobile. I said that I would sell up his burdening belongings, consolidate his resources into something simple that might not bring optimal income but optimised his ability to be free and happy, and then live his dream life. The problem, though, was that he could not face the implications of doing that, which were effectively a death.

A few years later we had lunch in Bedfordview and, forgetting our conversations in Thailand, he told me about the "worst day in his life" when the owner of the American mother company of the South African office he had left to start his own rival service provider flew to Johannesburg to buy him out and stop him "kicking them in the shins." The deal went through overnight and he had his dreamed-of nest egg, but, found himself in an unexpected crisis: he also had nowhere to go in the mornings, no staff to give him status, and no phone ringing all day.

He had to face himself, which was something he hadn't the wherewithal to do. Since then, he said, he had kept himself busy with maintaining and renovating properties and running small enterprises so that he could sidestep the void and escape having to answer questions too terrifying to contemplate. Those were the very questions I had been taking on in Thailand during our synchronised holidays. Not many people, it seems, get to ask and answer them, despite their age or financial resources. Even with money, this is what most people do. Don't let it be you.

Let it go and see what's left. What's left is what's real.

Imagine having, instead of multiple properties and paperwork up to your eyeballs, a safe-enough sum in a simple arrangement that lets you live exactly as you choose by being in tune with who you are, what stage you are at in life, and happily resident in the present moment. Imagine being relaxed in your whole being, humming like a happy engine, and pulsating like an inspired author, writing and creating for the love of it but thriving holistically as a result, having more to live for than ever but being detached from it, doing your best work without strain or struggle, coming from a transcendent place but loving the grit and glory of the unfolding and wonderful world, and glowing with grace. Imagine everything being simple, easy to run, an unencumbering when it comes to living your best life. You can live it.

Arthur and Colleen believe that they are going to heaven when they die, but isn't heaven a hope based on an incomplete life, an antidote to a perceived hell, and a conceptual relief from the hollowness that can't be filled by anything you own? Isn't the real answer to drop beliefs, encounter the void with lucid and sincere interest, let yourself fill with emptiness rather than run from it, and allow heaven to arise as things are here and now? Then you needn't be going anywhere because it is all already available.

There's a parable about an old man on his deathbed hearing his three sons standing around him discussing their steps after he goes. The first-born suggests an expensive coffin to honour the good man, the middle son proposes a mid-priced casket to pay due respect while saving on cost, and the youngest says that he's happy with the cheapest box since the old man will be dead and they will be paying with what is their money. From what seems like a coma, the old man suddenly opens his eyes and asks for his shoes. The sons are shocked and assert that he cannot possibly stand up or get dressed in his state.

"Give me my shoes," he insists, and with that puts them on his feet, walks to the cemetery, digs his own grave, lies his body down in it, and dies. Although this is unlikely to be a factual, it is a story of true courage that show someone who is prepared to be thoroughly responsible for himself, content in his aloneness, rigorously organised and baggage-free, and ready to see what's next.

Aristotle was ready to go in a similar way when he presented with the choice between withholding his disruptive wisdom to preserve social stupidity, and drinking poison as terminal punishment for being so intelligent. He chose the death sentence with pleasure and without compromise, saying that he had lived fully while here and was ready to enter the mystery with the same enthused curiosity with which he had approached everything else so far. Exemplary.

Chapter 43:

Come On!

Lao Tzu, one of the greatest teachers of all time and one of the few who were true, refused to write down any of his teachings. One of his famous quotes is, "Those who know do not say. Those who say do not know." That explains why he wouldn't formalise anything, and it is indicative of the consciousness from which he spoke. When he eventually did write a book, just before his death, his opening statement was that what he is speaking of cannot be written and what is written isn't what he was speaking of. Nonetheless, he kept writing. The semi-legendary narrative goes that, at a ripe old age, his time to die had come and he had headed from his home country of China west to the Himalayas to slip away in solitude and the powerful surroundings of the ancient mountains. Whether this actually happened or whether he even existed as recorded are up for debate, but those are not as important as the enduring point of the possibly factual, definitely mythical and most meaningful account.

He arrived at the border, and the guard, knowing the purpose of his crossing, would not let him through the checkpoint without the famous teacher recording his wisdom. And so, under duress, Lao Tzu wrote the Tao Te Ching, saying what couldn't be said, and coming from and pointing to transcendent awareness. It's the closest a book can get to enlightenment, and of the few sprinkled in human history it is one. It's not easily readable, partly because it was written so long ago and also because the inexpressible inherently comes articulated with a koan-like quality. A koan is a riddle-like statement or paradoxical parable, a Zen device, to provoke enlightenment through presenting a problem unsolvable to the mind. When thinking finally tires and drops, the unutterable truth remains.

Lao Tzu wrote only as his rite of passage out of this world, and his full message, both worded and lived, stands thousands of years later for anyone with eyes to see. Another great teacher of that calibre was Buddha. I am impartial to him (that's a joke!) but the truth is the truth and he portrayed it exceptionally. He was rational and congruent, saying it like it is, doing it by living it, and thereby showing it while he spoke it. He didn't write either but stated plenty, although he preferred not to, for the same reason Lao Tzu refused to write. Knowing that he really had no choice in the conundrum that is worldliness and human communication, he taught unreservedly with little if any hope of succeeding.

Buddha's disciples wrote his words down, certainly misplacing more of the essence in translation. The light is not in the words but the being using them, and that is largely lost in language, especially when less illuminated minds try to make sense of it.

291

Nonetheless, the two legends did their best, which is all any of us can do. As much as Buddha told people not to idolise him, there are more statues of him on earth than of anyone else. That's humanity for you. What can a man do? Jesus had similar struggles getting through to people and was executed by his own tribe, as the famous tale goes (although there are accounts of him living on into old age in the East where he had first absorbed his teachings and had his insights.)

Another teacher of the highest calibre, and a contemporary one, was Osho, who died in 1990 at the age of fifty nine. Perhaps he is even the best of the bunch, certainly in his ability to speak a modern and poetic language, to challenge the system fearlessly, and to combine opposites into a vision for humanity that promotes integration and transcendence with style. With his idea of the emerging human being as "Zorba the Buddha", he expressed a balance between worldliness and otherworldliness, a happy harmony between celebrating the physical while going ever-deeper into the mystical. My concept of BEntrepreneurING is similar, with the word 'BEING' referring to the natural, spiritual and ever-present, the word 'Entrepreneur' denoting the practical, functional and tactile, and the grey and black logo on white signifying the Yin and Yang.

Osho was born a Taranpanthi Jain in India in 1931, named Chandra Mohan Jain, nicknamed Rajneesh in his childhood, renamed Bhagwan Shree Rajneesh when he became recognised as a spiritual teacher, and then ultimately called Osho to refer to his oceanic consciousness. He credits his fierce intelligence to dying consciously in his past life, which is my suggestion in this book, and then not being subjected to discipline and social conditioning in his first seven years of life, which is not a bad idea either. Thus, he said, his spirit was never broken. He was raised rurally by his maternal grandparents, a wise and insightful grandmother and a less enlightened grandfather who revered her and bowed to her better judgement, and allowed to be himself and to commune with his surroundings without interference.

Similar to Eckhart Tolle, who is renamed from Ulrich Tölle after his hero, the thirteenth and fourteenth century mystic Eckhart von Hochheim, or Meister Eckhart, Osho describes an experience in his twenties of inner transformation or enlightenment, a seismic shift into a state of lucid awareness and untouchable bliss. From there he combined being awakened with penetrating intellect, vast knowledge from famously reading at least 120 000 books, and a lyrical way, which meant that he could convey so much so well. Tolle, too, to my mind, is one of the most important teachers of our time owing to his ability to convey the power of presence so simply, and link it accessibly to all the major teachings in history.

These first three teachers knew, and the fourth is still physically here and, thus, aged seventy at the time of writing, knows in the now. Lao Tzu personified Taoism; Buddha was the first and last real Buddhist; Osho articulated a religion for a new humanity, which is, of course, not a religion at all and still to kick in fully as we all catch up; and, Tolle is quietly taking us all up in the modern vernacular of the timeless now. I am working on something similar, an existential shift through my art, my business and my being, and making it contemporary, catchy, and a fuck-load of fun. I *am* writing, which is because I am a writer, like Eckhart has done, by divine inspiration, or the power of presence, if you prefer. It's one of my ways. Osho spoke, and his talks were recorded and transcribed, resulting in around six hundred books, more and more of which have been edited for the western palate and published worldwide. I have read at least seventy of them, some a number of times, since 2003, when I first discovered his stuff in Paul's bookcase in London. In 2015 I went to the International Meditation Resort that he founded in Pune, India, a city and country where Osho is big. His body of work is towering and truly inspiring, notwithstanding his cultic goings-on. The work of these four fellows goes to show what we are all capable of.

Lao Tzu wrote only under ultimate duress, taking everything so vast and unspeakable and saying it straight for the good of the community so that he could proceed to his solitary destiny. That takes profound preparation, some doing, and boundless being. He distilled it all under those conditions and found a way to voice it simply, succinctly and precisely, and then he went on to his death. Like we all can, he paid his substantial dues, did his singular job, and left a living legacy, all by just going all the way into who he was within. His death was as matter-of-fact and, at the same time, as sublime as anything else that perfect. He was in bliss, and famous yet anonymous ('Lao Tzu' means 'old man' or 'old master' and isn't his real name, which remains unknown). To head into the crags consciously and deliberately to relish your death and leave your body to be absorbed into the wilderness is like a breath of clean mountain air. You can't even call it courage because there was no fear there, only knowing. There was no tension, only flowing by being. There was no attachment, only the moment. What joy.

I am also writing under duress. How do you think all of this has descended onto paper in just a few months? Where does it all come from and how does it gain sculpted form so fucking fast? The answer is simple: I have been working on it my whole life and I am under profound pressure, in a do-or-die situation. I was reflecting on that last night and discussing it with Resheka over dinner. She continuously expresses amazement. The book and the ability to produce it have been brewing in me, accumulating over decades and getting ready to manifest, with a recent intensification of tension in Johannesburg and then a precipitation in Thailand and a royal release ever since. The meeting with Simon brought the topic to my lips, and I grabbed it and ran with it, devoting myself to and ultimately delivering it. I was looking for it (as you should also do) and when I found it (as you will) I knew what to do (like you will) and I just did it (like you can too). It's in us all. The new earth is streaming out of our holy hands. Let's give a fuck with all we have, shall we? Let's live it.

If you commissioned such a book, say as a publisher or a spiritual teacher, or both, it might take someone twenty five years or more to write. This one has taken that long at least, if you add it up. I've been at the keyboard for four months (at the time of the second edit) but it too took me a quarter of a century and most of my adult life to develop my writing talent and craft, and to work on my wisdom. You could say that my whole life is in this. Van Gogh taught himself to paint very quickly so that he could capture a sunrise on canvas as it was happening before his eyes, almost photographically. You see it and you say it, as efficiently and effectively as possible, so that soul can speak, whether with words, palate-knife smudges, or living paint.

Without duress you might not manage to grab it, or see it through. The pressure is part of the product. (Undeniably I like alliteration.) Creative tension and high stakes give you the impetus to perform seeming miracles. Impetus is just a game, like all the others, and you must play along with it. If the universe wants to dance, you do the fandango. Writing is dancing and playing under life-or-death pressure, and all of it together is a kind of rebirth. Writing is in the moment, where we need to be. It is the key that unlocks the mystery. Lao Tzu wrote to be free. It's the same for you and me.

My job is to integrate. Each strand of the story expresses aspects of it, and together they form a big picture of the experience I am communicating. There are many ways to articulate it and many metaphors into it, and there are many ways to reach out and resonate. There are multiple methods to commune. One is on the level of myth. Myth is what Lao Tsu fulfilled. Myth is what Bruce Springsteen and George Michael have followed and found. Myth is what I am living out here. Myth is what I'm speaking to in you. Myth brings us together.

The living within each of us is an inner phenomenon, a stirring structure stitched into our subjectivity. It's where we express ourselves from, and also how we make sense of our outer world. It integrates our evolving experiences. I'm not sure where it comes from but we seem to be born with it and it is the language of meaning we carry inside and project onto events and happenings around us. It's the story we come with and live out in real time, thereby advancing and resolving it and fulfilling our function in the social and broader fabric of co-existence. We have to live on this level along with the other levels in our being, and we want to do so.

The level of myth is interpretive, and as convincing as the hologram of material form. Both are part of the picture and in need of proper attention. Living our myth is by nature an epic challenge and also a great honour. And so we have to engage it with convincing passion yet learn how to do so from beyond it by being our higher selves. It is a great gift and a big pleasure, a serious story and also just a bundle of dramatic fun, and so the trick is to find and follow that understanding, and relish the multi-dimensional experience, while watching the whole hoo-ha as a detached witness. This witness is who one day will watch you die. Grow your roots in it.

It's simple and just needs a knack, which can be difficult to get. The ability involves timeless presence along with understanding and working with myth. It's multi-levelled and concurrent. The one stratum is the intuitive sense of the narrative seeded inside us, of how we need to manifest ourselves in the world. We know what our story needs to be, and our deadly yet playful task on earth is to find how to live it out on the knife's edge of the present moment.

We are all challenged in our respective interiorities to be the heroes of our own lives, and charged with the opportunity to do so in the theatre of our current circumstance. It must be for the good of everyone, too, whether they appreciate it or not. We are in the arena and we have to engage the drama in all seriousness while knowing that it's all just costumes, make-up and clever lighting. It's what the Hindu text the *Bhagavad Gita* addresses in the hero protagonist Arjuna's struggle be both true to himself and at the same time participative in the life and death tragi-comedy of life, relationship and death. He is in anguish over how to reconcile the two, and Lord Krishna, disguised as Arjuna's charioteer, tells him not to overanalyse but to live! Get in the ring. The myth will reveal itself and resolve as you go, but you cannot shy away from the battleground. It is the furnace in which you forge yourself.

Myth is like a blueprint in us. Bruce Springsteen needed to be a rock star and them some, and George Michael needed to take pop music and celebrity to a revolutionary new level. Simon Napier-Bell needs to do his thing, Robin Wheeler needs to do his, and you need to do what you need to do. It needn't be out front and in your face. Resheka isn't writing this book but she is doing her life's work in it. Amanda has been seminal all the way through and reaching you through it. How do you bring yourself into full expression and make your mark on the world (however low-key or high profile that may be) by giving your gift and living truly richly along the way?

How do you die satisfied and thrilled with your imminent experience? That is our rhetorical question that answers itself in how we live our lives.

Myth is on the inner level and in the outer story. It links the two. You are rivals with someone and then become lifelong friends, which has a mythic quality that would be quite at home in Ancient Greece. You both grow as you live out the heroic story. Steve Jobs started Apple at a young age on courage and soul, got ousted at thirty years old by the CEO he had brought in to run it for him, processed the betrayal and loss, realised the blessing in disguise, returned to his creative roots, took a second passion-company Pixar to the top of its game, became CEO of Apple again through a remarkable turn of events, led that to legendary status, and then died at fifty six. That's more living in a short lifetime than most people could imagine. It's the stuff of classic mythology.

As a hero, you get called to adventure and, at first, you react in fear. It's natural to resist. A mentor appears at the right time, though, and gives you the confidence to go, and you realise that you are ready. Spurred by having no other option, you take the risk and the leap. New life floods you with magic and rewards your courage, and you wonder why you didn't make the move sooner. Then you face increasing challenges on the road to the opportunity to claim the prize you came all this way for. You face death, better the threshold guardian, slay the dragon by outgrowing your old self, seize the elixir in transcendent triumph, and skip home in the nick of time, with lightning at your heels, to a rapturous return.

Transformed and inspired, you set about sharing your secrets with the tribe through your blossoming relationships and revitalised art, thereby fulfilling your collective function and self-actualisation in one. As a shamanic figure, you perform a priceless role in the fabric of friendship, family and broader community by being yourself in service. Having found your truth, you introduce others to theirs, and give your gifts to the world in your singular presence. And then, probably, you do the next trip, with another book or cycle of adventure, or even another lifetime.

The best way to talk about this level of living is through the language of myth. It's the vernacular of the soul. The succinct run-through that I've just given is informed and inspired by the empowering work of Joseph Campbell, particularly his book *The Hero with a Thousand Faces* (Pantheon Books, 1949) and how it has helped me make sense of my story and express it as my life's work. *The Writer's Journey: Mythic Structure for Writers* by Christopher Vogler (Michael Wiese Productions, 1998), which is based on Campbell's work, has helped me too. Both link in to Jung's contribution to our understanding of the individual and collective psyche using archetypes and mythic narratives.

My myth is in Wimbledon, Irene, Bedfordview and Phuket. My myth is in these words and in you reading there. My myth is in living out my lifelong intuition and inspiring everyone to be themselves for a living. We interpret our lives on this powerful level, and doing so deliberately changes the game. Doing so consciously transforms the players and the planet.

Chapter 44

Where Did Your Heart Go?

So, one aspect of being who you are, and one aspect of dying, is living through your myth. Do you go out in a blaze of glory or with reclining style? Do you do it not on the sofa, not in the hall, not on the kitchen table, and not even outside, but in your bed on Christmas morning? Do you triumph over adversity to live out your inner story, or does your narrative end tragically? It all has its place on the level of the unspoken made manifest in story and experience, and it all ultimately makes sense, especially when you work with it consciously.

We cannot avoid the unfolding drama, we have to play along, and everything is enhanced by awareness. Even enlightenment does not absolve us from physical being. A spiritual master still eats, sweats and goes to the toilet. Similarly, on an emotional level, we all need to laugh and cry to be whole and healthy. Consciousness is not the freedom from these things but the freedom to enjoy them more, to be in harmony with them and the overall intelligence of which they are functioning parts. Similarly, the myths we live through still

301

keep unfolding when we have insight into them. The awareness transforms but the theatre continues.

Alexander the Great's myth might have been to conquer the known world, but tucked into that was his self-induced encounter with Diogenes, which brought a transformative twist. That leaves his real message for the world. Some might see him as an admirable warlord but wiser souls get the more penetrating message. Diogenes too had his story, and it is said that he died the same day that Alexander did, owing to their connectedness. Whether that is factual or mythical is less important than the meaning in it. What does it mean to you? The story is what stands throughout history because the message is what life wants us all to hear. Historical facts are empty compared to legendary truths.

Parables articulate otherwise inexplicable understandings, and poetry and music are the ways to voice inner experiences. This is why movies, novels and plays are created to resonate with the structures and struggles we all work and grapple with. Thus they express and reflect our deep inner lives to us, giving us comfort and confronting us to progress. People relate to the protagonists and the stories they live out, because we are all heroes, and we each have a unique myth to embody fully before we die, whether we like it or not. We live and die rightly when we work and play along with this deep-seated narrative. It's fun, for fuck's sake!

A second major 'M' word in the mix is 'meditation'. Death and meditation go together. They are, in a way, the same thing, a dissolving of the self, a disappearing into the unifying field, and a release of tension. Meditation is an increase in awareness with the surrender of rigidity and form, which is what death is too, perhaps one level up or on a bigger scale. We will all have to wait to see if I am right with regards to the final freedom from body as we know it, but all other deaths discussed are clearly applicable already. Meditation is conscious death, and death is forced mediation, unless you consciously ride the wave, in which case death is your unbridled and glorious coming across the universe, without losing your cool.

You go into mediation intentionally and it reveals what you need to know at the time, and you go into death regardless of will, and that reveals all. Mediation transmutes present energies into insight as you sink deeper and deeper through the levels of tension by getting in touch with those tensions and letting them go. By doing this daily you encounter death and its gifts, and prepare for the big day. Also, of course, you enormously enhance your current living.

Meditation is the accessing of awareness outside of mind and beneath the noise of daily activity. It means stopping doing and attending to being, and then letting doing happen with relish. It is finding stillness inside by letting the thoughts come and go without acting on them, and watching as they subside. It is feeling feelings and allowing them to be as they are, following them into their origins and seeing what they are saying, and descending through layers of tautness into the timeless truth of pure space. Here we inhabit who we are and develop our access to higher awareness for increasing inclusion in our day-to-day living.

Meditation is a device (the practice) and a destination (the way of being). Meditativeness arises from the practice and becomes part of your way of being, your consciousness and presence, which brings the deathless into the realm of the living and dying, and prepares us for the day when we shift from the predominant sense of form to the integrated and boundless. Living your myth on earth is one layer, and transcending it is beyond layers. Both are part of being yourself for a living.

Meditation takes us out of the head, through the heart, past the soul and into awareness as the backdrop to everything. With it we become deathless and able to watch our bodies die. Without it we are attached to form, stuck in thinking, out of touch with feeling, unconsciously acting out inner structures, and sadly missing out almost entirely on what life can and should be. We are figments lost in a hostile hologram, searching for God, endlessly pursuing pleasure to counteract the pain, and feeling powerless to fill the emptiness.

With it, however, we make the most of life and know how to live with appreciation, wisdom and joy. To get it we need to die while we are still alive, and set ourselves free. Without it we are a bundle of animalistic instincts, biological urges, psychological precedents, unfulfilled desires, clouding illusions, and rootless existence. With it we have a perspective on all of these factors, which gives us a gap from which to act consciously and responsibly, and a source that is essential and untouchable. With it we become grace itself.

Mind is the stream of thoughts and the most superficial aspect of our being, the circumference. Heart is deeper, the seat of feeling and loving, and closer to our core. Soul is a construct that we carry deeper still and work on as we enact myth, creating and forging it for ourselves from the work we do in engaging our lives. And consciousness is the domain of the true self, the one that watches everything happening down in the valley from the top of the hill, just as we have seen our hands go from chunky and childlike to brittle and wrinkled with the observer being unaffected. The more we move from thinking to being, from mind to higher awareness, the more we can see and understand and the less oblivious we are to what is actually going on. The more, too, we are ready to die anytime and when the time comes. When that happens we are in tune, aligned and ready. A new ecstatic humanity is afoot.

Meditation is a soft but bottomless orgasm. You start feeling better as you face rather than fight your thoughts and feelings, and feel better still as you find and release the strains in the system. Then you feel even better as you settle into source energy, and feel subtly sublime as you inhabit a serene and steady subtext to all surface-level activity. You reconnect with love and bring it to bear in all you see and do, often with a streak of sexiness and straight-faced mischief. When the big orgasm comes you are in familiar territory that is now simply taking over, so you lie back, relax and do what you came here for. Yes, this is what you have come all this way for...

There is another 'M' word involved but first I am going to touch on a 'T' word, because it is a sidecar to meditation: Tantra. Do you know that word? Does it make you think of sex? There's a lot more to it, and a lot more than I know, but the bottom line is basic. Be in your body and, through that, be on all levels of your being in alignment and harmony, and, through that, be the beyond.

Let me put it like this: It's almost late afternoon and I'm at home in Bedfordview lying on my couch with sunbeams streaking across the room from the open sliding door, the distant and almost inaudible hush of rush-hour speckled with more nearby sounds of birds and neighbours, and silence shrouded around me in the room. This is all I need. It's a symphony. This is Tantra.

I have a pull to eat something sweet following Chinese chicken soup, Indian samoosas and masala tea for late lunch, and I am loving the longing as much as I would the sugar. I am still relishing the fine food I ate in the afterglow it has left me with, and I don't have to indulge in a dessert to appreciate it. It doesn't matter whether it's something or nothing, absence or presence, you can savour it. Savouring is the art of presence, presence is life, and life is all you need. This is Tantra.

The silence reminds me of a quiet spot I found once in Phuket and always visit when I'm on the island. It's just outside Patong, a few kilometres on the bike along a winding south beach road and then unexpectedly left up the hill into the chunky jungle. It's overgrown and lush and thoroughly still, although only a few hundred metres away from human activity. When I first went there, which was towards the end of my second trip when I felt ready to rent a bike for the first time, I just followed my instincts as I explored the island, and they took me along this tarred path up to a gate that closed off private property that reminded me of Irene. So I stopped and switched off the scooter and instantly felt the stillness descend like a loving and sacred cloth soothing body and soul. By the time I was unclipping my helmet, I was transfixed. Just a few moments there were like being reborn.

On this recent trip I rode Resheka up there, having mentioned it to her a few times, and almost missed the turning because the previously secluded beach road has a few small businesses along it now. The spot was still silent, though, and she felt the full effect as we dismounted. "Wow," she mouthed without making a sound. You don't speak there. It's too enchanted and too sacred, like a tropical church. You just beam at each other and gaze around listening to everything and nothing at the same time, and hearing yourself. A few minutes are enough to remember the truth of who you are, and to recharge, like a night of the deepest sleep. In no time you are ready to keep going with renewed knowing. It's like an orgasm up there, a quick pit stop in the loving arms of death.

It's the fullest feeling of life. Your whole being responds to the realness and you become instantly vital in naked recognition of your nature. You feel everything, sensory and spiritual, and reintegrate with the earth while watching from above it. It's totally existential, simply spiritual, utterly aligned, and effortlessly ecstatic. This is Tantra.

Tantra could be called an ancient set of techniques, but ultimately it is a state of consciousness, the highest one available to us. It is awareness of body, acceptance of polarity and, through this, awareness of all. It's all about being and using the body as a base to access the beyond. Our bodies are our home and we cannot go anywhere healthy or happy while out of harmony with them. We are above our bodies but we will get to that via them, not in any form of rejection or denial. Be bodily. Physical form is presence, and inhabiting it brings you home. The body is also sensual and here to enjoy reverently. The body is a most intelligent biological structure that carries in its simple wisdom the most sophisticated accumulation of evolution. The body is pure genius, and our overall intelligence is based in embracing it.

Listen to your body. If it wants to sleep, like mine did earlier, let it. Life is a treat when you are in tune and friends with yourself, and that couch loves you too. Go for a walk at dusk like I did yesterday, or stay in to rest and grab the writing as it kicks in for the day. Listen to the inspiration shining like fine sound. Voyage along with a compilation of music from the lounge while you type under warm ceiling lights in the study and watch the green garden go grey outside through the Venetian window. Feel your feet firmly in socks for the first time in a while, and beautifully wrapped in fitting shoes tied just right. Feel your firm ass in soft jeans on the supportive chair, and watch your tanned arms extend organically from your black T-shirt sleeves and type out these appearing words. Rub your palms together at the end of the sentence. Bring your one hand up to your mouth and read what you've written while your nostrils gently bellow warm wet air onto your index finger. Feel your heart beating...

Love your body like it's a living work (in progress) of art (in motion). Fill it with stillness and goodness, use it thoroughly and keep it happy like a cross between a puppy and a finely-tuned organic automobile. Make love to the world just by the way you inhabit yourself, with tender and sexy grace and a firm thrust. Start slowly and finish strong. This is Tantra.

It is the key, the door, and the great outdoors. It is the pathway to the inner, the hum of the whole, and the view from the sky.

Chapter 45

Blue (Armed with Love)

And now for the third 'M' word: 'mourning'. For a few of the seven years in the last cycle I felt like a failure. When I set out in 1996 I was drawn by a white-light vision and fuelled by associated dreams and inspiration. The dream was of everyone in the world being ourselves for a living and me doing so en route, inspiring and helping and, thereby, manifesting the intuition I had as a child and again even clearer as a twenty seven year old making a monumental career choice under duress. I was galvanised into place and knew what to do, even though it was a combined big leap and baby steps to start. It meant the death of my old life back then and, in a big way, the birth of who I had always been. As time passed, though, the pressures seemed to take over and the spirit of what I was doing became more sparing with the enthusiasm it spread to me. Anguish took over (although always held together and on track by a vein of pure gold). The job felt too vast, the response to my extensive efforts felt less encouraging, and the whole 'being yourself for a living' experience seemed not to be working. I became increasingly disheartened and weighed down by struggle.

Around the twenty year mark I saw an interview with Elon Musk in which he said something to the effect of, when you start your business you are very happy, then you get very unhappy for a long time, and then, if you survive and succeed, which is extremely unlikely, you become very happy again. I related to that! It had been a protracted struggle, precious people had come and gone, I had always stayed on course, and my time to be happy again was arriving. The dungeon years were behind me at last. I was not fully out of the woods yet but I could see the sunny clearing through the shimmering trees and feel the welcoming warmth on my skin.

I had been through an inverted phase where I had felt one way when the reality was another. I felt like I was failing when I was successful and breaking new ground steadily while I kept building a base and working on my inner world. I was enduring remarkably but I felt like I was barely functioning and stuck in a situation that seemed insistent not to budge. That was largely a function of being in pain. It was the arrival of Resheka in my life and her reflection as she got to know me that helped me see that I was not the way I saw myself and that the hurt I was handling was understandable but not definitive. I began to perceive myself and my position in a new way and make my way into the sunlight.

There was still a weighty grief that I needed move through and shake off. I had come out of a hurtful relationship breakup without any closure, and I was learning in leaps on that front, which was certainly part of the problem but not the core of it. I was writing two or three books a year, and so creativity and productivity were far from absent. I had great friends, like Amanda and my old school buddy Greg, hearing and supporting me when I needed them, which was priceless and cause for sober appreciation. I had a beautiful home and an ideal lifestyle with the power to make changes if I wanted them. But still I felt stuck, which was a function of choices I had made and kept making but predominantly because I was compelled to stick to my path regardless and the road was really rocky and agonising at times.

What I began to see was that I was unhappy in what I was doing, and as a whole, and that I could not winch myself out of the mire as I seemed too deeply sucked under and too sore to surface. My mom suggested antidepressants, as she is quick to do instead of working on issues and developing awareness, and I felt so down that I wanted the relief of the drugs, but I was adamant to face my feelings and not employ any leverage that was not absolutely necessary. I had the support of the little bottle of pills she gave me, but did not want to go there if I could help it, and I stuck with my gut feeling, forging forward one gruelling moment at a time.

What I realised then was that I was mourning, and that the grief was partly about those early dreams not coming true to the degree that I wanted or expected them to. This was a pivotal insight. Grieving your lost reveries is real, and a serious block until you get through it. When Springsteen's autobiography came out Resheka suggested that I write mine, which seemed absurd at first but soon precipitated into sixty thousand words produced in one month. It was waiting to be put down on paper and it dropped like a bomb, blasting me out of my past by allowing me to systematically revisit, work through and release it.

It also gave me perspective on what I had done in the preceding twenty years, which brought me into more alignment with my success. When I was reading the new writing to Resheka over a few nights, she picked up on the feeling in the section from the early business years and pointed out that I had been happy and confident back then. She wondered out loud what had been accountable for that and what might have changed since. Sitting with that made me see the spirit with which I had set out, and that I had become weighed down by a feeling of compounded frustration because I was not getting my needs met. The accumulation over time was crushing. Mixed in there was the sadness, which, I saw, was an enormous factor. Giving up my own requirements for a bigger picture and processing a perceived loss of dreams was like handling double deaths.

There was nothing wrong with my dreams, in fact, as they were expressions and extensions of my calling in life and echoes of my inner myth. Perhaps, if anything, they were too small. They have since come back into revived prominence, more expansively and accessibly than ever, after I shifted the rock of grief out of the way. Since I died to the old self in a bonfire of alchemic release, a new me has been born from the ashes, and this energy is much more of what brought me all this way in the first place. It is the right stuff, which was there all along but the reason, in the context of perceived failure, it was tough to make sense of the feelings at the time.

Since I shed my skin I am more myself than ever, which also points to a conundrum. The mind cannot understand these experiences much of the time, like when the big picture is beyond its inherent limits or when matters of the heart take natural precedence. Sometimes the myth is too intense to get your head around, which is part of the hero's plight, for a patch anyway. When the emotion shifts, though, the landscape clears and the prevailing truth can ring clearly again from the hills, more beautifully than ever. The story becomes clear again. You can't just think yourself though the storm, though, you have to fight and cry it out. You have to express the emotion, scream and shout! That's what it's all about. You have to see things through in the arena and cannot discuss them from the grandstands. You are the gladiator in the drama and must undergo catharsis. You must be cleansed, over and over as life reveals itself. Death is the ultimate cleanser and it happens often along the way.

What was wrong for me is that I felt like I was losing at something profound that I had already acquiesced to two decades before and had no choice in changing. I felt that it was taking all I had to keep going without me going anywhere. I couldn't see my way clear to proceed when the way was in front of me behind a heavy cloud. The problem was the perceived death of my dreams and associated grief and huge emotional weight that came with that sense of loss. I needed to mourn until I was clear, and I needed to address my frustration until I returned to being in the flow. I needed to move through the end of an era, find a new one, and be happy again, and this is exactly what happened. As there is no set time span for grief, we have to go through the motions of it and learn what it has to teach, including things like patience and grace. We sometimes wonder if and how we will survive but we come through with understanding and are always wholly better for the experience.

I stuck it out without drugs and can testify to the rebirth. When our trip to Thailand finally arrived with the end of the year, I was stripped bare in ways you wouldn't believe, and primed for renewal, with not a pocket of attachment to distract me from the present moment. A midnight stop in Doha soon turned into a sunset in Patong, a brand spanking new fuel-injected scooter with fewer than five kilometres on the clock, a private hotel tucked towards the back of town, three rousing trips to nearby ports of inspiration, and five weeks of island life together for the two of us. We had kind friends across the road, who are super-connected travel agents, a laundry around the corner, a coffee shop a short spin away for our favourite breakfasts, restaurants of choice down on the beach for day-and-night delights, the mall and the market within walking distance, and a ticket to ride wherever we wanted to go.

We had happiness! That's what Thailand has always meant to me and now means to Resheka too. Most of South Africa's stresses are removed and replaced by freedom, natural beauty and a feast of humanity that keeps you endlessly entertained. The first week was gone in a flash and we had already seen forty kilometres of the west coast of Phuket when we thought it best to visit the nearby Phi Phi islands for a night in that early gap in our expansive yet tight schedule. We had flights booked to Kuala Lumpur on Christmas Day, just before the middle of the five weeks away, plus we had a possible plan for going up country in early January. A packed ferry powered us across the water one morning to the scenic paradise that was equally a party destination, and so we soaked up the beauty, piled on the epic photographs, swam in the sea, walked the entire inhabited area, and then lay sleepless until the early hours when the thumping music finally stopped and the last of the revellers rumbled past our room at 4am. We were in one of the better hotels and yet far from the sounds of silence. In the morning we took a long tail boat to the smaller island through choppy waters, I communed with exotic fish in deep and breath-taking waters on one of our stops, and we returned enriched but ready to go home to Patong. The boat and the minibus taxi were torturous but part of the whole picture of being in bliss. Life is a package deal.

The flight to Malaysia also came with an early morning, a taxi spree, a busy airport, and expectable tensions, but brought treasures of other types, like a happy hotel right next to the superlative Pavilion shopping mall, fulfilling meals, the sense and promise of global projects, cosmopolitan encouragement, and respectful and responsible cab drivers. It can be done, you Thai mothertruckers! The international trip also renewed our immigration stamps on re-entry, and so we were set for the rest of our stay in the land of smiles. We were back on Phuket for the world-famous party of the year coming up on the 31 December 2017. Crowds and craziness were not our preferred scene but a phenomenon worth immersing ourselves in once a decade. The signs were up when we cruised down the beach front on our scooter: Patong 2018.

The seasonal hordes had pulled in during our three days away and the sense of increased pandemonium was palpable for that week between Christmas and New Year and then a few days after... We adjusted to it and got back to appreciating our precious piece of perfection, sticking to a loose plan while staying open to the way it fell into place. This brought us, after a long walk, to our swimming spot towards the top of the bay at sunset on the last day of a year that had been extreme in its trials and lessons, and now in its highs. The water was flat and the sky was filling with silent lanterns leaving the land as the night fell and the two of us floated joyfully, sometimes in each other's' arms, weaving everything together in soft conversation and feeling the calm rise of the future.

After that timely and transformative Thailand trip, the emergence of this book in the first week of January, I am a new man. A new surge is taking us somewhere more exciting than the original plan, and being yourself for a living is breaking new ground. Death has had a central role to play every turn of the way.

There's a fourth 'M' word and it's 'magic'. This is where all the 'M's come together. It is M to the power of M, the centre that everything can find in itself and, thus, find in everything else. Your centre is the same centre as the centre of all things, and the centre of nothing, which is the nature of everything, and so finding yourself makes everything available to you and brings it together. The centre is enchanted.

The centre is calm when a storm can be raging around it. The centre is the source and the destination. The centre has no beginning and no end, and it has no substance, and yet it is solid and immovable, while being utterly abstract. It can take any form or none, and be neutral either way or both. The centre is Tantra. It is your family history culminating through you and, at the same time, it is your total individuality. The centre is your death while still alive and the future for humanity here and now. The centre orgasmic.

While we are at it, there is one more. 'M' is also for 'mischief'. Unofficially, it's also on the list. A happy human is full of fun. Mischief is magical and magic is mythical. Mourning brings joy, and when all the 'M's are in the mix, you have existential bliss. It's where we need to be. When we are in it we can go to death and be ready, and we can revere the magnificence of being alive.

Chapter 46:

It Doesn't Really Matter

I woke this morning to a message from Simon. "In the language Setswana, there is a saying: the greatest laughter is death." Setswana is a Southern African language from a region not far from Johannesburg, and the quote, which I looked up, is from an article in The Guardian online yesterday (19 Feb 2018) called "Why, as a woman, do I laugh at misogynistic jokes?" by Siyanda Mohutsiwa, a satirical writer and speaker from Botswana, South Africa's neighbour to the north. Her point is that sometimes life is so horrific that all you can do is laugh in the face of it, as an instinctive coping mechanism but also from the irony and absurdity confronting you. Perhaps laughter is the best response to death in its various forms, too. What else are we to do? Take it too seriously?

Laughter is itself a form of death. It shakes off the disease of solemnity and keeps the wheels of life turning fluidly. It sheds the shackles of accumulated pain, releases pressure, and slips out of the straightjacket of social appropriateness. It lets us see, and helps us settle into and say the unthinkable and the intolerable. It is what Buddha said we will burst into when we finally see things as they are. We will throw or heads back and roar with our whole being at the cosmic joke as well as our self-obsession and its silly trappings. With that, our spirits will soar free. We will have found the truth and realised that it was here all along while we obsessed with ourselves in silliness. Death is definitely in that mix: the death of the ego-based hell we clung to, and death of the mirrored world as we knew it.

Do you think you could laugh at the time of your death? Might it be the only fitting response? Certainly it would a sign of a life well lived and a wonderful way to go, even if everyone else might find it odd. They may find it emancipating! We die a little every time we laugh, and so it would make a certain sense to take it all the way on our crowning day. Life's tensions tumble away with mirth and we are born afresh right there, just like that, without even leaving the body. It's a reboot through merriment, a restoration to default settings without passing begin or paying two hundred dollars. In fact, it's absolutely free, and equally freeing. The profound stuff can be that simple and usually is. Laughing is a kind of orgasm too. Keep shuddering there in happy liberty.

It looks like we have a picture coming together here, and coming together is a kind of shared death. Funny, that! Isn't it what we long for, to be with each other when we live and die? How beautiful it can be. So much love.

Another essential step on the path is comfort in solitude and joy in aloneness, which is the primary position in life. Start here and learn to love it. What's there not to love? Find the bliss in being you and in your natural state. We come into the world and leave it alone, and we are each an unavoidable subjectivity, and so we must begin and stay here. Get to know the great mysteries and the ways of the world through it. Get to know the brimming emptiness that you are. It's pure divinity. Rather than fear the void and try to fill it with fake substitutes, let go into the nothingness and feel it rise. Relish your infinite nature and be at home in your direct relationship with existence. This is residence in a state of unconditional and undirected love, which, as we all know, is who we are, where we come from, and where we go. It's all there is, and we are back where we belong, having gone nowhere.

Then, from this state rooted in individuality and source energy, you feel a longing to share generously and commune creatively, and you reach out lovingly in playful intimacy. It will probably even be mischievously because you are so happy and can't help being naughty. Infinity itself is impish. You connect in shared aloneness, or all-oneness, and something more arises from the coming together, making you and everyone else even richer, with a good laugh along the way. As you discovered who you are in solitude, so you do again in relationship, in communion of the heart not the mind, and, thus, you encounter yourself from both sides. You are rich in both directions and an integration of opposites, going up with every layer of awakening. You are forever something more, which is even more magical than before, and you are always the watcher of all of this transpiring. This is real richness and life giving infinitely. Love keeps growing. What more could you possibly ask for?

After Frank died, my learning about love and death continued, both on the earthly plane and in the beyond. He didn't have a satisfactorily updated will when he fell ill and so, when it seemed prudent, I proposed working through one together, which he welcomed. My lawyer friend from school days, Claudio, kindly sent me a template and I sat at Frank's bedside one evening and combed through every clause until it was, in our mutual styles, impeccable. My dad also made it clear to me verbally what his simple wishes were for his estate. As he was an expert in financial and legal matters, and owing also to his rigorous disposition, I trusted his stance and decisions. Although he was incapacitated physically and suffering intensely, he lay patiently and addressed every detail in every clause, either approving or altering the standard document before we moved on to the next sentence. I saw how it is done, as it was all largely new to me. Death can thrust acute learning into your path.

He appointed an executor whom he had worked with, insisting that it was the best way to manage matters. The fee was more than worth it, he said, both in terms of the significant administrative workload and the fairness between my sister and me. He couldn't sign the document at that point because he had a gammy arm, the result of what was suspected to be a stroke he suffered in the hospital, and so he made the best mark he could to authorise it.

My mom, who is a commissioner of oaths, officiated the anomaly, which she could do owing to not being a beneficiary of the settlement. Their divorce in the mid-nineties had defined the agreement between them and they were not close at that point more than ten years later. From what Frank said, it was clear that he assumed that the maintenance component would fall away with his death and, of course, I went along with that.

A few weeks after he was gone, I went to see the executor, a lawyer in her own practice specialising in deceased estates. She didn't seem particularly together but gave me a list of things to do, and so I left unimpressed and somewhat frustrated but ready to resolve matters without delay. A couple of weeks after that I returned with all the items ticked off but she had forgotten most of her instructions and began issuing them again. At that point I became confrontational and driven to work out what was going on and how to handle it. No-one tells you these things, particularly the people paid to do so, and I was in a decent position relative to people dealing with banks or other impersonal administrators. It's a tough lesson to learn that comes at a high price.

By the end of the settlement nearly three years later I had taught myself all I needed to know in the field, and managed the process while this woman drew her commission. The work I had done to get the estate settled would have paid me as much as what my father bequeathed to me had I done it in my business. Money, even when it's technically yours, has to be systematically pried out of people's claws.

The big picture that I eventually figured out is relatively simple: first, the exact extent of the estate needs to be assessed; second, the nature of all liabilities and claims against it need to be determined for payment; third, the assets need to be mobilised and allocated; fourth, the administrative fees and government taxes need to be deducted; and, finally, the beneficiaries can be paid what's left. If the executor had given me this overview upfront I would have understood what lay ahead and taken the tasks in context, but she just hurled instructions at me haphazardly as if I worked for her, until I took charge and taught her a few things about fucking around the wrong person. Still, what load of nonsense.

Eventually I was emailing three or four parties at a time – one person at the bank, another at the one stockbroker, someone else at another trader, plus our esteemed executor - having liaised with all of them by telephone, and driving the project through to completion. Heather was overseas, and so almost all of the responsibility fell on my shoulders. This is the kind of experience to expect when someone close to you dies or for those people close to you when you do. Also, in our case, Beth began to deal with the implications of Frank's death for her survival and looking into the terms of the settlement and her claim against the estate. Heather and I were working out how we could look after her while she was working out on her own how to take care of herself. In the end we came to the right arrangement but it could have become nasty and, in most cases, does. Death and the redistribution of assets can bring all sorts of dark and hidden personal characteristics out of the woodwork and wreak havoc in families and close relationships. Our situation was relatively simple but still instructive, and my education noteworthy, and so I am sharing them with you.

Another insight worth considering is the inheritance of ancestral issues and the successive struggle with these in the resolution of the shared story. My parents' marriage began to collapse in the late eighties when I was leaving school, which was part of why I chose psychology as a career at the time. During my first degree particularly but up until I left home at twenty three to backpack around Europe, I worked to help the two of them get on. It didn't work and the passive aggressiveness continued for many more years until eventually they parted in the most silently violent way. It wasn't my problem to solve in the first place but, in a few ways, I had been a parent to them from birth, and this was just a continuation of that inverted dynamic.

In time I came to distance myself from it and then attempt to get right what they couldn't by giving my marriage my best effort. Ultimately and probably inevitably that failed too, and the two divorces still stand as the most painful experiences of my life. The point is that I was faced with the relationship dynamics handed down through the generations, whether I wanted them or not. When Frank died, I was still left to finish sorting out his divorce agreement with my mother. He had no conscious intention of leaving me with that but I was left with it nonetheless. Death does not always resolve or release tensions but often intensifies them and confronts related people with discovering a way through the struggles that the previous generations before could not find.

All of this is part of processing death. You can understand it and plan accordingly, getting your affairs in order and leaving the people left behind with the least problems possible. They might still face challenges and be compelled to grow, though. If you die intestate, without a valid will, you will certainly leave problems in your wake. Personal property and the notion of ownership are really just ongoing battles with the state for control, which becomes shockingly clear when settling estates. Prudence takes this into account when preparing for departure. Although living and dying have nothing to do with the law, the law makes them its business, and everyone is faced with dealing with its agents and fighting through the legalities when someone close to them moves on. Human madness. We live and learn.

On another level altogether, soon after Frank's death, I went to see a Family Constellation Therapist, a man called Richard, who shares his name with Frank's father and happens to be an old boy from the same high school I went to a good decade older than me. I had heard about his work from a few people but not been drawn to it until my mom suggested a session to help me with feeling depleted and listless, and in need of serving myself instead of over-giving to others. I am cautious when subjecting myself to healing of any kind, mindful always to retain authority over my own being and to employ the help of others from my power. Also, though, I am open, to hearing what my body, psyche and soul are saying and benefiting from the talents of my community. I have been enriched by therapies of various kinds over the years and been able to refer friends and clients to them with existential insight.

Family Constellation work was founded by Bert Hellinger in the twentieth century by combining family systems therapy from psychology, existential phenomenology from philosophy, and African spirituality. The basis as I experienced it is to tune in to the undercurrents of significant interpersonal relationships, with people living or dead, and have the soul conversations that are otherwise impossible but significant for your wellbeing and spiritual untangling. This is usually done in a therapy group, but can be done alone with the practitioner, which is how I preferred and went ahead with Richard.

He began with some background information before we met and had a picture of me and my situation by the time I arrived for the session. We spoke at first, connecting and getting the story into the room, and I told him about Frank's recent death, which was the angle into the work ahead. Technically it was a little soon after that to make the connection, Richard said, but owing to my level of awareness, we were able to proceed. Working with small mats on the floor, with one in the centre representing me, we arranged key relationships all around and, while I stood on my spot, Richard moved from one to the other to access and articulate the presence and issues of my significant others.

Most significant, of course, was Frank. Then there was his father, who was important in my picture but mostly in his relationship to mine. He had been hard on his firstborn son, which had extended to me in the lineage, and, with the help of this amazing work, I was able to understand the reasons for it, process the emotions around it, have the conversations between the people, and free us all from the hurtful misunderstandings and blockages. Therapist Richard intuitively accessed the existential space of each deceased man and immersed himself in it to speak on their behalf to me speaking for myself. Catharsis indeed. Then we swopped mats and I inhabited Frank and Richard Wheeler, understood their subjectivities, and saw myself from their perspectives. We all said what we couldn't voice or share during the living years and reconciled on the most profound level, which had a most liberating and healing effect.

One could debate or dispute what was going down but what mattered was the deep inner knowing and positive outcome. I have no need to explain exactly what happened, but I can say that it was transformative work. The Wheeler side of my family shifted again, as it had done on other significant occasions over the years, like when I agreed to my calling in 1995 or discovered my grandfather's diary in 2000. I returned to see Richard soon after that, to work on my mother's side of the family, which facilitated shifts in other unresolved relationships at the time. And then I felt that I was done with Family Constellation Therapy. It worked for me and became part of understanding life, death and interpersonal connection via blood and other bonds.

More recently, during my dark time last year, I went to a friend, Lucy, for a session of her brand of intuitive healing, on her suggestion. Once again it was when I needed desperately to receive instead of give out all the time. I was uncertain about going, right up to the morning of the appointment, when I sensed inside that it was the right thing to do. Sometimes feeling our way is that delicate, and that in the moment. Lucy was confident, though, that it was the right thing at the right time, and she was right. I hadn't the insight from seeing her socially that she was capable of such sublime work, but it soon became clear after I lay down in her healing room. It was a cool morning, so she covered me with a blanket and then cleared the energies with the chime of a brass bell. I felt the presence shift and clarity overcame the sacred space.

Moving her hands around my aura, a few inches away from my body, starting at my feet and slowly progressing up to my head, she tuned in to my stuff and voiced where I was at, what I needed, and what the guides, as she calls them, advised for my way forward. Apparently she is in constant touch with these loving leaders on their plane, which has led her to leave her previous job and go into this work as her vocation. My scepticism was converted to quite the opposite as she did her work, which was at once soothing, nurturing, assuring, stimulating and inspiring. I had never felt heard like that in my life, and I didn't say a word! Everything was unspoken in the energies, she felt it with amazing precision, and then voiced it with the utmost eloquence, speaking to elements of my being that no-one else had ever accessed, no matter how much I had attempted to share them.

Who knows what is going on in this mysterious world? We all have our individual experiences, we are all lost in illusion, we all have access to a unique aspect of the truth, and we all struggle to connect and communicate clearly. And yet we all know and understand fully on some level, and that level is here right now. We are all on the journey, and we are all going to die. Whatever the twists and turns, love awaits us on every corner. What a trip.

Chapter 47:

Hand to Mouth

After a long weekend in Durban with Resheka and a few days either side adjusting, I am back at the burger joint to write. I like things coming around, coming full circle and coming together. I like it when a trip takes you home. That's one reason we set out in the first place. It's part of the point to go out into the great wilderness of wonder to come back to where we began with new insight and experience. There's something inherent about the return, something ever-present with every step we take. That's the implied message in my book *Heading Home* (2001), an account of my backpacking experiences around Europe in 1992 and a metaphor for the ultimate journey of life.

Wherever we venture, we are destined to come home, and whatever we seek and find is essentially always ourselves. Whatever we discover was within us already and the delight is in exactly that, among many splendored other things. We see who we are in the reflections of the voyage and we stumble in satisfaction upon the familiar with fresh eyes and an open heart, and a tale to tell. Maybe this is what we long for most, to die as destined having blown open and filled up with an expanded capacity to love.

How much does traveling the world mean if you do not venture into who you are and get to know the traveller? How skewed is science when it looks only at the observed and not the observer, especially in light of quantum awareness that the two are inseparable? How uninformed is it to not know the knower first? How far can you go with only an outward view?

I'll tell you. You will end up with technology that far outweighs our maturity to use it wisely. You'll find yourself on a planet racked with stupidity while intelligence is at our fingertips. You'll sit with a species that is effectively an infant with a loaded gun in its hand pointed at its head and its sticky fingers fumbling with the trigger. You'll have oceans of pollution and storming seas of alienated people lost in corporations and fighting to uphold their own slavery, and Elon Musk striving to colonise a not-so-nearby planet as a last resort for the survival of the human race. Even if he succeeds, the problem remains with us, though, because who will go to Mars, and who will decide who goes? The madness will go with us and the solution will be no solution at all, perhaps just a bigger problem. Location is hardly the issue, as we have a perfect one already. Our lack of consciousness is the problem. Our awakening is the only solution. It's a do-or-die situation.

Are we so unhappy with fucking up one home in paradise that we have to send the human virus out into the solar system do the same to a substitute of red sand? We take ourselves wherever we go and we do not know ourselves at all, which, along with nuclear weapons, spells pure danger, or at least a little Greek drama mixed with science fiction. And all the while the rivers and the trees are here waiting for us to come back to earth, for fuck's sake. Why not fix ourselves first and see how that fixes everything? Then we can go to Mars for fun rather than trying unsuccessfully to escape the human conditions, or not go at all. We can stay here now, where everything has always been, and make sexual love to each other, or write from the soul to the music of falling rain, and sip red wine in a cardigan to Buddha Bar beats. What a world that will be...

Wise, awakened people, reverent in the face of definite death and blessed life, sustainably resourced through intelligent technology in harmony with the rest of nature, mobile around the world, pollution-free, sharing the best of themselves in an ever-enriched global community, all being themselves for a living happily. Present people, not living in the corrupted head and lost in the past and the future but connected through the heart, rooted in the transcendent, and fully occupying our being on all levels in the timeless moment. Not consumed by ambition but realised in the now and unfolding more than ever. Not competitive but co-creative, not fearful but love-filled, not twisted and money-mad but spirited and sensitively sane. You and me, baby. The rest is history.

The ability to live this way is elementary and within us. It is neither difficult nor complicated, but the road to it may seem to be from a resistant perspective. The road is the release of resistance. The key is the evolutionary and revolutionary removal of who we are not, and this can be terribly troublesome until we get the knack, especially without the guidance or example of those who can see and work with it. But whether we have a teacher or not we are still on course, still set for success, and surrounded by teachers. Universal intelligence is at work through us and we are becoming able to flow with it consciously having returned to unity after exploring the illusion of independence and sampling its consequences. Realignment is our awakening, our enlightenment, and our coming home with the wisdom of having been wayward, which was part of our prerogative and the cosmic plan. It's prodigal and all very rock 'n roll, if you ask me. The rebel gets rich and famous and grows up along the way.

Our linear pursuits came up from behind to bite us and we were forced by our own myopic hand to become systemic, strategic and, ultimately, surrendered to greater intelligence. In this, we reintegrated. We died to our individual egos, let go of the illusion and rediscovered our oneness, innocence and wellness, with insight from the dark side, all of which were essential yet incidental. We are at peace within now and, thus, in harmony with each other. Creative tension is our wave to surf and the cosmos is our canvas.

Resheka and I went for dinner last night to one of our local Italian restaurants and saw some friends from the Bedfordview community, Larry and Daniela, who ordering take-aways and then came and sat with us at our counter while they waited. We all spoke about Larry's recent loss of his father, as I'd seen a post on Facebook a few days ago about it, sent him a text message of support, and kept an eye out for them around town. If it was meant to be, we would certainly see them, and there they were. By the time they left with pizza to feed the family, Larry had mentioned twice that he would have liked a manual on how to handle the situation he had suddenly found himself in.

How does he deal with flood of emotions when feeling is not his forte? How does he handle his stirred-up family now heaped on him while already taking care of his vulnerable mother? How does he face the undertakers in the morning while managing the usual pressures of running his business? And the funeral? A round of golf took his mind off the muddiness but there's more to face. Love will show the way.

"At least they taught you the difference between cumulus and cumulonimbus clouds at school," I joked, "and none of the important stuff."

Nothing on earth can prepare you for your father's death, though. For everyone, but perhaps particularly for a man, losing your father is likely to be one of the most significant shifts in your life.

"Let me know if you need to talk," I offered Larry, along with some stories from my experience that might fortify and equip him in the intense time ahead. In the ten years since Frank died, I have always reached out to people when it's happened to them, knowing that they might need some resonance and insight.

If it's a manual you need, maybe you have one here in your hands. Life is not like that, though, and wouldn't be life if it were. We are thrown in head first while our little bodies wrestle through the birth canal, and our forgetting is formative in where we are going. Growing pains are par for the course, and duality is the mechanism of creation with which we have to contend, while love and awareness transcend it all and take us home one way or another. Suffering is here to teach us what not to do until we wake up to what's meant to be and what works holistically. That means spiritually and physically in one, otherworldly and worldly together, yin and yang, masculine and feminine, business and personal, creative and destructive, light and dark, and, most important, in full acceptance and understanding, resident in transcendence. Transcendence is maturity, and our destiny.

After our friends left, Sheke ended up talking about and processing her father's death, revisiting what happened sixteen years ago, what she did, her emotions then and now, and her two brothers' experiences and actions then, which she could understand now looking back. A death in the community spread ripples of love and release across the lake of relationships, reaching across time and space to you too.

Interlude 5:

The Strangest Thing

Two or three years ago I was helping a friend from the community, named Savina, write her first book, and she leant me her copy of Anita Moorjani's *Dying To Be Me* (Hay House, 2014) about the author's near-death experience and subsequent full recovery from severe illness. Basically her body had been riddled with cancer, beyond any level seen by medical doctors, with lemon-sized tumours on her spine, when she had begun to leave it and die. She describes being able to see herself on the hospital bed, as if from above, with her heartbroken husband by her side begging her not to go. At the same time she was able to witness a conversation that the doctor was having down the hall, plus see her brother making his way frantically from India to Hong Kong to try to reach her at the news of her condition. These events were actually happening at the time and she was conscious of them all simultaneously despite being physically restricted and medically at death's door.

Her perception was altered and her consciousness expanded to transcend customary or assumed boundaries, and she was overcome with a feeling of unalterable wellness. She describes it as a state of unconditional love and pure knowing that was always available to her and part of her being but somehow shut off from her conscious awareness by fear, false assumptions and social conditioning. She suggests that we are all in this disconnected state to some degree, and a shift in awareness away from true knowing. (George has just come on the stereo.)

Anita explains in the book that she drifted further towards death, away from her body and this physical realm and into the light, so to speak, as it had a light-like quality in terms of perception and feel. She kept feeling better and better as she approached this following a natural attraction, and then she encountered her deceased father, who embraced her lovingly and let her know that she was at a point of choice where she could still return to her body, but that moving any further away would be irreversible. He urged her to stay alive because she still had work to do in her bodily form, but he left it up to her. She decided to delay dying, as overwhelmingly appealing as it felt at the time, to stick around on this mortal coil, and return to fully inhabiting her body, bringing with her the sense of transcendence and the distinct flavour of unconditional love that she had tasted on the brink of the beyond.

Her body began to show immediate changes and soon defied all medical precedent and explanation with the extent and speed of its healing. She still underwent certain medical treatments but knew that she was over needing them, which proved correct. Inexplicably, other than through her convincing account, she rehabilitated way beyond previous levels of health and happiness and found herself writing about the experience, then producing her book by having it commissioned by Hay House, and doing talks around the world. She's quite a brand now. Shifted by a near-death experience, she began being herself for a living and helping others with her unique perspective, triggered like I was all those years ago by a life-changing event. That's how it happens.

When Resheka found out that she was afflicted with something similar to Anita last year, I bought her a copy of *Dying To Be Me*, which she soaked up with resonance. It explained not only what she felt to be her predicament, but the way out of it too. So far, so good: she is well and getting more so, growing spiritually and turning insight into education. She isn't speaking on stages globally yet, but it's likely, and she is spreading a distinct wisdom in her job and related dealings directly from her healing, plus she is in this book and writing more and more of her own. Like with everything else, we'll see. The knock of death has certainly sent us into new realms of feeling, seeing and being. We are so happy these days, and the magic of our work is unfolding before us.

What matters most to me from Anita's account and work is that it opens our awareness to possibility and spreads a sentiment to which we almost all certainly relate. How factually accurate it is interests me, of course, but that is secondary to what it achieves experientially. The testimony seems sincere and I have no reason to doubt it. Perhaps her understanding is representative of what we will all encounter on our way. Either way, it keeps us all available to options and in touch with wholesome goodness. We may be meat on one level, managed via a biological computer, but we are much more than that, and then some. All we need to do is expand into our capacity for awareness and see for ourselves. Most significant is the feeling that Anita brings with her story. When she speaks, we know what she is saying is true. It resonates with what we have perhaps forgotten but certainly never lost.

Something distinct comes across when she testifies to her experience, and you can clearly feel where she is coming from. It is a palpable place in her that speaks to one in you, even though it has been dormant or neglected for a lifetime. Her energies resonate with ours because they speak to something in us that we know well, and her vocational calling on earth is to remind us of this. Similarly, when Eckhart Tolle speaks or writes, there is a tangible sense of his unusual presence. He speaks of nothing more than presence, with that particular presence, and when he does so you feel it and know it, because something in you recognises it as real.

He, too, is teaching us something universal via his individuality, and being himself for a living, like George, Simon, Resheka, Amanda, you and me. Explanations aside, resonance reins. This is higher knowing rekindled in us. Something timeless rings like a quiet clarion call across the hills. Best we hear its chime, for it chimes for us. We each have our voice but the sound is the same.

Is death perhaps an interlude between lifetimes, or are lifetimes interludes away from a form of higher consciousness that, for the lack of a better term or understanding, we call death?

Writing this book has been a rapid transition into a new life and a new me. I was ready and responsive, the old stuff was over, and, when the new dropped out of the air, I jumped on this chariot and rode it all the way to where it wanted to go. Four months ago we were about to leave for Thailand, Resheka was still to set foot in famed Phuket, and I was so overdue to go back that I didn't care anymore. That's how ready I was. When you are primed like that, a lot can transpire very quickly.

Another four more months later and this book is going to print next week. Then Sheke and I are flying to London to set up the launch and publicity there ahead of Christmas 2018. *Death is the Ultimate Orgasm* will be released worldwide at the end of October, with occasions and promotions in Johannesburg and Cape Town, and then the two of us will return to London to do the same there. This is my first trip in nine years to the city where I first arrived, and it is fittingly significant. My physical birth was there in 1968, a few days late, in distress, and via Caesarean section, and fifty years later, having come full circle, I am returning, this time giving birth to myself. I am exercising a man's prerogative to self-actualise. I am calm, excited, and in my power. This completes the healing for me and gives it to the world. I am going home, and Sheke is taking the trip with me, integral to it and thriving through it. Amanda is here supporting us both as her story unfolds like a rose in the spring sunshine. We are all in this together.

Sheke and I are meeting up with Larry and Daniela and travelling north to Bedfordshire to see Van Morrison in concert on 31 August, which happens to be his seventy third birthday. He is supported by The Waterboys, and between them, these artists two of the few left on earth that I still want to experience live. We are seeing them both on one night in Wrest Park, a heritage site set for a fitting occasion at a moment of transition. My sense a month ago was that we would get to the UK in spring next year, but then I bumped into Larry and Daniela at another of our Italian restaurants, called Ottimo, which translates to 'Optimum', and they reminded me that they were off to Italy, where Daniela's from, for the trip they mentioned when we saw them just after Larry's dad's death. They added that they were crossing to England and seeing Van in concert, a lifetime high for music fan Larry, and told me that they had two spare tickets.

It was if the gods orchestrated this occasion into the story so that it could culminate in this way. I told Sheke about the synchronicity, remembered my intuition at the beginning of the year to have *Death is the Ultimate Orgasm* 'the most talked about book in the UK for Christmas 2018', and found the picture swirling together with remarkable sexiness. At short notice we pulled together the trip and fly on Tuesday. A beautiful and budding global business in India is doing much of the publishing work for us, and we are meeting with a British crew on Pall Mall in the first week of September to arrange the campaign for the Isles. Wow! Even I am amazed, and I have seen a few spiritual spectacles in my time. This is what happens when you make the commitment, follow the call, take the ride, do the work, trust the flow, and be yourself for a living. The ultimate orgasm keeps coming.

One shift from this book journey has been towards greater trust and attention to what is happening within me and guiding me from here. I have a much more crystalised sense of transcendent self, and a stronger intent in occupying it. I am less distracted by and susceptible to manipulation from outside interests, while being far less frustrated and much more congenial as a result. It's working well. A proper book transforms the author as it comes into form, and then goes on to transform the reader. I needed this to catapult me into who I have had the capacity to be, and now I can continue my work better than ever. Write that book you have brewing in you.

From being all things to all people and feeling depleted and torn, I have found how to be more resident in my subjective being. From having my sense of self tangled up in others and the tethers of business, I am at home where I have longed and worked to be. Paradoxically, this has allowed me to get flowing interpersonally, and business is taking off on all fronts. I have been getting out of my own way, allowing the success of a lifetime to flow, and keeping a balance between the inner and the outer that feeds me on both levels. I am also getting the collaboration with key people right. You need to be happy, enthused, self-contained and thoroughly connected while the story storms into cathartic climax in and around you. All of the strands described in this book keep weaving together and bringing you to this profoundly pleasurable place.

"Don't move from your focus," Sheke said to me. "Nothing is more important than this."

Chapter 48

Look at Your Hands

One of Carlos Castaneda's later books, the ninth in his series of twelve, is called *The Art of Dreaming* (1993, five years before his death, although he would not have used that term, as sorcerers of his lineage talk of leaving the body in deliberate and transformative terms). This book expands on something referred to throughout the earlier titles but brought to the fore in this advanced instalment because of its importance and its full emergence in the author's awareness. It took decades of space-time for him to grasp and be able to write about it. 'Dreaming', according to the shamans in the Toltec heredity represented by Don Juan, is also called the 'second attention', which is one we are able to access and then develop through a set of techniques described in the book. From Castaneda's books and from my experience, I am able to describe something of significance to human consciousness, and of help when learning to live and die.

The 'first attention' is this one that we know well, the familiar if not only reality to most of our minds. However, it is regarded as reality by shamans and seers (as they call themselves) only because we all apply our attention to it, while there are many other options to perceive when we make ourselves available to them. This one, like any other, is not so much a physical reality as it is a shared perception based on collective application of awareness to it, which creates and upholds it and maintains our sense of form within it. Reality, then, is a function of attention and shared perception, which can, does, and should shift. It is a cluster of energies from which we can extricate ourselves through saving inner resources that are otherwise consumed in upholding it.

With work we can begin to experience awareness outside of the intense grasp of collective consciousness, and realise our true nature, plus begin to play with it. 'Play' is perhaps not the most appropriate word, since the shift and exploration are a deadly voyage into the unknown, yet that sobriety is tempered by a spirit of light-heartedness along with the rigour required, or the impeccability, as the shamans call it. The first attention is the one we have been conditioned into and take to be all of reality when it is far from that. The first attention also correlates with the mind. The second attention is another dimension of consciousness to which we can develop our access and apply ourselves, thus opening it up and coagulating it as an alternative reality as convincing and as practical as the familiar one. The one way to find and follow it is through dreaming.

The contention is that our dreams are another form of attention to which we can apply ourselves in largely the same way we do to this first attention, just more deliberately since our application to the first is now routine and unconscious. When we first entered this world, we did not have a mind, which is the inner cognitive structure that mirrors the outer form with which we engage. With no mind there was also no solid form out there, just an amorphous experience full of texture and colour stimulating our inner fascination, similar perhaps to a strong acid or mushroom trip or ayahuasca journey. The repeated exposure we have to agents of conditioning, namely people already familiar with form, like parents and other protagonists of worldliness, eventually leads to the setting of outer experiences into solid things in our perception, which is accompanied by the crystallisation of cognition, bringing outer and inner reality into synchronisation.

The world out there and our identification with it thus slot into place, and with that we lose our sense of wonder. We succumb to the limited assumption that nothing exists outside of this perceived form, and agents of this agreed reality consume our attentive energy to such a degree that are unavailable to recognise anything outside of it. From that young age onwards, first attention awareness works all the time to block out anomalous perceptions, of which there are many, and uphold familiar and shared structure, at the expense of much, including our overall intelligence and experiential richness. It keeps us from the possibilities of perception and, most important, from who we actually are.

We encounter another band of attention in our dreams, but we haven't the wherewithal to make it solid. The shamans work to free up perceptual energy in themselves and their apprentices so as to make it available for the transformative task of entering and developing this second and separate reality. In time and with extensive work, the awareness of the practitioner becomes such that they fulfil the formidable task of finding their hands in their dreams and, in that, shift to the second awareness. The job presented to them has been to try to remember to look at their hands, and thereby become conscious that they are dreaming and invoke intent in that realm, and eventually they have managed to remember to do so and unexpectedly achieve the goal. Usually at this point they wake up, tricked away from the second attention by the relentless mind, but with more practice they become increasingly active in the dreaming awareness, and able to operate on that plane more or less as we all do on this one.

This is an instructive insight in its own right, but also in disposing us to awakening or any change in consciousness. In managing ourselves during a spell of anger, perhaps, we might have a hook in place put there when we were calm, one that can help us remember our wiser selves. Anger is a kind of drunkenness on the adrenalin and other chemicals rushing through our bloodstream, and when it wears off we might regret our behaviour under the influence. Remorse is the other side of rage, unless we deny that too and insist on our ego's justification for our behaviour. Otherwise, though, we will be keen at some point to be less enslaved to our rage and even interested in its nature and reason for existence. If we have access to feeling the fury, which comes in cycles, and the relative state of sanity, we can resolve in sobriety to attempt to stay conscious when the cycle repeats. Much like looking for our hands in our dreams, we can look for the tell-tale signs that we have become possessed. We will eventually awaken from that anger.

Many cycles may come and go before we catch ourselves. Rage convinces us over that we are in the right, and the other or the outside is to blame and responsible for some wrongdoing. And so we act out the drama again and again, but each time we become a little more aware, and perhaps, too, we are spurred by the severity of outer consequences to be more mindful. Slowly we surface, and one day find ourselves angry but aware that we are angry. The watcher has activated enough to offer us the chance to remain resident in it while the emotion rages on without controlling us. Steadily we establish ourselves in a state of higher consciousness, and free from our destructive behaviour.

Another application of the 'second attention' insight could be to consider that death is a frequency running parallel to the awareness we have, and that there are many more. Like radio waves, they are running invisibly through everything as we see it, or next to it, and are available to our perception via the right tuning. We can, with application of our attention, find the frequencies. Perhaps we will find the domain of the ancestors, or the gods, or the guides, or simply the ever-present formless ether or unmanifest realm. All of these and more are a shift in perception away. We can dispose ourselves to perceiving them, familiarise ourselves with their worlds, and thrive in a world of wonder. Look for your hands, and find your other dimensions of awareness.

Waking up generally in life, and being more conscious as a whole, is the same as becoming ready for death, because death is really just a waking up from the collective dream. The lessons of these shamans are profound indeed, in their specific teaching but generically too because of their opening us up to possibility. Like with the distinction between facts and truth, the important insight is that we are beyond what the head holds onto as actual. It is this openness that is paramount, because everything possible proceeds from there.

I tried the dreaming exercise for a while in the early 2000s, when I was working through the Castaneda books, which I read in sequence, usually two or three times per title before proceeding. I even began writing a book about it back then, called *Dreaming*, which resides in my archives now probably having served its purpose. I wrote about how I tried to become lucid in my dreams, by intending before I slept to look for my hands, and being on the lookout for signs or anomalies that were trying to catch my dreamy eye. I knew that this may have happened quickly or taken ages, but should have work eventually, even though the mind does all it can to avoid and resist the shift. It doesn't want us to find the second attention and will trick us out of it by making us wake up if we do ever remember to look directly at our hands. It will ultimately be overcome, though, by intent and persistence.

And so, intently, I persisted. In the introductory chapters of my book, I recount the time when it happened for me. I had been trying for months without success when one night I found myself on the upper deck of a London bus, surprised to be in the special city, sensing that I was dreaming, and watching the tree tops and first-storey windows pass by outside as we drove. I was alone with the rows of empty seats, the scented texture of the scene, and the distinct oddness of dreaming that somehow normally eludes us. Something felt unusually accessible about it, as if there was a twitch in the matrix trying to get my attention. I knew that I knew, but I couldn't quite get a grip on my knowing.

Then I looked down at my wrist to see the time, and noticed that my watch had the logo for the band Oasis on its face rather than its own branding. I had spent much of the previous decade enjoying their era of reign, and so this caught my attention. Oasis watch, I remember thinking, like it should mean something to me. Oasis watch. I'm wearing an Oasis watch. I looked at it more closely, almost scrutinising the familiar font but still not registering that it was a crafty call to look at my hands, which were right there. And then it occurred to me. Look at your hands, I thought as I realised that the watch was what I had looking out for, presenting itself to me seductively. I flipped my wrists to see my palms and felt the realness of dreaming galvanise for moment. And then I woke up back in my bed.

This second attention, according to Castaneda's books, can be entered, as described, and then solidified in the same way as the first attention has been, through repeated exposure. We can become comfortable in it, and able to navigate it. Once you have found your hands and activated your conscious second self, you can get up from your bed and see yourself still lying there asleep. You can move around just by intending it so that, instead of walking through the house, getting into your car and driving to the restaurant on the edge of town, you can just think of the place with intent and you appear there instantly. Time is not linear in dreams, and our bodies and other objects are not solid. My understanding is that this is how shamans can famously be in two places at the same time, although not in exactly the same form, with one self able to eat food and the other not. They appear as if from nowhere and take the shape of other living creatures, like birds, and fly.

More important to me here than whether that is actually the case is, first, the possibility that it is, and second, what it teaches about awareness on the whole. It also shows us how to prepare for and deal with death. How, in the context of such possibilities of awareness, could we settle for Quincy Jones' curt contention?

Can you deal, even conceptually, with the possibility that dreaming attention can be accessed, managed and mastered? You dream, of course, so you know that the realm exists. From there you should be able to imagine what I have just described, even if you don't accept or haven't experienced it. Can you contemplate that it is another form of consciousness just like this one that can be entered into more substantially than you know so far? Can you sense that it can make us aware of another side of ourselves usually obscured from view? If so, then that allows for possibilities, and once we are open, we are available to awareness. Perhaps you have experienced all of this before and can teach me a few things.

How do you feel about the probability that cognitive awareness severely limits us and can be loosened to make us available to much more perception? If 'we don't know what we don't know', then the strong suggestion, if not the primary point, becomes to know that we don't know, before we set out to know. Be aware that you are unaware and then seek awareness. From acceptance you can make yourself available to greater knowing, and begin to venture into new territory. With insight and guidance, you can navigate the sometimes bumpy ride into increased consciousness, one way or another. The Toltec shamans regard it as a journey of no return into domains of danger and incomparable profundity.

The outcome is the ability to negotiate realms beyond our wildest imaginings, the pinnacle of which is optimal living here and now in harmony with the magnificent earth. This, to me, is the point! The result is not just expanded knowing but better being, which is the ultimate attainment. It is the meeting of spirit and soil, the orgasm of being fully alive. It is the existential space from which the solution to our pressing problems is likely to ensue, and where our gift of life and death can crest for everyone. This is the new humanity being born, you and me being free from form while revering having it, and us thriving on a whole new level of integrated intelligence. It's possible and worth exploring, don't you feel?

Chapter 49:

Kissing a Fool

Today is Saturday, seven weeks since the meeting with Simon. Seven times seven days is forty nine, which, in years, is my age at the moment, and also the number, in thousands, of words I have written of this book. That's roughly halfway. I have averaged a thousand words a day and reached the end of the first draft. (Two weeks and the first edit later, we are at sixty five thousand words; four months in and we are nearing the end of the second edit and anticipated one hundred thousand words; and, eight months later we are going to print.)

The numbers are slotting now from all of their spinning, lining up magically, and we are winning. We may have ourselves a jackpot here. Stay calm, it's all in day's work. We have come far to enjoy this reward, from stardust to this fine day. All of existence is culminating in this moment and there is nothing to do but enjoy it and, if so inclined, write about it as we do. We are at home in ourselves, and we have our loyal deaths to keep us company. We have a song of longing in the ever-changing air, a loving heart broken open to the elements, and a clear mind in service of our soulful presence. Is anything more required? I reckon that we are doing quite sweetly, thank you.

I let Resheka and Amanda know the numbers earlier, and kept them posted as we went, and they are both rapturous with excitement and supportive in awe. Well, when you have been working on something your whole life as a natural extension of who you are, it is second nature to bring it to bear when the blessed inspiration descends. Wherever it comes from is good, and it's good to go along with it. This is the work of the new way and the way of everyone who has ever walked it. Alignment. Flow. Self-acceptance, self-love, self-expression, and higher awareness articulated using careful craft and love and devotion. Where does it come from? I'm writing this and I'm telling you that it's not from me, although it's not not from me either. The beyond is the big boss but I am of the beyond, and so where is the line? I am not it, but I am here saying that, which contradicts it. Perhaps the self is simply a meeting place, a membrane of magical manifestation. Death might wipe away the membrane, but the meeting and the magic go on forever.

I am writing with a new compilation playing, one I finished making last week and have had on repeat pretty much since. That's how these ribbons of magic form and weave their way into the transient fabric of permanent presence. Such superb sound fills the sentiment I share. There is a George Michael track in the mix, a lesser-known song from his dance album that was due to become *Listen Without Prejudice Vol 2* but never did, and came out instead on the charity album *Red Hot & Dance* in the early 90s. It's just been released again on the companion disc with the reissue last year of *Listen Without Prejudice Vol 1*. Oh, and there is an old Wham! song on there, too, the B-side of "Club Tropicana", that's a bit blue but not at all bad. George is among us, bringing in his talent and inspiring soul. Might I also linger after I'm gone? I am already gone, and this is the moment speaking to you through a keyboard with a soundtrack.

Today is also the first anniversary of Resheka receiving the diagnosis from the biopsy she had on her hip that led to the treatment that filled the following six months of last year. We had dinner tonight and she told me about her reflective revisiting earlier of the encounters with doctors at the time, one in particular who went well out of his way to ensure that what she was complaining of was attended to satisfactorily. She was still processing the symptoms, investigations and unclear results when he took personal ownership of getting to the root of it.

It was he who, at no charge, made sure that they found out what was wrong, and wrote to the professor of oncology to ensure that she received his due attention. A year later now she felt moved today to write to him and acknowledge all he did back then, much of which she had come to appreciate fully only since. She expressed her gratitude for his help and care, he responded quickly, remembered her well, and was thankful for her message, more, I would imagine, than he voiced. Today was a big day for her having come so far, and for me too, having come all this way with her.

Synchronistically Sheke was buying some supplements at the health shop in the mall this afternoon when she spoke to the attendant there, a medical student who had advised her a year back to look more deeply into some of the test results she'd received. The two of them also took stock of the journey since, and shared a moment of realness and resonance.

"And here you are now," he told her, "well again."

"Yes," she said, glowing with goodness. Well and then some.

The healing has been far-reaching. Check-ups and maintenance treatments are still frightening for us, but they keep coming up positively and the relief brings a fresh rush of humble thankfulness. Tonight she reflected on all she faced and achieved in the past year, and on her blessing for being here alive and well. An ordeal with death changed her life, and affected those around her, not least of all me. One year after I had gone to her house with Thai take-aways for dinner to sit with her news from earlier in the day, we were eating out on the town with quite a story to share and tell. Love and life have taken us to new levels and the wheels of fortune have spun into a winning sequence, albeit with more modesty than ever. There were no lights flashing or coins clinking, but we were celebrating. It was a quiet orgasm of joy together in the outside corner of our regular Italian restaurant. Just the two of us knew the secret chime of our special occasion.

Sometimes life works with tension to shift us into new realms. Perhaps life itself is such a catapulting action. The notion that earthly existence is some sort of purgatory is not without resonance either. To have the odyssey, we face the package deal, with birth and death and the whole bang shoot in between. Of course, its primary value is intrinsic, but there is more to be found wherever we turn, whether that is a turning away, a turning towards, or turning in a dervish spin. The bottom line is that we have bought the ticket and taken the ride. The only way out is through, and being here is the biggest blessing. When we fully occupy the present, everything takes care of itself and even our folly makes sense in the comical mystery. A page turns, a new day dawns, and the next level appears under our feet. The rich myth makes itself apparent once again, and we step forward into the story one more time.

As the last week of our stay in Thailand began, Resheka and I set off for Pattaya to follow a feeling and allow what we were looking for to find us. The well-planned day brought an unexpected addition to our adventure, though, which pushed us into some preparatory insight. First, the taxi driver was straight from hell and gave us a death ride to Phuket airport, as if we needed the rude awakening. He was a wiry-eyed mafia-type, aggressive for some reason at that early hour, inept at English when we attempted to communicate and yet able to understand us clearly even when we spoke softly between the two of us. As if the playfully provocative gods had read our inner myths ahead of time, and engineered his place in the story, this lunatic seemed driven to make the testing trip much more so than justifiable under any sane circumstances. Relieved to arrive at domestic departures and stirred into alertness, we were primed by the build-up to what then happened with our flight, which those same gods would have had a hand in too.

We made it through airport security a little less offended than we were on the Kuala Lumpur trip, only because we were prepared for it and not because they were less offensive with how they handled us. With our fingered toothpaste tubes back in our toiletry bags and our serenity restored, we appreciated not having to pay for a grossly overpriced breakfast, because we had eaten earlier, and then we queued for the plane at the gate specified on the departures screen while keeping an ear out for our names, owing to the approaching time of the flight.

On our legs to and from KL ten days before, on the same airline, we had been delayed by over an hour on the way out and then took off twenty minutes late on the return. So this time we were alert to variances but equally distracted by those recent experiences. The screen above the boarding pass check-in counter had our flight number displayed on it, but the queue of passengers was static, right up to the time for our flight, at which point they opened the gate and the people began to move forward. When we arrived at the counter, though, the attendant told us that the plane door was closed and our flight was already on its way. What? There was only one a day, they told us coldly, as if it was our fault, and we would have to "come back at the same time tomorrow."

We had done nothing wrong and were having none of it, feeling outraged at the situation and more so at their rude way of handling of it. All the while they were wasting time on the phone when they could have slipped us on board instead. They kept giving us an argument of why they couldn't do that, and then absconding to call a supervisor to tell us the same nonsense but never returning with one.

"We walked past with a board with your names on it four times," they asserted as an offensively pathetic retort, and then asked hostilely, "You want to see security camera?"

"You are responsible for this, not us," I insisted unwaveringly, "and now you are making it worse. We have a meeting in Pattaya tomorrow, we are going to be there, and you are going to do whatever it takes to make that happen," I stated as firm fact.

"If our luggage was checked in on the plane," I pointed out, "it would never leave without us."

"Yes," they agreed, "for security."

"Exactly," I said, "but now you claim the doors are closed, which means security means more to you than service. Just get us on the plane now. We are going to Pattaya today."

They fucked us around for almost another hour but eventually resorted to changing our outbound ticket to one for the more frequent flights to Bangkok, which would get us up country, as required, but to Don Mueang, the alternative airport across town, instead of Suvarnabhumi, the main one in the big city. This would add a three hour taxi drive through the capital and on to Pattaya, at our expense, of course, but we took it and left the chaos behind us. Flicking through some photographs on my phone, I saw that the ATM we had stopped at to draw cash on our way to breakfast that morning was outside a branch of Bangkok Bank. We realised then that the sign had pointed to our detour ahead of time, like a flash of premonition, and served as affirmation that all was meant to be and unfolding perfectly.

On the flight, still relieved that we were going to get to our goal as planned, albeit with a sizable delay and some unscheduled sight-seeing, we reflected on the meaning of the experience and extracted insights from it. We laughed at how resolve can kick in when you are uncompromisingly committed to something, and how much an unbending intent can influence events. It can take a touch of crisis to bring out the best in us. Never back down unduly, we conferred, employ your resourcefulness, and stay open to the seemingly bad leading to surprising good. And keep a lookout! Everything points to where you really want to go.

Fired up by the frustration and eventual resolution, and shifted by the catharsis, we accessed some more answers to big questions at the root of what we were working on. For one, I remembered my ability from youth to negotiate a deal and be patiently resolute until the right arrangement falls into place. I felt rekindled by this for the future and primed for the ensuing day and evening with Simon, which would contain an element of such negotiation. The universe has everything perfectly engineered and yet, in this, we have free will. Intelligence is in exercising heart and soul, and raw guts and versatility, and tempering these with best judgement by inhabiting the present.

The whole first day of the trip turned into a navigation through such rocky and revealing terrain, with the hotel into which we had booked from Phuket laying on more nonsense at reception when we eventually arrived, by pretending not to understand our straightforward questions about extra items on the account. Then they put us in a room with a noisy air conditioner unit outside the door and ignored us when we complained. They got the message, though, when I walked into reception in my baby-blue sleeping shorts and white T-shirt holding my phone blaring a recording of the offensive racket.

I stood at the counter glaring at them without saying a word until they figured out a solution, which meant shunting us to a replacement room way across the building at 1am and leaving behind our luggage without considering the implications of that for us in the morning. Having salvaged only a few hours of sleep from the wreckage of the night, and keeping our grumpiness in check to stay on course for our reason for being there, we strode self-consciously but shamelessly down the corridors and through reception in our dressing gowns at 8am like celebrities, back to the original room to shower and shape up. Along the way we were relocated to a third suite that looked like it was going to work for us at last.

After a reasonable but equally shambolic breakfast, we were sleep deprived and ruffled, but still unfazed and excited, and in the foyer on time as arranged when I saw a familiar figure cross the bridge on the level above and enter the elevator. One floor down we were waiting when the silver doors slid open and the visitor stepped out to meet us.

"Hi Simon," I said smiling and extending my right hand, "I'm Robin and this is Resheka."

We were primed for a flood of progress and a perfect day.

Interlude 6:

Understand

There are two things that matter here: how we live and how we die. Yes, they are the same thing, but they deserve separate mention and attention too. How we live is on this side of the great divide, and how we die takes us into the other, and neither makes sense on its own. We are here to live and we are going to die, and we need to know how to do both. That is the job at hand, otherwise we have wasted our time. To live rightly, know that you are going to die, and to die rightly, know that you need to live. This may well mean waking up and entering a new realm. That's what happened when you were born, and being born is on the other side of dying. They are one experience. Separateness exists only in the mind, and we are speaking, in part, to the mind.

First, this is how you live: you trust yourself, follow your calling, listen to your ancestry, materialise your intuition, create your ideal life, use your talents, express your love, discover yourself, enjoy good taste, grow all the time, be who you are, live in the now, create as a way of life, stand your ground, have a good laugh, align with the light, go with the flow, use your best intelligence, keep it simple, engage fully, remain detached, resolve the paradox, share the passion, write the books, do the dance, be the fool, be your own boss, drink the wine, have the sex, drop the sex, embrace your age, befriend the end, love the lot, guzzle the grappa, sip the espresso, make the music, renovate the house, take the trip, swim at sunset, ride the bike, change the world, be yourself, personify the spiritual, finance the essential, welcome the financial, deserve the reciprocal, savour the tranquil, walk in the afternoons, ride the islands, take the photographs, watch your words, smell the roses, weep and scream, roar with glee, sleep a lot, adore your solitude, feed your roots, grow your trees, cuss and swear, minimise the paperwork, outsmart the snakes, earn some respect, go it alone, lean on others, never compromise, always add spice, mix the colours, wink at the guilt, proceed regardless, resolve the issues, indulge the process, give it space, appreciate the anger, drop the desire, see the sky, watch the clouds, be the blue, soak in the sun, listen to the ocean, stay up late, get up early, do whatever you want, double the word count without warning, take an expected turn or two, love your neighbour's neighbour, inhabit the globe, pen your own scriptures, inhabit holy blasphemy, forget spirituality, enlighten existentially, have a go with me, throw a silent party, celebrate endlessly, and don't blame me for your ecstasy.

That's if you like lists. Here's one on how to die: accept endings, dissolve boundaries, brave beginnings, jettison conditionings, dismiss charlatans, take responsibility, sleep blissfully, awake gratefully, exude mystery, proceed consciously, seduce playfully, cry regularly, rise gracefully, rock relentlessly, surrender willingly, trust totally, sing innocently, laugh uproariously, stay ordinary, dance with me, organise efficiently, plan practically, subsist spontaneously, rave richly, endure economically, merge musically, make melody, look lucidly, stay friendly, hear clearly, be with me, love indefinitely, cry unconditionally, speak non-verbally, move openly, give rapturously, receive graciously, offend politely, travel extensively, reside joyfully, depart discerningly, create unreservedly, use a dictionary, eat ravishingly, forget nothing, remember everything, forgive freely, expect accountability, retain integrity, be funny, perceive poetically, move mythically, and go gracefully.

Most important, access your being beyond mind and reside here, watching the wonders of the world. See things as they are. Let go of the illusions because they make you cling and clinging makes you miss. Don't miss! To truly live, die before your death, and when the day comes, go into it relaxed and friendly. Do not cling or resist. Be at ease, accepting and happy. Flow with the river of life into the ocean of love. Everything is perfect.

As for business, this chapter from book eighteen in the series, HAPPIER INSIGHTS, says it succinctly. I wrote it exactly one month before George died, and was drawn back to it for inclusion in this book by an enthused comment about it on my blog this week. As we draw to a close, it becomes the earliest piece of writing here, the one that unwittingly kicked things off. It also reminds me of the very first Wham! single, "Wham Rap! (Enjoy What You Do?)", in which the visionary young North Londoner (who has just come onto the stereo again) outlined his value system for living this life. No job, thank you. Be yourself, retain dignity, find your groove, stay stylish, be happy, be soulful, defy society, enjoy yourself, and fucking go for it! Those formative sentiments spoke to me then, have stayed with me ever since, and apply now more than ever. Here's my take thirty five years later:

Business is in bad taste. It is beneath us. Of course we all need to earn a living, so to speak, but the universe brought us here without us selling ourselves, did it not? We are in good hands. We are, in fact, those hands, inseparable from the big picture. So why make ourselves small and sell out? Stay in tune instead and let the whole do what it does. Stay integrated and see. Business is petty and we are quite the opposite. There is no need to trade for a few pennies what is priceless.

We all need to earn a living, so to speak, because the world is upside down. The planet provides for us, we have just turned everything inside out. We are, as a result, inverted in ourselves, making a case for what we do not want. Tell someone that earning a living is a red herring and they will argue with you, insisting that you are out of touch with reality. They want to be free but they build a prison instead. That's why we all need to earn a living: we won't have it any other way. It's time to have it another way. A better, more enlightened and happier way.

In a global scenario where business rules the roost and exploits every individual out there, of course earning a living will be viewed as non-negotiable. But in a situation where robots and artificial intelligence are taking over most jobs when those jobs have been alienating people for decades, is the idea of earning a living even valid anymore? Aren't we all going out of the old way of doing business? Do we not need a revolutionary approach? In such a new setting, would people not be taken care of on a basic level, with food and housing and transport, all provided sustainably and pollution-free, and thus be able to share their talents and love and joy and creativity in a blooming, awakened world? Wouldn't the human contribution be prized instead of repressed? Wouldn't we be empowered to be ourselves?

Here we will not have to earn our living, we will have it automatically provided as a matter of trust, dignity and respect, and what we give will just make it all the richer. Being yourself for a living will not be a business, it will be way above that. We will not be reduced to the lowest common denominator controlled from behind the curtain by corruption. We will have awakened and claimed our power.

Well, stand your ground, because this future is here.

We are living and thriving on a new earth.

Chapter 50:

A Ray of Sunshine

"Wanna hear some of what I've written in my book today, inspired by you?" I asked.

"I'd love to," she beamed back.

"OK, here we go... 'If I were into younger women, you'd get very lucky.'"

"I like that!" she said sitting down next to me.

"Really?" I asked almost in disbelief.

"Really," she repeated.

You know where I am. It's Monday, one of my favourite days of the week, and happy hour, one of my favourite times of the day. The one waitress, Leandra, is halfway through my first INSIGHTS book and loving it, she tells me, stopping by my bench to talk at length, and the other waitress, Letitia, the one serving me, is Indian. Say no more. She's also returning to talk, after I read her that piece of my latest writing, which makes me feel so blessed. It's a pleasure to be an author. Keeps death at bay. Worth writing for.

I am *so* into younger women. I can't think of anything I'm more into at this time. And I love this burger joint. Great food and beer.

Luckily Resheka sees the funny side, most of the time, although she has to keep an eye out. These younger women can be fairly forward! Luckily, too, Resheka looks half her age, which is a wonderful combination, being wise and well-formed with a sense of humour. Leandra is also amazingly wise for her age of twenty one. She's just been back and I am struck again by her insight. I'm not being facetious!

I told the two of them together that they are in my new book and they approved enthusiastically in unison, like a choir of angels to my ears. It might be a ploy to get me to drink more beer, so I'd better watch myself, although the one cherub doesn't have serving me as her excuse. There may be more than beverage sales at play here, in my head anyway. Dreams keep coming true, you know. Love like you are going to die, write a book, live the life, do your thing.

I feel like a thirty-five-year-younger version of Quincy Jones. Both waitresses are joining me for a shooter now. How did that happen? I do recall expressing distinct consent, I must admit. A party for three, all in this book and on my tab. Remarkably like Thailand, actually. What would we do without cinnamon-flavoured whisky? That was unexpectedly pleasant, actually. What's the cliché in situations like this? I remember now. Fuck, I love my job.

My old friend, Greg, a leading estate agent in the area, who went to primary school with me up the road, and high school with me over the road, lives next door, and is as mischievous as they come, has just arrived for wine and a bite. He expected to see me here, just like I had expected to see him. I didn't go as far as making contact, though, but I didn't need to because here he is. He introduced me to this place six months ago and we have often met up or bumped into each other here since. During my low last year he did an evaluation on my house with the view to selling it, but encouraged me instead to get away and find some new inspiration, insisting that I meet Simon Napier-Bell if given half the chance.

His friendship meant a lot to me at the time and his help gave me something to hold onto until the Thailand trip when the shifts happened. Dark times have their place and the tide turns in good time. We've been chatting tonight, to a rock 'n roll soundtrack, about the status of my current writing and the plans for it. He brought along an article from the Sunday Times that he'd kept for me from October last year when George's documentary *Freedom* came out and was covered in the press. It's titled "A Song for the Dying" by Neil McCormick, from The Daily Telegraph in the UK. When I linked it to the title of this book, Greg's mouth dropped open in amazement. This is the energy at work here. This is the powerful magic we partake in and the fun to be had.

Resheka noticed in Thailand and remarked since then how I can make things manifest just by being in the flow and sticking to my intent with detached relish. As the end of 2017 drew closer and the famed New Year party in Patong gathered momentum, I said in the sea one evening that I had been thinking that I could dash up to Pattaya on my own the following week and see Simon efficiently, rather than organise and incur the expense of a trip for two. It was one option that had occurred to me based on considerations we had worked through up to that point. She could stay in town for the day, I said, and I'd be back by the evening. I could even ride up to the airport and avoid those pesky taxis. She listened and then responded a few days later saying that she wanted to come with me and be part of the occasion. She wanted to witness what happened, and felt that it was more than worth the effort and the investment. I was more than happy to hear that and sketched a scene of how it could work, and we set out towards it, with no expectations. On the first of January I felt alignment in the air and wrote to Simon, who had time available on the coming weekend. And so Resheka and I researched travel options, made decisions, and set the wheels in motion.

It felt right, like it wanted to happen, and we wanted it to happen, so we went with it. That's how manifestation works without effort. I had ideas of what to do but these were inspired and not contrived, and so I was open to any changes that further inspiration may have brought. Manifestation means flowing with inspiration and adapting to variation, all of which keeps getting better. I had needs, and the more I sat with these the more I was able to honour them and allow them to get met. Manifestation arises in response to needs. I had intent, which I could apply to whatever I chose or found most prudent. I had my wits about me, all my experience to draw on, my flair for adventure (with a touch of drama), my mischief, and my sincerity to work with. Manifestation draws on our whole intelligence and takes it into new territory. Most important, I had my presence to bring these all together creatively and in the moment. I was ready and the iron was hot.

We moved through the manifestation like plain-clothes magicians, bringing about exactly what we described in the sea before we set out. As it was said, so it came to pass. Currents converged and we had ourselves a fertile delta of flow and formation. When we were back in Johannesburg a few weeks later, Resheka had a flash of insight about it and felt the compulsion to tell me the message for my benefit. "You can bring into being anything that you want to in exactly that way," she said, affirming what was apparent to her but not to me, although I immediately knew what she was referring to and ran with it. The shift transferred from her to me and I was more mobilised than ever. This is fun. Pure fun.

Usually we try to manifest for the wrong reasons and in the wrong way, and so we suffer through it. We have insecurities we want to compensate for and desires that we want fulfilled, both of which are the deficient and distorted way to approach life. By having these as a base, we create discord and have to fight for materialisations, which bring further dissonance rather than delight. The price they come at is high but we don't learn from it, and so we try again, repeating the process without the insight. And then once we have achieved, we are emptier than ever.

But when we manifest in harmony and flow, we work with what wants to happen, which is entirely different in origin and outcome. There is creative tension involved but it polishes the rough edges of our inner sword and makes us sharper. This makes us more incisive and primed for opportunity, which will come and which we will take with effortless class and style, and without expectation. The experience of spirited manifestation opens us even more and empowers us to make more of it happen, and the crescendos keep taking us up in waves of incremental wholesomeness. We need nothing more than to let go into living this way. Everything is taken care of as we go and we can work with whatever transpires.

A week later I am at the burger joint again and Shannon, the waitress from a few weeks ago, has just been over and talked to me quite extensively, considering that she is at work and juggling the demands of her duties. We picked up where we left off about creativity and being true to yourself and, uncannily, she began saying exactly what I was writing about just before I came out for a break. We are certainly all in tune on levels that are not usually acknowledged or discussed, but which are invigorating to explore and mutually enriching to bring into the open. She was amazed and enthralled, and then had to run off for a while, so I wrote for a bit until she came back again.

Speaking about success, which is what she says she wants in life, she explained with trepidation, for her, it means financial and, more important, emotional independence. She wants to be her own person and have an established centre in herself from which goodness flows. It's an instinct and it is a discerning insight too, especially at twenty one. It's phenomenal, yet to be expected. Everything hangs together when you are in tune, regardless of age.

The trick is to be aware, regardless of age. Death can help with that. Her perfumed scent still lingers on my shirt from the goodbye hug, sending dreaminess through me with each inhalation.

For a day now I have felt ready to let Paul in London know about this book but sensed that he would be in touch, which he was, sending me a photo of his side of the city shrouded in snow following a cold spell in Europe. I wrote back saying, "Been thinking of you. I'm writing a new book sparked by my meeting with Simon Napier-Bell. Working on the second draft. It mentions you and your ayahuasca chapter. It's called: *Death is the Ultimate Orgasm.*"

He replied, "I thought you might be up to something! Very you, that title. Sounds intriguing. Happy to be associated with it! I'm going to Ecuador in August for more jungle adventures. The tale continues..."

"Amazing!" I wrote. "Can't wait for progress reports."

"There's a book in there somewhere," he said. "Been simmering for years."

"For sure," I agreed. That's going to be quite a book.

I saw that Simon was online this morning and so I wrote to him as planned. "Two months today, 60 000 words, finishing first edit."

"Looking forward to reading it," he reiterated.

"Glad, thanks," I said, adding, "It's full of you and looking strong. Starts with our meeting, and that story carries throughout."

"Intrigued," he answered.

I rejoiced at the sixty-thousand-words-in-two-months mark with Resheka and Amanda via text, with each of them at their respective offices, and said that I was celebrating by working. These close companions have been with me all the way. Their backing means the world. We need support when we create, however solitary the pursuit may be. Everything is always collaborative too.

"Your work is your love," Sheke said. "Celebrating with you here, too. Feeling the joy and having a great day." The rising energy is so strong.

"Robin!" Amanda exclaimed, having followed every numeric update with glee. "Congratulations!"

"Thanks so much for supporting and sharing, A," I said in heartfelt understatement.

"What a privilege it is," she replied with a heart.

What I'm saying with this book is: Be ready. Don't believe, be willing to find out. Be comfortable not knowing and just watching. Don't be afraid, be aware. Be present. Don't live in denial but in truth, and then die the same way. Live to the full, in the moment, and be ready to die any moment, and then, when you do die, remember all that you have been open to and let it serve you. How can death be anything but good? It has to be the greatest experience of all. Living accordingly must ensure that we will die rightly. Be clear and relaxed, lucid and receptive, and non-resistant. Be free and keen to see. Create as you go and live out your myth, but remain detached. But then you know that already because you've just read it.

Fifty chapters, fifty years, and fifty million copies sold. And then another fifty. Spread the goodness.

"Three months. Nearly there..." my message to Simon read this afternoon. I sent it spontaneously having had the date dawn on me when I read an email from Amanda that spoke encouragingly about my writing and put a skip in my step. I wasn't sure if I would mark the date I had predicted in Pattaya on that Saturday night, and wasn't even looking out for it, but when I read her words I remembered the occasion and wondered for a moment if I had missed it. I worked backwards from my haircut appointment next week, which was on my mind because the salon called me this morning, and my calculations brought me to today. I checked my phone and sure enough, three months to the day.

I reflected for a second, considered the time, which was just after 3 pm here and 8pm there, and then sent the note, which he read shortly afterwards. Then I forwarded the message to Resheka and Amanda. Sheke texted straight back, saying, "Wow! Yeah...We were with Simon on Walking Street around this time three months ago. You have achieved so much since that momentous and monumental evening. Awesome to hear. So happy for you. So proud of you and all the work you have done on yourself and the book. Supporting and loving you all the way!"

There's some cosmic timing, synchronicity and myth-realisation for you right there. In that spirit, I have come to the burger joint on this late Friday afternoon, with the yellow sunshine blasting onto surrounding buildings and silhouetting the trees outside and making the folding doors frame the scene. The beer and nachos are going down well, Thando, the manageress, has just come over and given me a hug that Sheke would disapprove of, and a response text from Amanda has just pinged in saying, "Love times infinity." That's my kind of mathematics, my kind of scenario, and my kind of story coming together. Glad you could join us.

Simon slipped on a wet bathroom tile this week and posted a picture online of himself pouting in the hospital with his left arm in a sling. That couldn't have been pleasant, stiff upper lip and playful coping mechanisms notwithstanding. A six week recovery time, he said. From my experience of the medical profession, you can double or even triple that period, which is enough time to write the bulk of a book. Maybe he should slow down a bit and be with himself, in the moment. Maybe I am making too much of it but life could be nudging him to face some issues, feel some feelings, embrace the ever-unfolding real deal, rest, and re-evaluate. He will, after all, be seventy nine this month. There's no need to push it. The second part of my message to him earlier today read, "Hope you are taking it easy and healing up." I'm a nurturer in these situations. We need to hear ourselves and feel for each other. Frailty is a blessing and a bond, and mortality is as close as the shower floor.

Four months after I started, I reached ninety six thousand words, and five days later, on a Friday afternoon similarly sunny to the one on which Franked slipped away, I sent a message to the three significant others signifying the home run of one hundred thousand. Festivities ensued and a feeling of such satisfaction followed that we spent the weekend basking in it, albeit in a state of exhaustion on my part. There is no feeling like doing your best work with all you have, integrating it effortlessly with being yourself, mixing it with rock 'n roll panache, growing to another level in yourself and your business, living in readiness to slip away while remaining resolute to harvest the absolute out of life.

Tonight my new book goes to print for preview copies, and these words constitute the end of the third edit, and the third reliving of the trip. This is the last week in August with new life about to burst into spring in Bedfordview. Tomorrow Sheke and I fly to London and I am on my last day of a long and focused run-up. Feeling raw as a result, I bumped into Andrico in the mall, a friend from the community and a local lawyer, who told me how to end this book without knowing that he was doing so.

"I'll tell you something, Rob," he said. "You are absolutely correct with your saying, with your new title. I was speaking to this old friend of mine, also from Cypress, who's about sixty now. He's a guy who has truly lived to the full, and he had a heart attack recently, from stress and family troubles, you know. It got to him, and he had a heart attack." All this while Andrico had been glancing around pensively as he spoke, paying for his doughnut and dropping some coins into the tip container, but then he looked me straight in the eye. "He was dead for two and a half minutes. And you know what he told me? He told me he had this feeling of all the tension being gone, no more stress and pain. Just peace and harmony, like he could completely let go. Pure bliss." And with that, I can go to print and to London.

I see death as the ultimate orgasm and I'm living by it. Are you coming with me?

A Last Request

(I Want Your Sex Part III)

This book is a seduction and so is my whole life. How else do you draw someone towards the spiritual and the mystical? How else do you entice people into living profoundly and poetically? How else do you introduce someone to themselves? It's the start of a lifelong romance that requires an appropriate approach. This is my gesture of courtship. Death is the ultimate seduction.

When Simon and I met, it was a mutual seduction. That's how Resheka described it afterwards, among other ways, having witnessed and been part of it. We were charming each other and checking each other out, we both knew it and were both enjoying it. It was the sophistication of the dance, the appreciation of nuance, and the mutual enchantment. Seduction can be most cultured, and must be for the more erudite and refined palate. We all want to be won over in spite of our sorrows, cynicism and stubborn insistence. We want to have our deep knowing that life is good validated on all levels. We want to feel fully alive and to tumble in love through outer and inner space. We want the sorrows and joys to weave together into song and carry us away on the magnificence of the moment. We want what we have been searching, working and longing for all this time: satisfaction.

We want to die because it is a return to oneness, and also because dying is how we live and we want more than anything to live. We want to feel experientially all that we have come here for. We want the myth and the meditation to culminate in our magical dream come true, to live out what we have always known as we give beautiful birth to ourselves again and again. We know we can do it and we are doing it. Death gives us all of this and more, and I am romancing you towards it.

It descended over me like a cool shirt, soothing my sunned skin with divinity, and blessing me with a long-awaited moment here now. I felt the clean cotton and the fresh benediction both, which slipped me straight into the distinct space, the one that has been inviting me indefinitely. With it, I came straight to the keyboard. My ancestors are ready and the path is opening up. I am ready, too, and the feeling lightness is showing the way.

Yesterday Resheka and I were in Irene, and we walked past the Wheeler house, as we do every few weeks late on a Sunday afternoon. This time Peter was there, outside on the front lawn, with a golf club in his hands, hacking a few plastic practice balls around in the fading light, like he has always done after a day in the workshop. We slowed down to see him, with me not having done so for a decade, since Frank's memorial, and Resheka doing so for the first time, transfixed by having anticipated this moment and now having it happen. A few months before we had caught a glimpse of him closing up the wooden garage doors, as he has done since I used to go there in my late teens, but he hadn't seen us. We hovered at the gate and considered calling out to him, but we left it for another time, trusting that there would come a right one. This was suddenly it.

Sheke and I had spoken about Irene all day, after I woke with a strong sense of my grandparents and had the place's presence hovering in the air since. On our way to eat at a new restaurant in central Bedfordview, where the corner Greek-owned café used to be in the eighties, we were passed in the parking lot by a most rare and well preserved Alpha Romeo Junior, and I had pointed out to her that it was like the one my uncle has. Over our supreme farm-style breakfast, we had discussed growing food on the family land one day, and then gone home to get walking clothes to head out there on an afternoon out.

A late lunch at a friend's pizzeria was as sublime as our food earlier, and we lingered there over coffee almost long enough to give Irene a miss and walk around a local suburb instead. But I still felt that I wanted to go, and that we should. We worked out that, with driving time, we would still have enough light for a decent walk, and so we set off, trusting the inner tug and changing route spontaneously from the planned highway to the old back roads that my family used to take when I was a child. This took little longer, winding us through my old suburbs, some industrial towns next to the railway line Frank used to travel to work, and through

English-countryside-like tree-lined roads into the green and rocky village between two big cities.

With sunset arriving early owing to autumn, we arrived way past dusk and parked in our usual place at The Oval, the central sports field in the fenced-off suburb where the community plays informal cricket or football. Sheke changed into her walking shoes and grabbed a bottle of water she'd brought along, and we chose our direction, oscillating for a moment and deciding to go with the intuitive sense of straight past the house rather than a longer and more logical way round. We would get our mileage done that way, and so we followed the spirited pull that was stronger than the reasoning mind. As if the whole day had been leading to it, we reached the corner of the property, looked over the low wall as we drew nearer, and then felt time stand still as we gazed at what we saw, galvanised by this frail figure on the lawn in the grey light.

Ten years can do much to a man, especially at that age. A stooped and bony Peter, familiar but foreign to my loving eyes, stood there at seventy seven (seven times seven is forty nine), two years younger than Frank and Simon. Was it the ghost of my grandfather or some stranger in front of the house? I couldn't quite place him, with such significant change and my intense emotion to process. Unable to move on, yet hesitant to stay, Resheka and I stood outside the gate for a few moments, until he looked up and saw us. When he did, my heart leapt, and then he waved, and I returned the gesture like a child, scared and thrilled at the same time. Assuming at that point that he still saw us as neighbours walking past, I stepped closer to the gate to show that I wanted to talk, and he started to make his way over. I watched his form become clearer and more familiar as it came closer, and I felt that I was seeing a long-lost friend, a dear brother, a façade of my father and a vision of myself, all at the same time. I would have started crying were it not so perfect an occasion, so orchestrated and meant to be that nothing but purity was appropriate or possible.

"Hi, Uncle Peter," I said, "it's been so long since I've seen you!" How else could I sum it all up? Was I happy or sad? So much was there in the moment: our respective lives, our relationship, our heritage and my long, long wait for this time to come.
"Hello, Robbie," he smiled, showing that he had seen who was there and was still the same man inside, just behind a body stripped back and buckled by a chunk of time. He had on the same khaki overall jacket I knew from ten, twenty and thirty years ago, one I had sourced for him from a clothing store I'd managed while at university. He walked the same and talked the same, and was still clear and fully aware, just a lot older. What a beautiful relief and joy to see him again, like seeing my dad, gran and grandfather after a lifetime alone. Were those ten years of isolation needed for him and me so that we could have this reunion?

I wanted to give him everything I have in this world, and at the same time felt a fullness and family resolution I had never known before. It was the one I had longed, and worked, and waited for, and then some. It was an occasion of such portent that I was struck still inside. There was nothing to do but inhabit it fully, the way life's meant to be. There was no push or pull in me, or between people, living or dead. There was a powerful and loving peace, a respect and an understanding. It was if my grandparents, who had been holding on to that house and the meaning it held for them, were now ready to work with me to take it somewhere new and better and, with that, back to where it all began. It was if the two of them had resolved their issues and were getting on again, grown up at last and responsible for their place in the shared and living legacy.

A few months before, with a concern for Peter and an urgency in the ether, I had handed everything over to them, trusting their timing totally and stepping away from any emotional charge related to the house, my uncle, their decisions, or the ancient tension surrounding us all. I left it where it belonged and awaited further notice, and now they had responded. I had also stood my ground, in my own dignity forged for myself on their shoulders and with their land in my heart, but by my own hand and from my individual soul. I respected them but I commanded their respect too. They had no choice but to honour what I have done with the myths and challenges I inherited like them and through them, and with my commanding place in the world, they could rise in their respective self-respect too, and come together as actualised adults.

This is the power of family. This is being yourself for a living. This is the gift of life, death and love. After my clear and silent stand in the affairs, it hadn't taken long for this precise orchestration to take place. In between, this book had begun and it was bringing together the whole story along with the people. Everything was contained in that perfect timing: a reconciliation, a resolution and release.

Resheka watched it happening, as she had done with Simon, and wove her powerful presence into the unfolding picture, supporting me and my manifesting mythology, and soaking in the richness for herself. A few months before she had walked those same Irene streets riveted by a vivid sense of my imminent future in that house, seeing for herself all I had spoken about and been guided by since I was a child or perhaps before. The gears had shifted, the cogs engaged, the big wheels turned and the levels aligned, and the three of us spoke for a few minutes more, standing at the gate.

"Are you still driving into Pretoria every day and running your business?" I asked Peter.
"Yes," he said. "Sometimes it's scary, when there's no money coming in, but we carry on."
"I know that feeling well," I told him.
I showed him some recent pictures of Heather's family, which he could see on my smartphone without spectacles, and we warmed up with an assuring sense of each other, at which point, as if my grandparents were expressing their blessings, a gentle rain began to fall, which sent him inside and us on our way.
"I know you switch your phone off over weekends," I ventured, "so we'll stick our heads over the wall next time we are come for a walk, and maybe see you." Leaving it loose, I then added, "I'm here if you need me, still on the same number."

As he turned to go, I gave my goodbye. "So good to see you, Uncle. Lots of love." Then I added, "Keep smiling," and he broke into a big Wheeler beam before heading back towards the house.
"Wait," I said softly to Sheke as I watched him walk away. "This may be the last time I see him."

He may also be in touch, or we may speak over the wall again one evening. He may need me at some point and I may even be there when he dies, like I was with Frank. Who knows? We'll see. Even if he chooses to go alone, I will honour that with reverence and love, and I will go into the patriarchal space to clear it and make it new. I will make it a thriving writer's ideal home and fill it with music, nurture the garden into a patch of paradise, do so with everyone's happy participation, without lifting a finger, and I will pay for it all with my pen.

I felt such respect for Peter seeing him again that day, for how he had lived in line with his own knowing, uncompromisingly and whatever the cost, because that has been my journey too. Each of us is breathing the family fire, facing the struggle and sculpting the legacy, and forging our dignity, individually and inseparably. We are living spirituality.

All will be as it should, with not the slightest error. All I have to do is stay in the moment. It's that simple, effortless and intense, and always has been. Everything is always perfectly part of the journey, forever culminating and climaxing in this moment. The following of the calling, the sticking at it, the sometimes torturous tension, the pain, the enduring struggle with money, the writing no matter what, the renovating and relishing of Frank's house in Bedfordview, the creation of twenty books in it, the quest with the wait for the Irene house, and now the return to Wimbledon exactly fifty years since the first time...

All of this was held in place by my ancestry and, above that, the great mystery, while I worked the earth here with my hands and heart. I can only continue being who I am and going where I am meant to. I can relax and enjoy it now. I have done well.

What's that cliché again? Everything is love and love is all. Something like that.

Waiting **(Reprise)**

A sound in the air

A song

A thumping drum

A heart beating in time

A string instrument singing

A wailing strand of bitter-sweet happiness

A longing, and a lingering scent of musical flavour

A mixed metaphor and a multimedia experience

A thrust of love going nowhere yet coming everywhere

We all call it being alive

We like using words

There are no words

Robin Wheeler

www.ingramcontent.com/pod-product-compliance
Lightning Source LLC
La Vergne TN
LVHW041313080426
835513LV00008B/444